LONE FATHERS AND MASCULINITIES

For Sue

Lone Fathers and Masculinities

RICHARD W. BARKER

Avebury

Aldershot · Brookfield USA · Hong Kong · Singapore · Sydney

Published by
Avebury
Ashgate Publishing Limited
Gower House
Croft Road
Aldershot
Hants GU11 3HR
England

Ashgate Publishing Company
Old Post Road
Brookfield
Vermont 05036
USA

British Library Cataloguing in Publication Data

Barker, Richard W.
    Lone Fathers and Masculinities
    I. Title
    362.82

ISBN 1 85628 522 7

Printed and Bound in Great Britain by
Athenaeum Press Ltd, Newcastle upon Tyne.

Contents

List of tables

Acknowledgements

I would like to thank a number of people. First and foremost, Sue Barker, without whose support, encouragement, and tolerance this end product would never have seen the light of day. More than anyone else she has paid the price, without reaping any benefits, of my doing part time postgraduate research, and then writing this book based on the research - for which she has my deepest thanks. Danny Barker and Jessica Barker have both taught me a great deal about parenting and fathering, and have coped patiently with the paradoxical position of having a father who was at (too many) times unavailable because he was writing about fathering. William and Margaret Barker, my parents, instilled in me from an early age the value of education, and this book is in part thanks for the experiences they gave me.

 Whilst completing the thesis on which this book is based I was extremely fortunate to have as supervisors Professor John Triseliotis and Dr. Lynne Jamieson. Their supervision and guidance was literally invaluable and I owe them great thanks; as do I also my examiners, Colin Bell and David Morgan. Newcastle Polytechnic has been supportive in offering sabbatical time and financial assistance with fees; colleagues in the Department of Social Work and Social Policy in the University of Northumbria at Newcastle have provided encouragement, particularly Stewart Mills, Iain Edgar and - not least because of his help with information technology - Andy Bilson. The DHSS, now DSS, facilitated access to a sample of lone fathers, for which key help I am very grateful. I am also immensely grateful to the lone fathers who agreed to be interviewed for this research, I hope that in presenting this study of their lives and experiences I am offering a fair representation of their views and situations.

Many other people have been supportive and of assistance - if their names are not included in this list that does not mean that their help was not appreciated both at the time and now - I thank them all. I have, of course, to accept sole personal responsibility for any errors that might be found in this book.

1 Introduction

This research is based on an examination and analysis of the lives of a sample of lone fathers living in the North of England.

The study is a description, analysis, and consideration of data obtained from 35 lone fathers living in the North of England, who were interviewed during the 1980s. The sample, which consisted of 19 divorcees and 16 widowers, was a random sample obtained via child benefit records. Both qualitative and quantitative data was obtained by means of structured interviews with the lone fathers.

Whilst the numbers of lone fathers have been increasing recently, little is known about the ways they define and live their lives. In relation to child care the norm is that mothers have a more important and vital part to play than men. The men in this sample had all had to face the crisis of becoming lone fathers, and the data considers the different ways in which they responded to this crisis. It is argued during this research that lone fathers are potentially in a paradoxical position, in that models of masculinities and models of fathering are not easily congruent. What transitions had the men undergone? How did they experience and negotiate masculinities, how did they experience and engage in patriarchal relations? How did they perceive themselves - as patriarchs who had the problem of child care to contend with, or as pioneers of new gender roles, or as neither of these? In what ways were different forms of masculinities pursued in the different structures of patriarchal relations? How did lone fathers balance the demands of paid and domestic labour, how far were those who engaged in domestic labour and not in paid employment different from those who were working in and outside the home? What were their perceptions of their gender role, and of gender roles in general, how did they relate to other men and to women? What were the different experiences of widowers and divorcees, and how might these differences be best understood? How were they involved in and what did they feel about child care? Were there social class differences that impacted on their lives? What were their experiences of the helping services - of social work agencies, of health agencies, of the voluntary sector? All these areas are explored and considered in this study.

In chapter two, the study begins with a consideration of the theoretical and research literature concerning gender and parenting, focusing particularly on masculinity, patriarchy and lone fatherhood. The incidence of lone parenthood and lone fatherhood is explored, and, following a brief discussion of sociological theories of the family in relation to fathers, the idea of parenthood, of motherhood and fatherhood, is examined. There is then a consideration of previous research into lone father families, and a discussion of the concept of role and role theory. Linked with this there follows a discussion of patriarchy, where it is argued that patriarchy can best be understood, and is most viable as a theoretical concept, as a series of different systems rather than as one system. This multiplicity is also applied to the concept of masculinity. It is argued that it is more appropriate to talk of masculinities rather than masculinity. Based on the theoretical material considered, and the data obtained in this study, the concept of a continuum of patriarchal masculinity is advanced, with traditional patriarchal orientations and pioneering gender orientations as the two poles of the continuum.

In chapter three, there is a detailed discussion of the research design and methodology. The disadvantages of previous research samples in relation to lone fathers, and the advantages of the methods devised in this study, are considered. The place of this study in the context of the social research literature is examined. The concepts relevant to understanding the positions of lone fathers, and how they were explored during the structured interviews are discussed. Data analysis and the reliability and validity of the data collected are considered.

Chapter four is concerned to consider, discuss, and explore the different routes into lone fatherhood of the members of the study. Amongst the sample, the routes into lone fatherhood differed substantially, and although the relationship was not a simple unilinear one, the ways in which men 'became' lone fathers had connections with the ways in which they performed and defined their roles as 'being' lone fathers.

Chapter five considers the lone fathers relationships with their children. A key area for all fathers, but particularly lone fathers, is that of their interactions with their children. This chapter considers lone fathers experiences of these relationships, and considers the meaning of the data in relation to parenting, masculinities, and patriarchy.

Chapter six examines the domestic labour of lone fathers, and relates the past and present experiences of the men in the study to a wider consideration of gender and domestic labour. It begins with a consideration of why the area of lone fathers and housework is of significance for this study, before examining briefly different sociological theories of the family in relation to housework. Following this, the chapter explores the members of the sample's involvement in housework when they were married and at the time of the study. It concludes with a brief discussion of the significance of the findings in relation to the nature of gender roles, masculinities, and parenting.

2

Chapter seven examines the lone fathers past and present experiences of paid employment. It describes and considers the previous and present paid employment and unemployment histories of the lone fathers in the research sample. Following a consideration of the significance of the area of paid employment for this study, the chapter briefly discusses different sociological theories of the family and of gender roles in relation to paid employment. The chapter then explores the members of the sample's involvement in employment, concluding with an analysis and discussion of the significance of the findings in relation to the nature of gender roles, particularly, as in earlier chapters, in relation to concepts of 'masculinity' and concepts of 'fathering.'

Chapter eight examines the economic positions of lone father families, within a wider discussion of the economic positions of single parents. To understand the position of lone fathers and their households it is necessary to consider their economic circumstances, both past and present, as the economic situations of different single parent households define boundaries within which the lives of the household members are pursued, and this chapter consider the ways in which lone father households are related to both general and specific economic circumstances.

Chapter nine explores lone fathers' relationships with kinfolk, and lone fathers sexual relationships. The relationships within individual households are, as will be shown in this study, of immense significance for the lives of lone fathers. However, lone fathers are not only members of the households of which they are the head, they are also members of a range of social networks. This chapter therefore considers the social networks of kinship. It also explores relationships with ex-partners, and relationships of sexuality in which the members of the sample were involved, and the nature and meaning of these relationships.

Chapter ten explores lone fathers relationships in their communities, specifically their relationships with the members of their local neighbourhoods. This chapter has a focus on two areas, the friendship and acquaintance relationships of the lone fathers in the sample, and the lone fathers relationships with the communities of which they were members.

Chapter eleven examines lone fathers' relationships and involvement with social workers and other professionals, particularly representatives of the law, health, and voluntary sector welfare agencies. It includes a consideration of the nature and meanings of these contacts for the lone father households, looking at similarities and differences between the experiences of widowers and divorcees, and patriarchs and pioneers. It concludes with a brief discussion of the implications of these findings for the services and professionals concerned with regard to parenting and masculinities.

Chapter twelve considers the conclusions that can be drawn from this study, including a consideration of the issues raised by this research for theories of masculinities and patriarchy.

This study moves from consideration of the literature and broad theoretical issues to a consideration of the research issues and methodology, following which there is a detailed examination of the data collected during the study and then a consideration of the main conclusions of this study. With regard to the structure, whilst substantial theoretical discussion is to be found in chapter two, there are also theoretical discussions at the start of the chapters in which data is presented, these discussions are intended to contextualise the data and introduce some of the main themes of each chapter.

The structure of the presentation of the material has been designed to start with the data on the establishment of lone father households, and to then consider the private activities of lone father households before moving into a consideration of the public activities of the households; concluding with a discussion of the data concerning the 'public' involvement in the 'private' household, that is agencies of the state's relationships with and interventions in lone father households.

2 Lone fathers, parenting and masculinities

This research is concerned to understand the different social and personal positions of lone father families, and to relate the evidence from this study to a wider discussion of parenting and masculinities, by examining a sample of one specific type of head of household - male single parents who head families with dependent children. Such men, and such families, are of interest for at least three interrelated reasons.

Firstly, they represent a particular form of family type which has been relatively underresearched; as will be shown later the number of one parent families, including families headed by men, has increased recently. However, little is known about lone father families. Therefore, this study provides data on a number of previously under researched areas.

Secondly, single parent families, including single father families, are sometimes seen to be 'social problem' families, deviating as they do from perceived norms of family life - being both problems in themselves, and problems for society. Alternatively, they are sometimes seen to contain examples of New Men, of men who have assumed and practice a new form of (to some) more socially acceptable male gender roles.

Finally, social science has in the last twenty years begun to develop a body of scholarship in the areas of gender, parenting, and patriarchy; both at the level of practice, and at the level of ideology. However, for understandable reasons, this largely feminist inspired scholarship has tended to focus particularly on issues related to female gender roles, motherhood, and the impact of patriarchy. Research knowledge about male gender roles, fatherhood, and the ways in which men are a force in, and experience, patriarchy, is less substantial, yet there is an increasing interest in this area. This research is one small part of the continuing process of developing more theoretical explanations and understandings about these areas, and is important in that it is concerned to relate this theoretical material to empirical data - much writing and theorising is speculative rather than 'grounded' in systematic data. (Glaser and Strauss, 1967.)

5

In this chapter it will be shown that lone fatherhood is not a modern development, and the incidence of lone parenthood and lone fatherhood will be explored. Following a brief discussion of sociological theories of the family in relation to fathers, the idea of parenthood will be examined. There will then be a consideration of previous research into lone father families, and a discussion of the concept of role and role theory. Linked with this there will then be a discussion of patriarchy. It will be argued that patriarchy can best be understood, and is most viable as a theoretical concept, as a series of different systems rather than as one system. This multiplicity also will be applied to the concept of masculinity. It will be argued that it is more appropriate to talk of masculinities rather than masculinity.

Sociological theories of the family and the position of fathers

Sociological theories do not adequately theorise the positions of men in families, and consequently cannot adequately explain lone fatherhood. In different ways functionalist, marxist, and feminist theories of the family and roles within them all tend to perceive men as fulfilling a marginal role in their families, because in the first instance society dictates it, in the second instance the needs of the economy dictate it, and in the third instance patriarchal power enables it.

Functionalist theorists, Talcott Parsons, (1949, 1953, 1956, 1980) being the most influential, argue that society's needs to socialise children, and maintain the stability of adults' personalities, leads to role differentiation within families by age and gender. Differentiation on the basis of age is related to adults having control of children, the gender differentiation of the adult family members is related to the 'need' to have males fulfilling 'instrumental' roles, and females fulfilling 'expressive' roles. This leads to men being primarily engaged outside the family in the world of paid work, with women taking the major responsibility for socialising the children and caring for the family generally. This approach would see women fulfilling the affective, caring roles within families because they had been better prepared for it via their socialisation than had men, and because in the division of labour within the family it is their responsibility and duty. Consequently, functionalism argues that lone fathers are ill-fitted to parent children in families where women are absent, and sees such family forms as being innately unstable and dysfunctional from the viewpoint of society's needs.

If functionalism has little to offer in relation to the analysis and understanding of lone father families, what of marxism? Marxist theory of the family, (Draper, 1970, Althusser, 1971, Gerstein, 1973, Zaretsky 1976) assigns a similar central role in society to the family, arguing that it is a form of 'ideological state apparatus'. Thus, family responsibilities encourage, motivate, and at times force society's members to strive for success, which for men is largely defined as success in the labour market. Men are thus engaged in paid labour outside the family, women in unpaid domestic labour (housework and child care) which supports and enables those engaged in paid labour. Seccombe (1974) has argued that domestic labour, whilst it is not a commodity which is sold, is nevertheless valuable, with a value equivalent to its production costs. Gender divisions operate in that women as housewives represent a relatively flexible 'reserve army of labour', (Beechey, 1977) to be called up or demobbed as the ups and downs of the economy necessitate (although Walby, 1989, has argued that the extent to which women are a reserve army of labour in late 20th century UK is exaggerated.)

Recently this process has been accentuated by the development of the dual labour market, with a division into a primary sector with secure, well paid jobs, and a secondary sector with more insecure, lower paid jobs. Gender divisions are central to the present functioning of this dual labour market in that men are more likely to be found in the primary sector and women in the secondary sector (possibly increasing the tendency for women to perceive the central meanings of their lives as 'family', and men to see the central meaning of their lives as 'work'.)

Gender differentiation, the dominance of adults over children, and the relegation of women to a supportive, nurturing role are thus general features that the Marxist model has in common with the functionalist model. Whilst the processes are seen to be similar, disagreement over the desirability of the outcome separates the two approaches, functionalists seeing these as positive, marxists as negative. Implicit in marxist theory therefore is the perception that:

> the (male) worker's life was structured by the demands made upon him by his employer: the household's survival depended on his fulfilling those demands. This, in turn, necessitated a domestic organisation designed to fulfil his needs. Just as the activity of the worker reflected the needs of capital, so the activity of the (female) houseworker reflected the needs of the (male) wage labourer. (p.199, Harris, 1983.)

In sum, marxist theory argues that families 'work best' for capital when men are freed by women from the majority of their domestic duties. The implications of this position are that lone father families will be likely to present difficulties in relation to the needs of capital and the needs of the families members being met.

The most influential force on the sociology of the family in the past twenty years has been feminism, which has highlighted and explored the disadvantaging of women in society in general and in the family in particular. Morgan (1985, p.257)) summarises the criticisms feminist theory raises of studies of the family

> - they often ignore questions of gender;
> - where they consider gender distortions often occur in relation to images of women;

- they have a male centred view of the world;
- women tend to be treated as more 'problematic' than men.

Just as there are ranges of functionalist and marxist theories that can be applied to the family, so there is a range of feminist theories (Oakley, 1981) However, Barrett and McIntosh reflect a general position when they write:

> Women's association with housekeeping and childcare is one of the keys to their oppression. The 'role differentiation' beloved of sociologists of the 1950s is nothing other than a very unequal division of labour. With the role of wife and mother goes housework. It is hard and exacting work...all the chores that men do can be done by women and often are..His contributions to the routine chores that go to make up housework are often seen as 'helping' his wife. The work properly belongs to her, but he will help her out if he has time and wants to. For her, the tasks are inescapable; for him they are not. (p.59-60, Barrett and McIntosh, 1982.)

Therefore, feminism argues that women are inextricably linked to the day to day maintenance of family life. Whilst feminist theories have understandably sought to make more visible women in families, they have understandably focused less on the different positions of men in families. McIntosh provides an example of this in her otherwise excellent chapter on sex, gender, and the family, when writing of lone parents she does not consider the possible positions of and issues for single parent families headed by men. (P.158, Worsley, ed., 1987.)

However, criticism of feminist theory is unfair, not least because feminism has done what functionalism and marxism have not done, namely, increased interest in the study of the family and of gender, thereby providing valuable ideas and material that can be used in relation to exploring and understanding lone father families.

It can be seen then that functionalist, marxist, and feminist theories of the family are somewhat lacking in offering explanations and analyses - or even descriptions - of how men live their lives within families. One major fact and factor that warrants consideration in relation to this process is parenthood, specifically ideologies of motherhood and fatherhood.

Motherhood and fatherhood

There has been a development, particularly but not exclusively in the past 100 years, of a strong ideology of motherhood, of a strong widely held perception, by ordinary members of society and by powerful decision makers, that mothers are central to families. It was thus no accident that George and Wilding's (1972) early work on single parent father households was called "Motherless Families", the concept of

8

'motherlessness' is directly related to the view that mothers occupy a central role in family's lives.

Numerous writers have written critically or approvingly of this central position of women in the family, and of the importance of 'mothering' for children. Bowlby (1951) and Rutter (1972) have written extensively on the problems of maternal deprivation, and Oakley, rightly lamenting the invisibility of women in much 20th century sociology, commented that:

> If women have no place of their own in much of sociology, they are firmly in possession of one haven: the family. In the family women come into their own, they *are* the family. (p.16, Oakley, 1974.)

Whilst he was clearly developing a perspective towards parenting that had existed prior to his research, Bowlby (1951) was particularly influential in shaping and echoing the hegemonic perspective that mothers were crucial to parenting success, assigning a much smaller position to the role of the father than the role of the mother. Parkinson has commented on the power of this paradigm of parenthood in noting that:

> Throughout this century, it has been generally assumed in Britain that women should be the primary caretakers of children and that women and children should be economically dependant on men. These assumptions are deeply rooted in patriarchal society and their influence can be traced in the concepts and practice of many different professional disciplines. (p.3, Parkinson, 1987.)

Government legislation and social policies have underpinned this paradigm, the post war system of social welfare benefits has been built on the foundation of the perspective of the 1942 Beveridge Report that men would engage in paid employment and women and children would be financially dependent on them.

Thus, during the lives of the men interviewed in this sample, the prevailing social ethos has been one in which child care has been seen to be the legitimate responsibility of the mother or a mother substitute with the father having a somewhat distant role in the family. Furthermore, the involvement of fathers with children is often perceived by those involved as 'helping' the mother. As one American study noted:

> (fathers) always assume that they are 'helping' their wives rather than 'sharing' the parental responsibility. Mothers are also likely to see fathers as surrogate parents, and, like their husbands, will use words such as 'helping' and 'baby-sitting' to denote the fathers contribution. (p.57, La Rossa and La Rossa, 1981)

In the United Kingdom, Kathryn Backett's pioneering interactionist study of middle class families in Scotland showed the central role of mothers in families and the relatively minor part played by fathers in actual day to day child care. She writes:

9

It was evident from my interviews that whereas many fundamental aspects of 'being a mother' were taken-for-granted, this did not apply in the same way to 'being a father'.... (motherhood) comprised , in essence, an involvement on a general level which was 'proved' by being constantly available and responsible for the children ...fatherhood was not perceived as having this fundamental and unchallengeable base. (p.195, Backett, 1982.)

She goes on to show how fatherhood often involved a relatively low level of involvement with the children of the family, having essentially three components:

a) dealing with the general administration of domestic and family matters
b) negotiating acceptable parental behaviour in relation to the mother and
c) developing a direct relationship with the child. (p.221, Backett, 1982.)

However, she concluded that in practice this latter element of fatherhood might not be major in terms of the time available or committed to it, often a good father was perceived to be someone who in principle would be involved in child care and in 'helping' his wife, even if in practice factors such as the demands of professional and executive careers meant that the 'help' was relatively infrequent.

Such a position represents a change from the 18th and 19th centuries, when, as Burgoyne, Ormod, Roger and Richards (1987) and Lowe (1982) have indicated, children were seen to be the property of the father, and it was seen to be his right to continue to control such property:

The 19th century abounds with cases demonstrating the strength of the father's so-called 'empire.'In R v de Manneville 1804, a father who had separated from his wife forcibly removed an eight month old child while it was actually at the breast, and carried it away almost naked in an open carriage in inclement weather. Despite this, the court said it could draw no inferences to the disadvantage of the father and upheld his right to custody. (p.27, Lowe, 1982).

By the middle of the 20th century the father's imperial legal rights over his children had been replaced by an ideological consensus that children's well being depended on mothers having similar rights - thus the justice (for fathers) rights of the 19th century were replaced by the welfare (for children's needs) rights of the 20th century. This position has an underpinning assumption in the latter period that mothers also have a right to have 'their children' ahead of fathers rights, and such perceptions are not simply common - sense perceptions, they have been reified and reinforced by 'experts'.

10

Burgoyne, Ormod, Roger and Richards (1987) have charted some of the changes that have taken place. Common law gave guardianship rights to fathers, and this, combined with the economic and financial advantages that men tended to have over women, meant that in disputed cases the fathers retained their children. Developing concepts of the 'welfare needs of children' led to the passing of the 1887 Guardianship of Infants Act, which, whilst it established the principle of viewing mothers as having equal right with fathers in deciding who should care for a child, did not affect decisions in practice. Even after the second Guardianship of Infants Act was passed in 1925, legal practices lagged behind, with judges tending to be hostile towards granting custody to 'guilty mothers' even if the child's welfare needs indicated such a decision would be appropriate.

Increasingly however, the ownership rights of fathers over 'their' children have been eroded, partly as the result of developing 'expert opinion' about the needs of children, and the consequences of these needs for mothers and fathers roles. Thus, Rapaport, Rapaport and Strelitz (1977), under the heading 'Social expectations of parenting-the impact of experts' argue that amongst the conceptions relating to parenthood that have dominated the mid period of the 20th century are that:

> the single crucial element in providing the essential kernel of constructive early experience is mothering...the mother child bond is biologically determined and is the best basis for sustaining the long term trials and tribulations of parenthood...mothers' needs and children's needs are complementary and the father is not directly important, only indirectly as the protector and provider of the mother - child couplet.(p.35, Rapaport, Rapaport and Strelitz, 1977)

The view expressed by Justice L.J.Salmon, in H.v.H. and C., 1969 that:

> From the point of view of common sense and ordinary humanity, all things being equal the best place for any small child is with its mother (p.1202, Clarke Hall and Morrison on Children, 1972.)

sums up the continuing dominant ideological paradigm on parenting, and implicitly define lone father families as being lacking and deviant.

Roles and fathering

Whilst analysis and explanation can proceed with some degree of sophistication at the micro or the macro level, social science research is still uncomfortably deficient in relation to what Merton (1957) has termed 'theories of the middle range.' Thus, specific detailed analyses of the individual personalities and life situations of lone fathers are possible, as are more general analyses of structural processes such as race, class, and gender in society. The problem for social researchers is to attempt to tease out interconnections between these levels, whilst acknowledging that the

11

paradigmatic shift has not yet taken place to enable the complete outcome of this process.

With regard to lone fathers therefore, how might social research seek to make these connections? Symbolic interactionism, offers one way of bridging the gap between daily individual acts and the structural forces in society. Mead (1934) developed the idea of the social self, that human beings are self aware, and monitor their behaviour in relation to how they perceive they should act in given social situations with regard to how their behaviour will be perceived and received by others. Thus, society can be seen as systems of interlocking interactions based on social actors' perceptions and expectations of each other. Blumer (1969) has argued that symbolic interactionism is based on three premises:

1   that humans act towards things on the basis of the meanings the things have for them
2   that social interactions lead to the development of the meanings that such things have for humans
3   that the meanings are sustained or negotiated through an interactive interpretive process.

Whilst such an approach stresses the power of the individual to define their situations, and the potential diversity of social roles, it also implies that stability and continuity will exist in society as the result of socialisation into institutionalised roles, which, in the form of social processes, form the bridge between the micro and the macro. The concept of roles has also been developed significantly by Goffman, (1968, 1971) to include such ideas as role strain - when the role performances perceived appropriate by an individual are not complementary, and role distance - when an individual is 'in role' but wanting to distance their 'self' from the performance of the role.

The concept of roles is not however unproblematic, Weeks (1989) has argued that analysis underpinned by symbolic interactionism can have an ahistorical bias. Nevertheless, Connell (1987) notes three advantages in using role theory in relation to the analysis of gender

1   It moves research into considerations of social differences rather than being biologically determinist.
2   It provides a link between personality formation and social structure.
3   It provides opportunities for change and reform in gender power relations - if roles are not biologically given but socially constructed there is therefore scope for social reconstruction.

However, he argues that the idea of the socially provided 'role script' inappropriately synthesises discussion of gender roles around ideas of stability, conformity, and social custom. (and as such has echoes of Parsonian functionalism.)

It is clear that there is a distinction that can be made between gender and sex, the latter referring to the biological division between men and women, the former to the social and cultural divisions. It is thus sometimes assumed that 'sex' is an innate attribute and 'gender' a social attribute, however, sexual categorisation can be a product of social construction - for example, children are assigned to a particular sex at birth, sometimes on the basis of unclear physical 'evidence' (Oakley, 1982). With regard to such a division, the danger of role theory is that:

> For an account of power role analysis substitutes a theory of norms..reducing all masculinities and femininities to one dualism, sweeping all women into one feminine role, which in turn is equated to being a housewife and located in the family. Most sex role theory is not constructed around problems raised by field observation, but as analysis of a normative standard case.(p.51, Connell, 1987.)

In (rightly) making these criticisms of conservative role theory, Connell implies that social research from a symbolic interactionist / role theory perspective, with an awareness of the overarching gender power relations in society, could be most acceptable. In fact such an approach meets his requirements to:

> focus on what people do by way of constituting the social relations they live in..(and pay) attention to the structure of social relations as a condition of all practice. (p.62, Connell, 1987.)

With regard to role theory in relation to parenting roles there is a clearer 'shared definition' about what is involved in mothering as opposed to fathering. This means that lone fatherhood can be seen to be a form of crisis, lone fathers can be expected to have difficulties in defining and performing their roles for two main reasons. Firstly, because the role and responsibility of father does not comprise a distinct, agreed set of behaviours in the way that the role of mother does in two parent families, secondly because in the absence of the mother, the role and responsibilities of men in 'motherless' families is uncertain. Therefore, if being a father is, as Backett (1982) and others imply, problematic, being a lone father is likely to be doubly problematic.

A further element to be considered is the possible regional variation in gender roles in the United Kingdom. This study has taken place in the North East of England, in a region in which generally there is still a clear division of sex and gender roles, and strong perceptions of what it is appropriate for men and women to do socially. Writing of research that she did in Hartlepool in the 1980s, Morris found that:

> across an age band spanning from 18 to 60, and across a wide variety of occupations - though all working class - I found a remarkable adherence to ideas about gender identity characteristic of the area...the development of the local economy has been such as to encourage a rigid division of labour between the sexes. A supporting

ideology seems to have grown up alongside this division and indeed seems to have survived the economy upon which it was based. Ideas about the man as the 'natural' provider and about his employment having priority over the woman's , are still strong across all age ranges and for *both* sexes. (p.192, Morris, 1987.)

It could be anticipated then that for the men in this sample, their involvement with their children pre lone fatherhood would be likely to have fallen within what could perhaps be termed a 'paradigm of minimalist fathering.' In contrast, it would seem to be the case that lone fathers - having sole care and custody of their children would be unable to adopt such a minimalist position towards parenting. However, as will be shown, it seems to be the case that some fathers do prove able to adopt such a position using help and assistance from others in relation to child care and domestic duties.

The implications of such perspectives are that the more significant the mother is seen to be, the more tragic and problematic it becomes for families to lose the mother, much more so than to lose the father.

Lone fathers are, like all social actors, both seeking to assert a form of control over, and to derive a form of meaning from, their social situations and circumstances. The results of this study argue that such processes are linked to the positions of parents, and ideologies of parenting, in 20th century British society. They are also linked to issues connected with patriarchy and masculinity, and a full understanding of lone fatherhood necessitates discussion of these two areas. To consider these issues fully it is first necessary to consider the concept of crisis, to consider how far lone fatherhood can be seen as a period of crisis.

Lone fatherhood and crisis

How far therefore can lone fatherhood be seen as a form of crisis? 'Crisis' is defined by the Collins Dictionary as both:

> A crucial stage or turning point, especially in a sequence of events' and 'an unstable period, especially one of extreme trouble or danger. (p.299, 1989)

How far is it useful to see lone fatherhood as either or both of these things? Crisis theory and crisis intervention has a relatively recent history in the helping professions. Writing in 1970, Rapaport notes that concepts of crisis have been developed largely in relation to individuals or groups facing extreme situations, such as natural disasters, or war, or individual difficulties such as major disablement. Noting the largely psychological background to the development of crisis theory, she argues that a crisis occurs when an individual's coping capacities are not adequate to meet the demands posed by threatening events or circumstances. However, the threat posed by a crisis, by the disruption of the 'steady state', also

14

contains the possibilities of change to a different, potentially more desirable, future 'steady state' - a crisis contains both dangers and opportunities, as every prospective MBA is now taught.

On the personal level therefore, it might be that lone fatherhood could be seen as a crisis. Lone fathers can be seen as men who were in two parent families who have, through the crisis of death or divorce, come to be in single parent families. Having entered a state as a result of crisis the state of lone fatherhood might also be seen to an unstable period - given the importance of mothers and women in relation to childcare and domestic work generally, then households containing children and fathers but no mothers could a priori be seen to be households in crisis. In relation to this psychological level of crisis it cannot be assumed that the nature or the duration of the crisis of lone fatherhood is the same for all lone fathers.

Alongside the individual psychological notion of crisis, crisis also can be seen to have a wider structural meaning - in relation to gender; and in relation to the family as the fundamental institution ensuring stability and continuity in society.

Connell (1987) has noted that there has, particularly in the second half of the 20th century, been a general historical dynamic which has been centred on the notion that the family is in crisis - because of such inter-related factors as the changing position of women, the increasing incidence of divorce, and the perceived increasing incidence of juvenile crime. Because of this there have been those who have perceived that the stability of modern industrial society is threatened. The New Right position in particular advances this view, (Mount, 1982), a position echoed and overstated by Margaret Thatcher when she said:

> There is no such thing as society. There are individual men and women and there are families. (1.11.87.)

What however does this notion of crisis mean? Connell sees that underlying talk of the crisis of the family and the crisis for society is the threat to:

> the major pattern of sexual politics, the overall subordination of women by men (p.159, Connell, 1987)

In similar vein, with regard to gender relations, Brittan has written of the 'crisis of masculinity', noting how it is popularly seen that, not least because of the changing position of women, men's power is threatened and has been diminished, and men:

> have lost their collective nerve, their self assurance, their sense of certainty. They are 'uncertain' about their potency, their hetero-sexuality, their status-worthiness. (p. 183, Brittan, 1989.)

From this more structural perspective therefore the crisis of lone fatherhood can be seen as part of a threat to a 'steady state', a steady state in which women are subordinate to men, and in which women are seen to lack competence in the public sphere, and men are seen to lack competence in the private sphere. Such a reading of the situation is nevertheless an oversimplification, as it rests on an assumption that all men have a similar sense of collective identity, which cannot accommodate positively the challenges of lone fatherhood. If however one moves from the concept of masculinity to the concept of masculinities, then lone fatherhood as crisis becomes a possibility, not a certainty - in that different expressions of masculinities might be able to maximise the opportunities, rather than the dangers, of lone fatherhood. In considering these issues further it will be necessary to explore the notion of patriarchy, and of masculinities, in more detail.

The paradigm of patriarchy and masculinities

By definition, lone fatherhood is inevitably a gendered experience. Concepts such as sex and gender are common place elements of social life whose taken-for-grantedness in many social situations disguises their complexity, and their power. Gender has however only fairly recently become the subject of detailed sociological analysis. Thus, if one examines a much used 1960s sociology textbook, Cotgrove's 'The Science of Society' (1967), such subjects as 'gender', 'feminism', 'sex', and 'women' do not appear in the index. 'Introducing Sociology', edited by Peter Worsley in 1970, and reprinted 9 times in the following 6 years, makes a brief reference to the subjects of sex and gender, but statements such as:

> **Man**, in fact is the least biologically determined of all species because **he** possesses features absent in other natural species. (p.25, Worsley, 1970, emphasis not in original)

are typical of the unconscious gender blindness and sexism of sociology up to that, and earlier, periods.

Sociology textbooks of the 1980s and 1990s are no longer so crudely sexist or genderblind. Thus, appearing less than 20 years after the original edition, 'The New Introductory Sociology' (1987) lists all the above areas, and Worsley notes in the introduction that new chapters, including one on sex and gender, have been included:

> to reflect changes and debates on the world around us, within the sociological profession and more widely.(p.9, Worsley, 1987.)

However, it is interesting - and significant - to note that this latter book indexes women as a subject but does not index men. For many years sociology was at best gender blind, recently the explosion of feminist scholarship has highlighted and begun to detail the past and present

16

positions of women in society. Therefore, as has been pointed out by writers such as Morgan (1981), it is necessary to 'take gender seriously' by considering anew the position of men, because, as McKee and O'Brien have argued:

> social researchers now need to study men, not by equating man with human, but instead by recognising the gender content of men's personal experiences and relationships with women, other men, and children. (p.196, McKee and O'Brien, 1983.)

How then might this process be undertaken? The starting point for such a consideration of the issues concerned is with the concept of patriarchy.

Men and patriarchy

As indicated, lone fathers do not operate within households, work settings, and neighbourhoods without being influenced by wider structural processes. As men and as fathers they operate within a patriarchal context, and therefore the meaning of patriarchy needs to be considered. Much of feminist scholarship has been related to, and has explored, the concept of patriarchy, (a subject which is indexed in 'The New Introductory Sociology',1987, but not in 'Introducing Sociology',1970), focusing particularly, and understandably, on the implications of patriarchy for women.

Whilst there is not universal agreement about what is the 'best' definition of patriarchy, Morgan (1985) has argued that the beginning of a definition is to see patriarchy as being a system of male oppression of women. He notes that whilst there is considerable evidence that systematic gender inequalities have been the rule rather than the exception in past and present societies, the ways in which these inequalities have been 'elaborated' are diverse. In the simplest terms then, patriarchy is about male power, about the ways in which such power is exerted and exercised in explicit and implicit ways, as individual events and as a system of oppression.

As part of the process of deconstructing patriarchy, Brittan (1989) has noted that there are two differing theoretical views of patriarchy. The first perceives patriarchy as resulting from and being inextricably related to the existence of social classes, particularly under capitalism. Thus, the economic base generates a patriarchal superstructure. The second sees patriarchy as being inextricably linked with, and flowing from, biological differences, with men taking advantage of the 'sexual division of labour' to establish and buttress their patriarchal power. In both cases the result is the division of society on power and authority lines.

This latter point leads to a question that macro views of patriarchy do not necessarily answer, namely, do all males benefit from patriarchy at the expense of all females? Viewing patriarchy as being not simply about maleness, but about the interconnections of maleness and power, it is possible to argue that they do not, as gender is not the only structural factor related to power and powerlessness, oppression and being oppressed. Thus, the variables of for example, race, class, health or disability, age, and sexuality, intertwine with gender issues and patriarchal relations placing men and women in different hierarchical positions.

Patriarchy then is a complicated and multi-faceted system of oppression, that interlocks and interconnects with other systems of oppression. Acker has noted that the concept of patriarchy is both:

> essential and problematic in the development of feminist thought (p.235, Acker, 1989.)

'Feminist thought' has to be framed in a wider sense than simply meaning those theories relating to women and the impact of structure and process on women, for, as Kimmel has argued:

> Definitions of masculinity are historically reactive to changing definitions of femininity. (p.123, Kimmel, 1987.)

and consequently patriarchy has potential as a concept to explain and explore the position of men as well as the position of women. It would be incorrect to argue that the process of developing the use of patriarchy in this way has been completed, patriarchy as a concept has been developed both as a 'macro theory' (e.g. Firestone, 1974; Brownmiller, 1976; Rich, 1980; Delphy, 1984, Lerner, 1986.) and as a theory to give a general explanation of specific events and situations at a micro level - each of the preceding authors can use their particular theory of patriarchy to attempt to explain specific individual events of female oppression, but, in doing so theories of the middle range that link the general to the specific are somewhat underdeveloped.

Recently, Walby (1986,1989) has made a significant contribution to theorising patriarchy, in arguing that:

> there are six main patriarchal structures which together constitute a system of patriarchy. These are;
> 1) a patriarchal mode of production in which women's labour is expropriated by their husbands;
> 2) patriarchal relations within waged labour;
> 3) the patriarchal state;
> 4) male violence;
> 5) patriarchal relations in sexuality; and
> 6) patriarchal culture. (p.220, Walby, 1989.)

She goes on to argue that patriarchal practices occur within these different patriarchal structures, and is thus suggesting that patriarchy is not a homogeneous entity, but rather it is a series. of practices and structures that can be analysed and understood. The logic of this approach is that some men can be more powerful in a patriarchal sense than others, depending on the nature and extent of their different interactions with the different structures and practices of patriarchy.

Therefore, whilst all men benefit from the **system** of patriarchy, not all men are engaged equally in all six patriarchal structures. One example of this which relates directly to this study is that some are lone fathers and are not expropriating their wives' labour. However, as this study has shown, some lone fathers who do not expropriate their wives' labour, are, via the systems of kinship obligations able to use/expropriate other women's labour. To take another of Walby's structures, some men are unemployed and are thus not directly involved in the patriarchal relations of paid employment - although they may be indirectly involved, for example as the recipients of other's expectations that 'proper' men go out to work.

Whereas Walby argues for a definition of patriarchal structures in terms of social relations rather than spatially located sites, the results of this study of lone fathers would suggest that a model of patriarchal structures that more directly incorporates both elements - the social and the spatial - is a more theoretically fruitful way of understanding the meaning of patriarchy. Walby argues that household is:

> merely a concrete place, not a high level theoretical concept. (p.220, Walby, 1989.)

This study argues that the meaning of domestic relationships are such that they warrant consideration as a separate patriarchal structure. The indications from this research are that from a theoretical and analytical perspective, patriarchal structures are better understood as having the following divisions:

1   the patriarchal relations of the domestic setting
2   the patriarchal relations of the economic setting
3   the patriarchal relations of the community and neighbourhood
4   the patriarchal relations of sexuality
5   the patriarchal relations of the State
6   patriarchal culture

Throughout this study data generated in relation to these processes of patriarchy will be considered. The nature of the methodological approach has been such that more direct data has been obtained on the first four patriarchal structures, although indirect data has also been obtained on the last two structures and lone fathers lives.

Patriarchy and masculinities

Interacting with the concept of different structures of patriarchy is the concept of different masculinities - as developed primarily by writers such as Franklin (1984), Connell(1987), and Brittan (1989).

Connell argues that oversimplistic scalar divisions into 'male ' and 'female' are neither theoretically nor empirically satisfactory, and that:

> The notion of distinct unitary sexual characters for women and men has been decisively refuted. (p.170, Connell, 1987.)

He goes on to argue that:

> The next step is to recognise that qualitatively different types are produced within the same social setting. (p. 176, Connell, 1987.)

Connell points to the fact that there are differences between versions of masculinity and femininity at the level of daily interaction and at the level of the 'whole society':

> The organisation of gender on the very large scale must be more skeletal and simplified than the human relationships in face-to-face milieux. The forms of femininity and masculinity constituted at this level are stylised and impoverished. Their interrelation is centred on a single structural fact, the global dominance of men over women. This structural fact provides the main basis for relationships among men that define a hegemonic form of masculinity in the society as a whole. 'Hegemonic masculinity' is always constructed in relation to various subordinated masculinities as well as in relation to women. The interplay between different forms of masculinity is an important part of how a patriarchal social order works. (p.183, Connell, 1987.)

Related to the concept of hegemonic masculinity is the concept of 'emphasised femininity' - which emphasises sociability, fragility, compliance with men's desires, child care etc. - if 'Rocky' or 'Rambo' are archetypical of hegemonic masculinity then Barbie dolls and many female characters in t.v. soap operas are examples of emphasised feminity.

Connell's analysis is important in that it clarifies that, in terms of masculinity, there is unlikely to be one single 'type' of lone father that fits the daily practices and experiences of even a small sample of single parent fathers.

Another writer who has postulated different types of masculinities is Franklin (1984.) Brittan (1989) summarises his typology:

> First there is Classical Man..the male chauvinist par excellence who believes that men and women are not only different, but unequal as

20

well...Secondly there is Routinely Masculinist Man. This man acknowledges the possibility that gender difference may be unfair and to his advantage, but this is as far as it goes..Thirdly there is Anomic Man... They are constantly searching for certainty and stability in a world which seems to have no clearly demarcated role for the traditional 'masculine virtues.' ..Fourthly there is Humanist Man 'who has constructed for himself the goal of sex role equality.'(p.181-182, Brittan, 1989.)

Brittan notes that whilst this categorisation is useful it is not necessarily the case that the four categories outlined can be accepted as proven, particularly as the research evidence in this area is limited. It is argued from the data generated in this study that, rather than Franklin's four fold division, there are two distinctively different forms of masculinities operating in the different patriarchal settings - a traditional patriarchal form of masculinity and a gender pioneering form of masculinity. This supports the point that:

A number of masculinities coexist within a given social dynamic. Some men are coping with this dynamic others are not. (p.183, Brittan,1989.)

Morgan (1990) has suggested that such a theoretical framing of masculinities rather than masculinity is congruent with post-modern theories of the:

slow but steady crumbling of gendered certainties and the strongly anchored identities of 'man' and 'woman'...(which) would seem to be a first, and essential, move in the critical deconstruction of models of men and masculinity. (p.1, Morgan, 1990.)

In the light of these ideas it can be seen how lone fathers are in potentially ambiguous positions in relation to parenting, in relation to patriarchy, and in relation to masculinity. How then are these uncertainties resolved in day to day practice and experience by lone fathers? One of the major issues that emerged in this research was to try to generate a synthesis in relation to patriarchy and masculinity that was viable with regard to the theoretical material and the data from this study. This synthesis has been developed by adopting a theoretical stance which allows for the possibility of individual men having different practices of masculinity in different patriarchal systems. Thus a man might be 'traditionally patriarchal' in relation to his orientation to one sphere of social life - for example,the patriarchal relations of the economic setting, and non-traditional or pioneering in his orientation to another sphere of social life - the patriarchal relations of the domestic setting.

A major theoretical conclusion of this study therefore is that masculinities are more adequately theorised in terms of a continuum with traditional patriarchal masculinities at one end of the continuum, and pioneering, progressive masculinities at the other end of the continuum, with men's behaviour being at different points of the continuum in relation to the different structures of patriarchy involved. In first considering the data from this study a more static model of masculinities was initially developed, with the assumption that men were either patriarchs or pioneers of new gender roles, but such an approach was not sustainable in relation to the data generated on the complexities of the samples' lives.

The traditional patriarchal orientation

The traditional patriarchal orientation involves a traditional perspective and approach to gender roles inside and outside families and households. Thus Parsons argues that to be effective families needed to have:

> the roles of mothers and fathers clearly differentiated with the mother providing a context for warmth and emotionality within the home, while the father, as a breadwinner, saw to its economic security by his activities, especially economic, in the world outside the home. (p.145, McIntosh, 1987.)

As shown elsewhere, writers such as Rapaport, Rapaport and Strelitz (1977) argued that until recently the first expectations that people had towards parenting was that mothers were the central actors involved in parenting, with fathers being peripheral. They argue that whilst there have been progressive changes to enable various possibilities for families, it remains true nevertheless, that the distinctively patriarchal role is one which most fathers adopt.

This patriarchal role in fact involves the non-patriarch - the woman - taking on duties within the family which enables the man to both retain his power within, but be freed from the day to day responsibilities of, the family - particularly child care responsibilities. Thus the traditional patriarchal orientation involves the exercise of power within the family, and having authority over family members, without assuming full day to day responsibility for family life. The traditional patriarchal orientation to lone fatherhood then consists of continuing to be involved in full time paid employment whilst ensuring that some one else - a woman - assumes most, if not all, of the responsibility for caring for the children and household generally. Thus, traditional male parenting roles continue, as do traditional male roles outside the family, with the impact of lone fatherhood being minimised. Such an orientation to lone fatherhood stresses continuity of role performance, the accent is on minimising change, in the domestic, the recreational, and the occupational settings, and on recruiting substitutes for the ex-partner.

The pioneers of new gender roles orientation

The so-called New Man - who challenges traditional patriarchal male gender roles - has become a figure much cited in the media but rarely sighted elsewhere. (Morris, 1990, Segal, 1990.) The theoretical studies of

22

masculinity discussed above are important as theoretical studies, but are not based on substantial research evidence. However, it does appear to be the case that there are some expressions of masculinities in relation to some patriarchal structures that can be seen to be forms of pioneering gender orientations. This may occur in an explicit way as a result of choice, or the process may not be so explicit and may be almost accidental, Jackson has written of lone fathers:

> the man may have to cope with an atmosphere in which his decision and his lifestyle are sensed as odd and peculiar. Every man is familiar with the back bar jokes here; and yet single-parent fathers could be amongst the unwitting and often unlucky heralds of a new sense of future parenthood.(p.167, Jackson, 1982.)

Clearly such a process involves the lone father taking more responsibility for the day to day running of the household, prioritising domestic activities as a more central activity in his life. Thus, it almost inevitably involves the single father seeking and embracing change, not necessarily seeking to maximise domestic support networks to enable him to be more active in the occupational or recreational spheres. Whilst the patriarch may seek a female figure to 'fill the gap' left by the ex-partner, a pioneer may not seek such possibilities as a result of being positively orientated to filling such gaps himself. The patriarch will be likely to be keen to return to or continue in paid employment, the pioneer will be more likely to wish to do so only if it does not conflict with his domestic and child care responsibilities, and will be likely not to wish to 'work at any price.' Such men will also be likely to rate the experience of single fatherhood positively rather than negatively, even if it has coincided with a decline in their material standards of living, and a reduction in their recreational and leisure activities.

It is thus being argued that whilst all men are the beneficiaries and exponents of patriarchal power, masculinities are most appropriately theorised in relation to patriarchal - pioneering dimensions. It is not being argued that the individual lone fathers in this study have adopted a single orientation throughout their lone fatherhood careers - their lives, and the interconnections between masculinities, patriarchy, parenthood, and wider social circumstances, are too complicated to be reduced to such a simplistic model. However, in general, in the different spheres of their lives the ways that they have engaged with the demands of lone fatherhood can be described and understood in terms of these different orientations.

Having established this theoretical framework the prevalence of lone fathers in Britain will now be considered, following which there will be a review of the research literature on lone fathers.

The prevalence of lone parenthood

It is a popular view that British society has changed in terms of family life, from being a society where the majority of people lived in multi-generational extended families, with large numbers of dependant children, to a society where the vast majority live in households consisting of father, mother, and one or two children.

This view, like many such 'commonsense views', is a myth. As writers such as Laslett (1972) and Anderson (1983) have shown, it is unlikely that the extended family has ever been the dominant form of family type in Britain - Anderson estimates that extended 3 generational families comprised 6% of families in 1821, with a maximum reached of 15-20% in industrial northern (English) towns in the mid 19th century.

There have always been a variety of different types of households in British society, including 3 generational, 2 generational, 1 generational; with and without dependant or adult children, families with servants, families with lodgers. Single parent or lone parent families have also been an enduring part of the British household scene throughout history (Anderson, 1971, 1980, Laslett, 1977).

Single parent families are not, therefore, a new type of family form peculiar to mid to late 20th Century Britain. It has been calculated that in 1851 18% of children were being raised in single parent households. In 1972 8% of children were being raised in such households; by 1989 the figure had almost doubled and at 15% was close to the rate of nearly 150 years before. In Europe in 1989, only Denmark had a higher proportion of single parent households at 31%, Italy, Spain and Greece had the lowest proportions at 7%, 6%, and 5%.

If single parent households are not new, the causes of single parenthood have changed. Death was the great creator of such family types in the past century, divorce has become a major contributor this century. Anderson has written:

> of couples who married at the average age in the 1860s, around one in three had their marriages broken by death within 20 years (which)..is remarkably close to the death - plus - divorce expectations of couples marrying today. (p.143, Anderson, 1983.)

and Burgoyne, Ormod, Roger and Richards (1987) have noted how the proportion of 'broken marriages' in the 1820s and the 1980s is remarkably similar, 'Dombey and Son' may have been replaced by 'Kramer v. Kramer' but the households examined in both are not dissimilar.

The 1981 census shows that in Great Britain on census night there were 414,298 households in which a lone adult was living with children under 16, containing a total of 721,211 children; of which total there were

24

45,151 single male adults living with 75,905 children, 5,561 of whom were under the age of 5. The OPCS Monitor in commenting on these figures states:

> Most of the 414,298 households will be one parent families. But, the total number of one parent families in Great Britain may be over twice that figure - the rest being in households with other people aged 16 or over.(O.P.C.S. Monitor, 29.6.82.)

The 1991 census figures indicates an increase in the number of lone parent households with children under 16 resident to 825,238. Of these, 61,013 were lone father households, in which there were 98,292 children resident, 16,954 of whom were under the age of 5. Thus, in this decade, whilst lone father households have become a proportionally smaller segment of all lone parent households, in absolute terms the numbers have increased significantly.

This data illustrates the extent of lone parenthood and lone fatherhood in the U.K., a number of research studies in the U.K. and elsewhere have provided other data on lone fathers and their households.

Research literature on lone father families

There have been a number of studies of lone fathers families, in this section the key ones will be highlighted and briefly discussed.

United Kingdom research studies

Lone fathers appear to have not been a major focus for social science research prior to the 1970s. The first major British study of lone father families, undertaken by George and Wilding (1972), had a sample size of 588 lone fathers (281 widowed, 307 divorced / separated / others) collected from Family Allowance and Supplementary Benefits records, and Children's, Education, Health and Probation departments. The sample was interviewed using a structured interview schedule via a panel of interviewers. The researchers focused on problems associated with 'motherlessness', the fathers emotional and social adjustment, the fathers perceptions of their children's experiences, occupation and income, and relationships with social services agencies. They found that widowers tended to be older and to have been married longer than divorcees, and that widowers tended to be more emotionally upset and feel generally more negative about the experiences of lone fatherhood than divorcees. Working class fathers were more likely to be unemployed than middle class fathers, and fathers on Supplementary Benefit were worse off in relation to health, housing, and income than other fathers. Partly reflecting the period in which the study was undertaken, George and Wilding's theoretical orientation and discussion was related more explicitly to income support and social policy issues, and, like the majority of subsequent research studies of lone fathers, there was little discussion of issues of gender and patriarchy.

Hunt (1973) obtained data on 600 lone fathers as part of a wider O.P.C.S. study on households in 5 areas of the U.K. Using survey interviews by a panel of interviewers, Hunt concluded that lone fathers tended to be in a median position between two-parent and lone mother families. Working class families were the most materially disadvantaged, divorced and separated lone fathers in most cases felt their wives had 'deserted them', and lone fathers tended to have fewer leisure activities than married men.

Murch (1973) considered 30 of the 42 lone fathers referred to the Motherless Families Project in Bristol in one year (23 described as deserted, 6 widowed, 1 separated.) Analysis indicated that those seeking therapeutic help tended to have been deserted, that one third of the sample had to cease paid employment for child care reasons, and that the most common worries of lone fathers were, in descending order of frequency, how to find a housekeeper, how to negotiate their wives return, child care arrangements, and financial and custody issues.

Ferri (1976) researched lone fathers as a subsample of part of a larger study of lone parents. Drawing on a national sample of children born in a single week in 1963, part of the National Child Development Study consisted of an analysis of the longitudinal data with regard to lone parent families. Information was obtained on 237 lone fathers via structured interviews by health visitors, and educational and medical data on the children. A major methodological flaw of the research was:

> that no attempt could be made to evaluate the extent to which any substitute parent was fulfilling the role of the missing..mother. (p.35, Ferri, 1976.)

The study considered lone parents' financial, employment, housing, and social situations. It found that children from lone father families were more at risk of coming into care than children from other families; and that working class fathers were more materially disadvantaged (although motherless families tended to be less materially disadvantaged than fatherless families.)

Hipgrave (1978, 1981, 1982) considered the positions of lone father families based on his study of 16 lone fathers (12 divorced/separated - including 2 remarried - 2 widowed, 1 single.) obtained via advertisements and media requests. His in-depth structured interview considered social, emotional and financial issues. He noted that material disadvantage and downward social mobility were associated with lone parenthood in general (but not necessarily all his sample). His argument for a 'non-pathological orientation' to issues of lone parenthood, and for a consideration of gender issues contributed to his conclusion that:

26

the individual personal and interpersonal difficulties that lone fathers (and mothers) face in reconstituting a social and parental role for themselves are compounded by cultural variables that make this potentially difficult process of transition even more stressful.(p.183, Hipgrave, 1982)

O'Brien's study (1983, 1984) considered 59 lone fathers (with some comparisons with married fathers) drawn largely from single parent and single father organisations (65%), with the remainder coming via advertisements, personal contacts, schools, and welfare agencies. Her single structured interviews with lone fathers revealed that there was a diversity of routes into lone fatherhood. With an essentially social psychological perspective, developing Mendes' (1975) typology, she argued for a categorisation of lone fathers into 'hostile seekers' - those who fought for the custody of their children, often against their wives' wishes; 'passive acceptors' - those who had lone parenthood forced on them by their wives desertion; and 'conciliatory negotiators' - those who negotiated the transition to lone fatherhood. Her study found equal proportions of these three groups amongst lone fathers, and argued that the manner of becoming a lone father was very important to the subsequent experience of lone fatherhood. Whilst O'Brien's study sensitively explores to a limited extent micro gender issues, particularly in relation to cross -gender interviewing of lone fathers, her data is not used to explore in any depth theoretical issues of gender and patriarchy.

Millar (1989) analysed official data on the economic circumstances of 1890 lone parents including 41 lone fathers. She concluded that lone fathers tended to be less likely to be poor than lone mothers. Her research sensitively considers the gendered experience of lone mothers and finance, but due to a lack of detailed data she was unable to consider the corresponding gendered experiences of lone fathers.

North American and Australian research studies

In the first major American study of lone fathers, Mendes (1975, 1976a, 1976b) focused on 32 lone fathers (25 divorced/separated, 7 widowed) obtained via single parent organisations, and education and health services. Using a semi-structured in depth single interview method, she focused particularly on the psychological aspect of, and transitions into, lone fatherhood. On this basis she developed a typology of 'seekers' - who had a positive orientation to parenthood, and who had been proactive in the process of becoming lone fathers; and 'assenters' - who did not enjoy lone parenthood, and who had acceded to rather than initiated the process of becoming single parents. Unemployment and material disadvantage were only minor elements in her sample's lives; she argued that counselling opportunities and practical parenting education were necessary to enable lone fathers to adjust to their roles. Thus, whilst she considered gender issues, the discussion was largely focused on micro and practical issues rather than with more general and theoretical issues.

In a Canadian study, Todres (1975) researched 72 lone fathers (15 widowed, the remainder divorced, separated, or deserted) by means of structured interviews. The study, using a sample drawn from single parent groups and volunteers obtained via the media, concluded that financial problems and feelings of social stigma were the most frequent concerns.

Gasser and Taylor (1976) considered 40 American single fathers (25 divorced, 15 widowed, sample source unknown). Their data, obtained via a structured questionnaire, indicated that divorced lone fathers felt 'better adjusted' to lone fatherhood than widowers.

Orthner, Brown and Ferguson (1976, 1977, USA) considered 20 lone fathers (15 separated/divorced, 3 widowed, 2 single, sample source unknown). Using semi-structured interviews, they obtained data that indicated that most of the sample had become lone fathers because their ex-partners did not wish to have, or were unable to care for, their children. Despite this, the majority of the sample felt confident in their role as lone father.

Keshet and Rosenthal (1978, USA) drew on an 'upwardly mobile' sample of 128 separated and divorced lone fathers in their study (sample source unknown). Structured interviews by trained male interviewers were used, with a more detailed interview of a sub sample of 10. The results concluded that the initial period of lone fatherhood was experienced as stressful, and that having sole responsibility for children was perceived by most men as 'inappropriate, strange, and even frightening.' (p.12, 1978)

Bartz and Witcher (1978, USA) considered 34 divorced lone fathers using a sample drawn from single parent groups and schools (research method not stated). They found that the men felt they had been highly involved in child care prior to their divorces, that their relationships with their children had become closer since the divorce, and that for the majority of lone fathers kinsfolk were experienced as supportive.

Gersick (1979, USA) interviewed 20 divorced lone fathers in a sample drawn from court records of men who had been awarded custody. Comparison with a group of fathers who had not got custody of children indicated no pre-divorce differences in child care involvement, and no differences in sex-role orientation. Custodial lone fathers had had less harmonious divorce experiences than non-custodial, and tended to be older and more middle class.

In a comparison of interviews with 19 divorced lone fathers and 16 lone mothers with custody, drawn from single parent groups, Santrock and Warshak (1979, 1983, USA) found that fathers had higher incomes, greater support, and more contact with their ex-partners than mothers.

Katz's 1979 American study obtained data on 409 lone fathers (80% separated/divorced) by sending a postal questionnaire to members of a national single parent organisation. Half the respondents reported working fewer hours or becoming unemployed as a result of becoming lone fathers, problems with child care and finance were reported to have increased, friendships to have decreased, and kin were the main source of support.

Beattie and Viney (1980, Australia) administered a range of psychological tests to 49 lone fathers and 52 lone mothers who were members of a single parents association. Two patterns of coping emerged: positive - associated with increased self esteem, better relationships with children, and general coping, and passive - associated with negative self preoccupation. The former approach was particularly associated with accepting help and 'resignation' to the situation; the latter with 'renunciation of an active, positive approach to problems'.(1980, p.343) Lone fathers valued their situation in terms of the opportunities presented for activities outside the family, such as leisure and sexual relationships, lone mothers valued their personal growth more.

Tedder, Libbee, and Scherman (1981, USA) interviewed 9 lone fathers (obtained via media adverts) and offered subsequent group support. Areas of difficulties uncovered and worked on in the group were loneliness, practical problems with child care, and general knowledge about children.

Pichinto (1983, USA) reviewed the research literature and found that lone fathers were increasing in number in the USA. He concluded that lone fathers undergo severe personal stress when they adopt the role, this stress can be coupled with feelings of loss, anger, and depression. However, he argued that the research showed that men do tend to become able to cope effectively with and be confident in lone fatherhood, that lone fathers tend to have been actively involved in child care prior to marital separation, and that they tend to be 'stable, rather traditional, established men'. (p.229, 1983.)

Greif (1985, USA) obtained data on 1,136 lone fathers via a questionnaire in a national lone parents magazine. He found that fathers who reported adapting better to lone fatherhood tended not to have financial problems, to have been involved in housework and child care prior to lone fatherhood, to be satisfied with their child care arrangements, and to have ex-partners who were involved with their children on a regular basis.

It can thus be seen that previous research on lone fathers in the United Kingdom, North America, and Australia indicates a number of areas that would appear to be relevant for future research, and areas that do not appear to have been covered extensively or adequately in these previous studies.

In relation to sampling methods, it can be seen that the majority of previous studies can be criticised for having obtained samples potentially biased towards those lone fathers who were members of lone parent organisations and / or who were predisposed to respond to media advertisements and requests for subjects interested in being the focus of research. The fact that divorced and separated lone fathers rather than widowers have been the subject of the majority of previous studies may be related to this bias in sampling methods.

The main areas of focus in previous studies include:

- the routes into lone fatherhood, and the impact of the different causes of lone fatherhood
- relationships with ex-partners and their meaning for lone fathers and their households
- involvement with and relationships with children
- relationships with kinfolk (including support from kinfolk)
- friendship patterns and leisure activities
- employment, unemployment, and economic factors
- contacts with social welfare and other agencies
- lone fathers feelings about lone fatherhood.

It can thus be seen that there is a useful body of previous research on lone fathers, and the main areas considered important in previous studies are considered in this study. However, an analysis of previous studies indicates areas that have not been covered adequately, with the consequence that there are gaps in the research literature that this study will begin to fill. Lone fatherhood in many studies is seen to be problematic, and potentially pathological - although some studies, particularly Hipgrave,(1978) O'Brien, (1983) and Greif (1985) argue for a more non-judgemental, social scientific perspective on lone fatherhood. Whilst studies have considered psychological factors e.g. Beattie and Viney, (1980) and a minority, structural and social policy factors e.g. Millar, (1989) there has been an absence in recent studies of research which has attempted to incorporate an understanding of micro and macro issues, apart from some limited reference to social class membership. Paradoxically, whilst lone fathers are defined as a group by their gender, there is an underrepresentation in research studies of detailed consideration of gender and sexuality issues, particularly in relation to the meaning of lone fatherhood for understandings of masculinities, and the location of lone fathers within the patriarchal relations of society. This is a major drawback of many of these previous studies, because, as argued earlier, it is essential to an understanding of lone fathers positions to consider issues related to patriarchy and masculinities.

In conclusion, in this chapter it has been argued that lone fatherhood is not a modern development, and the incidence of lone parenthood and lone fatherhood has been explored. The idea of parenthood, of motherhood and fatherhood, has been examined, as has the concept of lone fatherhood and crisis, following which there has been a discussion of patriarchy. It has been argued that patriarchy can best be understood, and is most viable as a theoretical concept, as a series of different systems rather than as one system. This multiplicity also has been applied to the concept of masculinity, and it has been argued that it is more appropriate to talk of

30

masculinities rather than masculinity. It has been suggested that two particular forms of masculinities, patriarchal and pioneering, represent potentially different orientations adopted by lone fathers in their relations within the different structures of patriarchy. These areas and ideas will be explored and considered further throughout this study. Previous research studies on lone fathers have been considered. The next chapter will look more closely at the research design and methodology of this study.

Lone Fatherhood during the 1960s?

3 Research design and methodology

This research considers one small group of lone fathers, and uses the examples of their lives to highlight larger issues, specifically issues of masculinities, of patriarchy, and of parenting. There are many issues to consider in relation to research into single parent families headed by men has to confront, including the appropriate theoretical and methodological perspective to adopt, the choice of the most appropriate research design, and operationalising the research design.

In relation to theoretical and methodological perspectives, as has been shown, there is evidence from the research and theoretical literature that lone fathers are influenced by the micro experiences of their daily lives, and by the wider social and cultural context within which they are located. Clearly therefore a theoretical perspective and research methodology which enables the exploration and understanding of the micro and the macro is desirable. To achieve this, it is most appropriate to adopt, as I have argued, a symbolic interactionist/phenomenological perspective informed by an awareness of structural factors. The research design seeks to explore and understand the meaning of the events lone fathers in their social situations experience, and the ways in which lone fathers interpret and reflect upon their experience and construct social reality.(Becker, 1963, 1970, Berger and Luckman, 1967, Blumer, 1969, Goffman, 1971, Bogdan and Biklen, 1982) Such a perspective can as argued, effectively be combined with an appreciation and understanding of the power and influence of structural factors, particularly gender, patriarchy, and social class. An interactionist perspective can overlook or underestimate the influence of structural factors, a structural perspective can underestimate the ways in which individuals in similar structural situations can shape and experience their lives in different ways. (Giddens, 1989). In commenting on Backett's (1982) analysis of parental roles, Morgan (1985) has noted that whilst the different sets of interactions produced some differences in understandings and interpretations of parental roles, they also produced some similarities, indicating that humans' lives consist of:

A very complex set of interactions between the social structural, the ideological, and the historical on the one hand, and the immediate, the experienced, and the day to day on the other.(p.204, Morgan,1985)

- hence the desirability of research that seeks to be aware of, and take account of, both perspectives.

Therefore this research represents a merging of 'traditions' which are sometimes wrongly seen to be epistomologically mutually exclusive - interactionist and structural theoretical perspectives, and qualitative and quantitative research methods. A number of recent writers have implicitly or explicitly argued for the adoption of such an approach, recent work on households and gender roles by Morris (1990) and Wheelock (1990) has illustrated the trend - and the necessity - to consider both the micro and the macro in sociological research and analysis. In relation to sociological theory Giddens has argued for such an approach in writing that:

theoretical diversity rescues us from dogma. Human behaviour is complicated and many sided, and it is very unlikely that a single theoretical perspective could cover all of its aspects.(p.715, Giddens, 1989.)

In relation to research epistomologies and methodologies Bryman has suggested:

the association of quantitative and qualitative research with different epistemological positions is largely assumed. There is much to suggest that the assumption is questionable when the practice of social research is examined. For example, a good deal of qualitative research shares an empiricist streak with quantitative research; much quantitative research shares a concern for subjects interpretations, which is supposedly the province of the qualitative researcher.(p.173, Bryman, 1988.)

With this theoretical and methodological approach, how then were the lone fathers represented in this research studied? In relation to research design, a major problem highlighted by previous studies is that of gaining access to those to be studied, there is a fundamental problem of finding an appropriate (however that is defined) group of single parent fathers to investigate and research. The importance of sampling in the research process has been stressed:

as the ad hoc survey is used increasingly for highly focused studies of particular social groups or narrowly defined issues, procedures for identifying and sampling minority groups become an integral part of survey design. The term minority group is used here to refer to any target population for a survey that is relatively rare because it has very specific characteristics or experiences and constitutes only a

33

small proportion of the whole population (such as one parent families).(p.51, Hakim, 1987.)

Indications of the drawbacks in the sampling strategies employed in previous lone father studies have been illustrated in the previous discussions of the research literature on lone fathers. George and Wilding summarise the difficulties experienced in previous studies in writing:

> we had to accept the fact that we could never secure a sample which we could prove to be representative,owing to our ignorance about the incidence of motherlessness and the characteristics of motherlessness. So there was no way of knowing what a representative sample of such families would look like.(p.9, George and Wilding, 1972.)

As a way of resolving this problem, the strategy adopted by researchers has tended to be that of obtaining a sample by any method deemed to be appropriate and economical, and then trying to determine how representative or biased the sample might be in relation to,for example, the age and class distribution of the wider population. (Race has not been a dimension that has figured explicitly or implicitly in much of the research reported.)

It is clear that the research process is not a linear activity,the choice of a method and a sample are intertwined,each having implications for the other. Given the interactionist/structural perspective adopted, in this research it was felt that it would be desirable to obtain data that was both qualitative and quantitative,with this aim in mind there were then implications for the sampling strategy.

The search for an appropriate sample

In this research I wished to consider the experiences of men who were single fathers, that is, who had the caring responsibilities for at least one child of 16 years or younger, and who were resident in households where no adult women - kinfolk or non kinfolk - were resident.

How then could the sample for a study such as this be obtained, given the desire to have a representative sample of single fathers, and the absence of any exhaustive national or regional list of single fathers? Clearly, this was the major research problem, to try and gain access to a sample of lone fathers which would be as representative of the wider population of lone fathers as possible. It could be anticipated that samples with in-built biases would be obtained if they were constructed via advertising, or via trawling health, social welfare, or education agencies, or by using lone parent organisations to make contact. In sum, sampling appeared to be an insurmountable problem, other than resorting to the methods used in the studies described above, which have, as indicated, faults.

Analysis of the problem led to the conclusion that there was one form of universal social welfare benefit that would provide a means of obtaining a truly representative sample of lone fathers, namely child benefit records. The policy in relation to child benefit records at this time was to automatically name the female who has responsibility for the child in the records and on the benefit book. Therefore, it was probable that any child benefit records which only named a male parent, with no female named, would be likely to indicate a lone father.

At the time of this research, an additional weekly payment could be claimed by single parents who were widowed, or divorced, or separated from their spouse for more than 13 weeks. At the time of the research interviews lone parents who were in these categories and who had claimed this lone parent benefit received an additional £4 child benefit for each child. However, it was decided not to access the data via the records of those receiving the additional lone parent allowance as it was possible that not all lone parents would have made the claim for this additional allowance. (In fact, all the lone fathers interviewed were receiving this addition.)

It thus appeared that obtaining a sample via child benefits records where only a male adult's name appeared in the records had at least two main advantages:

1   Child benefit was a universal benefit paid to all social classes and sections of the population that have parental responsibility for a child, therefore it is not likely to lead to a sample biased in relation to social class or other structural variables.

2   Child benefit had a cash payment as its raison d'etre, therefore individuals were likely to claim it; and it was seen to be an acceptable, and not a stigmatising, benefit to receive. Thus, there is some evidence that even where other welfare benefits are not claimed child benefit will still be claimed (Community Care, 8.5.86, p.3.)

Consequently, obtaining a sample of lone fathers via child benefits records is likely to lead to a more representative sample of lone fathers than obtaining a sample via other sources or methods. Moser and Kalton, writing about sample design, say that:

two major principles underlie all sample design. the first is the desire to avoid bias in the selection procedure, the second broadly to achieve the maximum precision for a given outlay of resources.(p.79, Moser and Kalton, 1971.)

In researching lone fathers, the difficulties in obtaining samples has meant that the majority of previous studies have been understandably influenced by the 'outlay of resources' element, and have thus pragmatically 'built' samples which are then likely to be intrinsically biased. The sampling method of using Child Benefit records leads to bias being avoided as far as possible. Therefore, the sample used in this study, obtained as it was via this method, is probably the most representative sample of lone fathers in Britain of any used in social research.

Agreement to have access to child benefit records was given by the DHSS,(which has subsequently become the DSS) with the condition that only people who had been approached by them and given the chance not to take part in the project would subsequently have their names forwarded to me. A letter explaining the aims of the research and requesting an interview was constructed, which asked for help, and briefly outlined the aims of the research, as being 'finding out more about the day to day experiences of fathers in one parent families, as it seems that very little is known about this important and expanding group.' The letter stressed the confidentiality of the research, and the fact that whether or not the men decided to take part their benefit would not be affected. It indicated that it was hoped that taking part would be interesting for the lone fathers, and asked them to reply within 3 weeks to the DHSS in the s.a.e. if they did not wish to participate.

The men contacted by the DHSS were drawn from a random 3% sample of child benefit recipients in the North East of England, in the postal districts centred on Newcastle upon Tyne, Northumberland, Durham, and Sunderland. This led to a total of 179 cases in which child benefits records listed only a male parent. Following contact by the DHSS, 19 men replied to them indicating that they did not wish to be involved with the research. Information from the DHSS was made available in relation to only 4 of these - one man had indicated that he would wish to be involved but would not be available because of work, one man had indicated that he was in hospital and could not be involved, one man had indicated that he was busy moving house but would have happily filled in a postal questionnaire, and one man had indicated that he was 'upset' to be asked - for reasons unknown and unstated - and did not wish to be involved. 3 letters were returned via the Dead Letter Office - indicating that the men had moved house but had not had their child benefit records updated. Thus the total sample was reduced from 179 to 157 lone fathers.

It is impossible to know how far the 22 men who were not available or who indicated their unavailability were distinctly different from the 157 men remaining, as little data is available on them. The slim evidence of the 4 cases quoted above is that in 3 of the cases there were practical difficulties in the men being involved, and in the remaining case a personal objection. It is impossible to guess how far then the 157 men who were sampled were different from their 22 peers. However, previous studies of lone fathers have by their nature been based on much more unrepresentative samples, thus the likelihood is that the 157 men who remained represented a closer approximation to a random sample than the majority of previous studies of lone fathers.

Having obtained the sampling frame, a table of random numbers was then used to select names from the sample, and small groups of the men were contacted by individually letter to remind them of the research and to suggest a possible date for a visit. By this means a number of lone fathers were interviewed. After the passage of some six months following the DHSS letter, a follow up letter was sent to those who had been randomly sampled reminding them of the research and asking them to specify in which parts of the week it would be convenient for them to be interviewed. Overall, two men were not available for interviewing despite three visits to attempt to see them, and they were thus left out of the sample, and one man was not interviewed because by the time of the follow up visit his dependent child had passed the age of 16 and did not thus meet the sample criteria. Finally then, a total of 35 fathers were then interviewed over an 18 month period.

Ideally, the men would have been interviewed over a shorter time period. However, the limitations imposed by the availability of researcher time made that impossible, and it does not seem that the passage of time between the start and the end of the interviewing phase had any impact on the process or outcomes of the individual interviews. No significant changes occurred in the general position of lone fathers nationally or regionally during the period between the start and the finish of the interviewing phase - the entitlement to social security and other welfare benefits remained the same, employment levels remained relatively constant, and the general definitions of, and relations between, the genders remained relatively unchanging during this period.

The sample of men who were interviewed are described in detail in the appendix. In relation to the cause of their lone fatherhood, the sample comprised 16 widowers and 19 divorcees - the results of interviewing the first appropriate 35 randomly selected individuals. In comparison with previous studies this is a higher proportion of widowers - many previous lone father studies have, as indicated, ignored widowers, and have been unrepresentative of lone fathers generally as a result. As will be shown, the members of the sample tended to have had relatively little involvement in single parent organisations, which throws doubt on the methods used in previous studies of obtaining samples via lone parent organisations lists, as such a method of sampling would have excluded the majority of the men in this study from this research.

It needs to be stressed that the sample was an all white sample, thus it should not be assumed that the conclusions of this study can be generalised in relation to the experiences of members of ethnic minorities. Clearly there is a need in relation to social science theories and social work and social welfare practices to understand and consider the experiences of other than white individuals and households, not least because it can be argued that masculinity is not a homogenous concept, but is influenced and related to a variety of social factors including ethnicity (Morgan, 1987.) This study therefore is a contribution to understanding some of the issues connected to masculinity drawing on a sample that was white and 'able bodied', other studies are clearly necessary to consider the positions of those who are not in these categories. This sample nevertheless was obtained by a method which appears to have presented the best possible guarantee of non-bias in relation to those who were sampled. It thus appears to be the case that the sampling method used in this study has solved the problems of obtaining access to a representative sample of lone fathers that have bedevilled and defeated previous researchers, and the method used in this research has produced the most representative small sample of lone fathers yet studied.

The method of data collection

The aim of the method of data collection was to obtain reliable, detailed data about the past and present experiences of the lone fathers interviewed within the limitations imposed by resource constraints. As such, a reading of the literature on gender and parenting, and the previous studies of lone fathers indicated that it would be likely to be the case that those experiences would have been diverse, and that lone fathers situations would be likely to vary considerably. It was also the intention that data would be obtained about quantitative and qualitative variables, as defined by Smith:

> A qualitative variable is a nominal classification of types of things which can be differentiated as alike or unlike. On the other hand, a quantitative variable can be differentiated by degrees or levels of continuous connections.(p.54, Smith, 1981.)

To obtain detailed data on lone fathers face to face interviews appeared to be more appropriate than the use of a postal questionnaire; Moser and Kalton have written that the postal questionnaire is unsuitable:

> where the respondent is being asked difficult questions or where it is desirable to probe deeply or get the respondents talking.(p.260, Moser and Kalton, 1971.)

In contrast, interviewing lone fathers appeared to be more likely to be productive of detailed qualitative and quantitative data about the interactional and structural positions of lone fathers , particularly if the interviews were in-depth. Hakim has written that using this approach:

> Individuals are interviewed in sufficient detail for the results to be taken as true, complete, and believable reports of their views and experiences.(p.27, Hakim, 1987.)

In choosing to conduct depth interviews, I was keen to allow the lone fathers I interviewed the space and flexibility to describe what I anticipated could be their diverse current and previous situations, but at the same time to be able to ensure that there was some similarity in covering appropriate areas in respect of each lone father. Research literature (Denzin, 1978, Hakim, 1987, Kane, 1985) and previous studies (e.g. Ford, 1982, Oakley, 1974, Wheelock, 1990), suggest that such aims

38

are achievable using in depth structured single interview methods. As Weller and Kimball Romney have written:

> The usefulness of collecting systematic interview data from subjects has been recognised for many years..and can be expected to produce results that are reliable and valid. In the areas that the methods have been applied the results have been very gratifying.(p.84, Kimball, Romney, 1988.)

I thus decided to organise the data collection in the form of a structured interview based on a pre prepared interview schedule, and so obtain both qualitative and quantitative data. To achieve this aim my intention was to use the interview schedule as the basis for the interview, but to only make brief notes during the course of each interview, and to subsequently transcribe the responses to each interview on a blank interview schedule on the basis the notes I had made and the tape recordings of each interview.

The piloting and operationalising of this method and the designing of the interview schedule that acted as the focus of the interviews took place in four stages

1   Unstructured interviews with three lone fathers
2   Interviews using pilot interview schedule with three lone fathers
3   Revised interview schedule piloted again with two lone fathers
4   Final design of interview schedule used with sample of thirty five lone fathers.

The unstructured interviews and piloting of the interview schedule took place with lone fathers who lived in the north of England outside the area from which the DHSS drew their figures. These 6 lone fathers were obtained via personal contacts through a community association (4 men) and a voluntary organisation that dealt with families (2 men). therefore, these lone fathers did not represent a totally random selection, in that they were, or had been involved with community groups - although their involvement with these groups was only minor, and not as a result of them being defined as having any particular problems.

All the unstructured interviews, and four of the five pilot interviews were tape recorded (the 5th case chose the offered option of not having the interview taped.)

For the three unstructured interviews, apart from briefly explaining the the purpose of the research - to find out more about lone fathers - and the bounds of confidentiality, the interviews were totally unfocused. These unstructured interviews were then transcribed. Following consideration of the tape recordings and transcripts, and the literature search, a draft interview schedule was then devised and piloted in two further stages.

Aims of the interview schedule

What then was this interview schedule seeking to explore? The overall aim was to obtain qualitative and quantitative data about the past and current situations of the lone fathers and their households. Thus the men were not simply asked to describe their current situations, they were also asked to recount and reflect upon their previous experiences as men and as fathers.

The interview schedule was also designed to examine, explore, and obtain data on areas previous studies had indicated might be important:

1   The routes into lone fatherhood, and the impact of the different causes of lone fatherhood (particularly indicated as potentially important by George and Wilding, 1972, Mendes, 1975, Gasser and Taylor, 1976, Keshet and Rosenthal, 1978, Pichinto, 1983, O'Brien, 1983, 1984,)

2   Relationships with ex-partners and their meaning for lone fathers and their households (particularly indicated as potentially important by George and Wilding, 1972, Murch, 1973, Mendes, 1975, Orthner, Brown and Ferguson, 1976, Hipgrave, 1978, Gersick 1979, Beattie and Viney, 1980, O'Brien, 1983, 1984, Greif, 1985)

3   Involvement with and relationships with children (indicated as particularly important by all previous studies.)

4   Relationships with kinfolk, including support from kinfolk, (particularly indicated as potentially important by George and Wilding, 1972, Ferri, 1976, Bartz and Witcher, 1978, Santrock and Warshak, 1979, 1983, O'Brien, 1983, 1984, Greif, 1985)

5   Friendship patterns and leisure activities (particularly indicated as potentially important by George and Wilding, 1972, Hunt, 1973, Hipgrave, 1978, Katz, 1979, Beattie and Viney, 1980, Tedder, Libbee, and Scherman, 1981, O'Brien, 1983, 1984,)

6   Employment, unemployment, and economic factors (particularly indicated as potentially important by George and Wilding 1972, Hunt, 1973, Murch, 1973, Todres, 1975, Ferri, 1976, Hipgrave, 1978, Santrock and Warshack, 1979, O'Brien, 1983, 1984, Greif, 1985, Millar, 1989.)

7   Contacts with social welfare and other agencies (particularly indicated as potentially important by George and Wilding, 1972, Murch, 1973, Ferri, 1976, but not an area featuring in most other studies)

8   Lone fathers feelings about lone fatherhood, fatherhood, and gender roles (mentioned in most studies but not a major area of focus or consideration.)

One hypothesis was that the changes the men had experienced in becoming lone fathers would be perceived by them as difficult and the cause of stress. The interviews were therefore designed to obtain the lone fathers accounts of the transitions they had experienced - including such factors as the types of changes, the speed of the changes, and the extent to which they had felt actively or passively involved in these changes. Thus, the interview schedule was designed to explore the mens' accounts of the causes of lone fatherhood. It was anticipated that some lone fathers would have sought actively the role of single parents, others, via death or divorce, would have had the role 'thrust upon them' and might see themselves as the passive recipients of a set of social circumstances and obligations not of their choosing - of their being reactive rather than proactive.

Another hypothesis was that the absence of support networks and structures would be a cause of difficulties with regard to child care, parenting, and paid employment, and the presence of such supports would make child care, parenting, and paid employment less difficult for the lone fathers and their households. Therefore, the interview schedule was designed to obtain indications of the friends, relatives, and support networks available to and negotiated by each of the lone fathers.

The interview schedule was also designed to obtain information on lone fathers' relationships with their children, and their experiences of domestic labour, paid employment, and gender and parenting roles.

In relation to their children, data was sought on the lone fathers perceptions of such areas as their relationships with their children prior to their becoming lone fathers, their childrens' experiences of the transitions into lone father families, and a detailed exploration of the men's performances of a range of child care tasks during their period as lone fathers. Indications were also sought on the meaning of children to the men in the sample - for example, whether their perceptions of the value and demands of child care changed.

With regard to domestic labour, it was felt that possibly previous studies have tended to underestimate the potential importance of this area. The interviews were designed to examine the ways in which the men in the sample, men who were not living in a marriage or a similar intimate relationship, who had the care of dependant children, got housework done. However, as well as the interest and significance of exploring housework in the lone father families at a micro level, it was intended that the data generated in the interviews would also have a significance for more macro theories of gender and parenting, of masculinities and fathering.

The interview schedule was designed to enable the interviews to explore the sample's experiences of paid employment. It was felt important to consider the nature, meaning, and contradictions related to such employment because the sample were men **and** because they were single parents. Linked to this, information was also sought on the economic positions of the households.

Questions were also included about the nature and meaning of the relationships that lone fathers experienced with non-household members, in relation to six areas:

1   Kinship relationships - with close, and extended family members, to consider how far such relationships were gendered, how far such relationships were experienced as supportive by lone fathers.

2   Ex partner relationships - it was likely that some of the divorcees in the sample had continuing relationships with their ex-partners; previous studies had indicated the potential importance of such relationships.

3   Sexual relationships - probably some lone fathers would have, or had have, sexual relationships, and the interviews were designed to obtain information on the extent and nature of such relationships, and attempt to consider the meaning of such relationships for lone fathers. Like the other forms of relationships, the non existence of sexual relations might be as influential as the existence of sexual relations.

4   Friendship, acquaintance and leisure relationships. The existence or non existence of these, and any changes in the patterns of these, might, as previous studies have indicated, be influential for lone fathers.

5   Community relationships - it could be anticipated that community membership might be of significance in their lives, one area to be considered for example, was how far lone fathers perceived themselves as 'different' from the rest of their communities.

6   Relationships with professionals and/or members of state agencies, in relation to lone fatherhood. The interview schedule was designed to explore lone fathers relationships and involvement with social workers and other professionals, particularly representatives of the law, health, and voluntary sector welfare agencies.

The interview schedule was also designed to obtain information on lone fathers perceptions of gender and parenting roles, specifically the ways in which they perceived masculinities and femininities, and parenting. Information was sought about their particular experiences of these areas, and about the ideological views they held - their 'world views' in these areas.

The interview schedule was thus divided into a number of specific sections:

1   Name and Family details
2   Becoming a lone father
3   Current relationships with ex-partner (if alive)
4   The children
5   Children and local authority care
6   Support systems
7   Friendships
8   Home, neighbourhood, community
9   Child care and domestic labour
10   Employment and unemployment
11   Lone father - past and present
12   Experiences of social work
13   Nurseries/childminders/schools
14   Contact with other professionals
15   Gender views
16   Views of the world.

In the design of the interview schedule care was taken to try to ensure that the sequence of the questions was appropriate in that questions to do with particular areas of the lone fathers lives were grouped together, and that there was a logic ordering in the sequences of questions. Attempts were made to avoid jargon in questions, to only ask one question at a time, and to make the questions, and the focus of each particular question, as clear as possible.

Redesigning the interview schedule following piloting

Piloting of this interview schedule showed that whilst the areas covered were fruitful in obtaining data, a number of changes would lead to an improvement in the interview schedule. The primary ones were the reordering of the sequences of the questioning, the changing of the wording of some questions, and the omission and addition of certain questions.

One substantial area of questioning was added as a result of suggestions made during this piloting, that of lone fathers sexual relationships. At the end of the unstructured interviews, and at the end of the draft interview schedule, the lone fathers were asked if the interview had not covered any areas that they felt were of significance to them, and the area of sexuality and sexual relationships was one which was raised. Out of a misguided sense of sensitivity this area had been consciously omitted from the draft interview schedule, as such perhaps the initial design of the interview schedule reflected what Foucault has written on the history of sexuality:

Sexuality was carefully confined, it moved into the (modern) home. The conjugal family took custody of it and absorbed it into the serious function of reproduction. On the subject of sex, silence became the rule.(p.3, Foucault, 1976.)

The indication from the piloting was that silence should not be the rule in the study, the omission of sexuality and sexual relationships was rectified in the final version of the interview schedule and interesting data was consequently obtained.

Thus, the revised interview schedule was prepared. This interview schedule was piloted in two further interviews and appeared to be effective, with further minor revisions to the wording of one or two questions to make them clearer. It was then used in the 35 interviews that followed with lone fathers.

The intention of this interview schedule therefore was obtain quantitative data and qualitative data about the past and present experiences of lone fathers both within and outside their households. Although the aims of the study, and a commitment to confidentiality had been contained in the letters which negotiated access to the lone fathers, before the interview schedule was administered each interview began with a reminder that the research was concerned to find out more about lone fathers and their lives, that eventually publications would be produced, and a stressing of the commitment to confidentiality and the anonymising of the results. The lone fathers were then asked if they would give permission for the interviews being tape recorded, which all did. The interviews lasted between 1.5 and 5 hours, the latter being the only interview which did not take place in a single session, but took two sessions separated by three days. The average time per interview was slightly in excess of 2.5 hours.

Issues raised by the interviewing process

In the process of doing the research interviews a number of interesting methodological issues arose which themselves are products of this research and merit further consideration.

The research interview process - the need to start with 'safe' subjects?

Much conventional research wisdom would argue that it is better to focus on areas that might be threatening to the respondent later on in the process, when a rapport has been achieved. Stock Whitaker and Archer have written that:

> not all factual questions are non-threatening, as for example 'when did your husband leave you.' Such questions are best introduced in the middle part of the interview. (p. 53, Stock Whitaker & Archer, 1989.)

Whilst there is some merit in this argument, as the men being interviewed knew from the negotiations to arrange the interviews what the focus of the research was, it seemed in this case appropriate to focus on the area of the men's experiences of how they had become lone fathers at the start of the interview. It did appear that all the men interviewed welcomed the chance to talk about this important - to them - area early in the interview. It could be argued that not to ask such questions early in the interview might have indicated either that the interviewer was out of touch with the respondent, in asking less than relevant questions, or was saving tricky questions until later and was thus potentially building up anxiety in the mind of the respondents as they waited for the questions about the more 'sensitive' areas. It is also not clear what non-sensitive or non-threatening questions are; there are no a priori objectively non-threatening or non-sensitive questions. For example, if one was to start with questions about housing, which might be perceived to be a 'safe' area, one might be asking someone who was about to be evicted because their gambling debts had led to them fall behind in rent or mortgage payments.

Gender and interviewing

There were some common strands in the research process with each lone father: all the interviews took place in the men's own homes, all the men were interviewed by the same person, and the race and gender of the sample was the same as the race and gender of the interviewer (white, male.) Some writers (Morgan, 1981, McKee and O'Brien, 1981, Scott, 1984.) have indicated that gender is a variable that impacts on the research interview process. Finch has argued that:

> the effectiveness of in-depth interviewing techniques when used by women researchers to study other women is undoubtedly a great asset in creating sociological knowledge which encompasses and expresses the experience of women.(p.81, Finch, 1984.)

Whilst it is difficult to quote 'hard' evidence, the impression gained was that the men in the sample disclosed more information because they were being interviewed by another man than they would have had they been interviewed by a woman, and that this information 'encompasses and expresses' their experiences as men more effectively as a consequence. Warren (1988) has noted that in some social research contexts same gender interviewing will be likely to lead to more honest disclosures than cross gender interviewing, Cressey, whom she quotes, argues more firmly in relation to social research interviewing that:

> It may be said that the 'anonymous confessional relationship' is a monosexual grouping..such an anonymous confidential relationship may exist between a man and a woman, although perhaps less frequently and less completely. (p.110, Cressey, 1983, quoted on p.43, Warren, 1988.)

That is not to say that interviewer and interviewee were in a patriarchal male bonding process during the interviews, and it is also true that in

45

general men may have a greater taboo in relation to the expression of 'intimate details' than women. However, the fact that a man was interviewing the lone fathers meant that they appeared to feel less need to 'put on a front' than they would have felt if they had been interviewed by a woman. Thus I would not agree with Dingwall's advice that better results:

> are made more readily available to personable young women...particularly in studies of older men.(p.881, Dingwall, 1980.)

If a 'personable young woman' were to interview lone fathers the likelihood is that they would feel more influenced to present a picture of themselves congruent with hegemonic masculinity rather than them describing their own particular form of masculinity and fathering.

Child sexual abuse and research issue

The sexual abuse of children within families by male adults is more widespread than had been thought to be the case until recently. At the time of designing this research and doing the fieldwork one concern therefore was the ethical and moral one of what to do if child sexual abuse was disclosed by a lone father perpetrator? Although this dilemma was resolved in practice because in the event there was no indication in any of the families studied that child sexual abuse was occurring, or had occurred, the ethical and moral dilemma remains - what are the boundaries of confidentiality? Punch has written that:

> settings and respondents should not be identifiable in print, and that they should not suffer harm or embarrassment as a result of the research. (p.45, Punch, 1986.)

Polsky (1971) has argued that confidentiality should not be breached even if the researcher becomes aware of criminal acts. In general, the subjects of research are seen to be relatively powerless as a result of the research process, and thus an assurance of confidentiality is seen to be a means of not exploiting this position. However, in relation to this dilemma, the situation would be that in relative terms the victim of child sexual abuse would have been in an ever more powerless position than the perpetrator. One solution would be to encourage the perpetrator to seek help from some appropriate professional or agency, on the basis that the respondents confession was an indication that he wished to change his behaviour. However, if the perpetrator refused to seek such further involvement, or if the interviewer suspected that he would not, the dilemma would remain. Then, given that the interview had been arranged on the basis of confidentiality, it could be argued that one of two choices would remain for the researcher. The first position would be that one would be unable ethically to do other than keep to the agreement of confidentiality, the second would be that one would decide whether the right of the respondent to confidentiality was greater or lesser than the

46

right of children to be protected from abuse. Each researcher would then have to make a choice on the basis of the contextual position and their own ethical and moral codes. It can be seen that this dilemma illustrates clearly that social research is not a neutral, scientific activity, but is part of human activity and is consequently enmeshed in ethical and moral dilemmas.

The use of interviewee completed rating cards

Use was made during the research process of cards which the lone fathers completed to provide information. Card 1, which was based on the data collected by Rutter (1967), asked lone fathers to record any problems experienced by their children. The rating card was introduced with the supplementary verbal information that it indicated common children's problems and thus illustrated the type of thing that ordinary children might experience, thus attempting to give the lone fathers permission to rate their children's behaviours without feeling that recording of problems was an admission of failure. The card served three purposes, it enabled the lone fathers to interact more proactively with the interview process at this point, and thus enabled the tempo of the interview process to be varied. It also was a small step in empowering the respondents, enabling them to rate and classify their children's problems - if they felt they had any - rather than that rating being done by the interviewer on the basis of the information they provided. It would also have been much more time consuming for the card's contents to have been administered verbally. Cards 2 and 3 sought measures of lone fathers' involvement in domestic activities and child care pre and post lone fatherhood. The domestic labour activities replicated those considered by Oakley (1974) in her study of housewives, with the addition of the category of DIY; whilst this categorisation proved very productive it would perhaps have been interesting to have subdivided the category of cleaning to see if gender impacted differentially on such areas as hoovering and toilet cleaning. The child care rating activities card was designed by Oakley in relation to young children, with hindsight, given the presence of teenage children in some lone father households the card could have been redesigned to accommodate the recording of the potentially different kinds of child care arrangements such children present. Cards 4 & 5 were designed to explore the lone fathers likes and dislikes in relation to domestic and child care work, again, partially based on those explored in relation to housewives.

Did such instruments prove useful? In relation to research methodology, it might have been anticipated that these five research instruments might have proved problematic, in that they were relatively complicated cards involving literacy and numeracy skills. In fact, they proved to be highly successful, the vast majority of lone fathers were able to complete them unaided, and the handful which were completed by the lone fathers with the interviewer's assistance were nevertheless clearly reflecting the lone fathers own assessments and opinions. Obviously, the process by which the sample had been negotiated made it likely that all the sample would be

47

literate. Nevertheless, on the basis of experience in relation to this method of data collection and other sections of the interview schedule it is possible to argue that the 'keep it short and simple' school of research design methodology underestimates the intelligence and abilities of respondents. If samples consist of people stopped in the street by market researches soliciting their views about matters in which they have little personal interest or investment, clearly to collect data the instruments have to be 'short and simple'. If however, the research considers and explores areas in which respondents are interested and have a personal investment, then relatively complex and lengthy research processes can be perceived by the respondents as meaningful rather than meaningless. Thus, participatory research can be seen to be not simply one type of research process, perhaps effective participation can occur and be structured into research processes which are not traditionally seen to be participatory.

The meaning of the research process to the respondents

Was the research process experienced by the men involved as a one way process, as a giving of information by them with no returns? It has been argued that there are significant differences between the social work and the social research process. (Stock Whitaker and Archer, 1989.) Conversely, it has been argued that there are similarities in the process, and the concept of the social work researcher:practitioner has been discussed. Whilst the aim of this research was not to generate a therapeutic process, viewed from the perspective of the respondent, in fact, there were some indications that the experience of the research process was perceived by some men as being 'therapeutic'. Such an evaluation was typified by the comments of Kevin GG, case no. 33, who said at the end of the interview:

> I've really enjoyed talking to you, you talk to your family and so on but they're not always interested - talking to you has been letting out a part of myself that's been stuck.

Analysis and writing up

The data obtained during the research interviews was transcribed onto the interview schedules. To obtain measures of the quantitative aspects of the data, results were then categorised and coded, and analysed by means of SPSS-X. Whilst statistical manipulation of the data obtained from relatively small samples can be an exercise in mystification rather than demystification, this process proved very useful as one method of analysing the data, and care has been taken to try to ensure that statistical results are not presented in a form which is misleading. Given the small size of the sample the main methodology has been the use of descriptive statistical procedures of data analysis, and then the use of judgement to consider the implications that emerge from such processes. Such a method is supported by Hakim, who has indicated that social science research can be too concerned to seek out small, statistically significant, relationships between variables:

> Unfortunately the statistical significance of research findings (which is determined in large part by the size of the sample used in the study) is, quite wrongly, regularly confused and conflated with the substantive or practical importance of research results, which is a matter for judgement and cannot be determined mechanically by statistical procedures. (p.7, Hakim, 1987.)

The other main method of analysis was via reading, thinking about, and rereading, the interview schedules. Thus, general reading of the interview schedules led inductively to ideas about potential categories and concepts and themes which appeared to be recurring in relation to the areas explored. Care had to be carefully exercised in being scrupulous in ensuring that the categorisation and subcategorisation of variables was on the basis of the actual responses, rather than what the responses might hopefully have been to get 'better' results - and in this the availability of the tape recordings of the actual interviews proved invaluable in relation to checking responses.

The results were considered by subdivision of the sample by two different methods of categorisation, causes of lone fatherhood and expressed orientations towards gender role relationships.

A number of previous studies have indicated the possible significance of the cause of lone fatherhood - divorce or death - as being a major influence on routes into, and the subsequent careers of, the lone fathers. By analysing the data from this study in terms of this variable explorations of the extent to which the divorce from or the death of the partner led to different outcomes, was possible. Whilst, as will be shown, in relation to some areas the differences between the two groups were less than the differences within the two groups, there were ways in which the situations of divorcees and widowers were substantially different. Thus, divorcees potentially, and in most cases in practice, had to negotiate and sustain a relationship with their ex-partner, widowers had to find ways of coming to terms with the permanent absence of their ex-partner.

As well as considering the sample in relation to the major difference of the cause of lone fatherhood, there were also differences in the sample's responses in relation to orientations and practices in the areas of gender and parenthood. However, it was not a simple matter to interpret this data in ways which allowed categories to emerge, rather than imposing a categorisation. It was clear that at times some fathers were acting, and defining their lives, in ways which could be seen to be traditionally 'patriarchal' and others were acting, and defining their lives in ways which could be seen to represent a more 'pioneering' orientation towards gender and parenting. However, it was also clear that because such attitudes and practices varied for members of the sample in relation to the different spheres of their lives, it was necessary to accommodate this variation in any analytical division of the sample. The use of the terms 'traditional patriarchs' and 'gender pioneers' is intended to reflect differences in expressed attitudes, whilst it is not intended to indicate any value judgement in relation to members of one group or the other by the use of these terms, it has to be noted that my personal preference is for attitudes and actions that seek to reduce inequalities.

As indicated, the categorisation that emerged that was most congruent with the differences within the sample was into traditional patriarchs and gender pioneers. This division was done on the basis of the sample members' responses with respect to attitudes towards gender roles and parenting, particularly with regard to the interface between the patriarchal relations of the domestic setting and the patriarchal relations of the economic setting. These attitudes and orientations had been determined by four key questions in the interview schedule:

1   What opinions the respondent had in relation to women being better at child care than men.
2   Whether the respondent felt that women should stay at home for child care reasons and men engage in paid employment, or whether there should be equal choices.
3   Whether being a lone father had affected the respondent's attitudes to gender issues.
4   Whether they agreed with the general practice of custody orders being made in favour of mothers.

The two groups emerged when the responses to these questions were examined. Patriarchs felt that women were better child carers than men, that men should have priority in relation to going out to paid employment, their attitudes to gender roles had not been changed by their experiences as lone fathers, and they felt in general that mothers should have custody rather than fathers. Pioneers felt that both sexes could care for children effectively, that there should be equal opportunities with regard to going out to paid employment for mothers and fathers, their attitudes to gender roles had changed as a result of lone fatherhood towards greater empathy for women's disadvantaged position, and they favoured custody decisions being made on the basis of the best interests of the child. To illustrate the differences the following two examples are random choices from each category. Cary M, no 13, was typical of the 'pioneers':

1   I think it would be up to the individual, it would be up to the circumstances, I do think it's wrong that men are brought up not to show feelings or emotions, you're brought up to work for a living to support them and be the breadwinner, I think there's something wrong there.

2   Providing they can decide something between the two of them that's suitable, if they can talk it through and decide that's OK - you've got to share haven't you, not just workwise but kiddywise as well.

50

3   ...I've realised that I never showed feelings as much as I should have done, I've realised it since I got the kids on my own. If there was a sad film on t.v., the wife would cry, you felt like it as well, but you'd be taking the mick, it wasn't right to show emotions - stiff upper lip, I think its all wrong.

4   When the kiddies are young, you've got to decide for the kiddies, even though there might be a moral thing involved like adultery.

Kev N, no 14, expressed typical 'patriarch's' views:

1   I would totally agree, (women) have got that motherly instinct that I think most men lack, certainly with younger children.

2   I definitely think that the better role is the women looking after the children, I'm not saying that it couldn't work the other way round, but that wouldn't be the best arrangement, I think that women are more able to cope (with children at home.)

3   No.

4   I think that any case has got to be looked at on its merits but I think that children are better off with their mother.

The above two sets of responses indicate the typical differences with regard to gender roles and the division of labour between the genders as expressed by pioneers and patriarchs. Therefore, by analysing the responses to these four questions, it was possible to see which men perceived gender and parenting in terms of traditional patriarchal attitudes, and which men perceived gender and parenting in terms of more 'pioneering' and equal relations. However, further analysis of the data indicates that with regard to their day to day practices there were times when some pioneers were traditionally patriarchal, and there were times when some patriarchs were pioneering. Therefore, by adopting this categorisation based on the sample's attitudes towards gender roles it was possible in the analysis to illustrate the differences between members of the samples' ideological orientations and daily practices. This solved the problem of how to define the different groups whilst at the same time accommodating the fact that in many cases in many areas of their lives the 'patriarchs' were not homogeneously 'patriarchal' and the 'pioneers' were not homogeneously 'pioneering'. On this basis, the sample divided into 10 pioneers and 25 patriarchs. The pioneers consisted cases numbers 4, 6, 10, 13, 16, 19, 26, 28, 31, 32, five of whom were widowers (numbers 6, 10, 13, 31, and 32 - numbers relate to descriptions in appendix). Thus the patriarchs comprised a group of 14 divorcees and 11 widowers. It can be seen therefore that as a proportion of the total sample widowers were a slightly larger proportion of the pioneers subcategory and divorcees a slightly larger proportion of the patriarchs subcategory.

This chapter has suggested that the sample of lone fathers selected for this study, and the means of investigation, has led to results which give some indication of the experiences of lone fathers in the UK. It has suggested that two particular factors to consider are the causes of lone fatherhood and orientations to masculinities; the former will be considered in more detail in the next chapter.

4 Routes into lone fatherhood

In this chapter brief details of the sample of lone fathers researched will be given, following which the different routes into lone fatherhood experienced by the men in the sample interviewed will be examined. Amongst the sample, the routes into lone fatherhood differed substantially, and although the relationship was not a simple unilinear one, the ways in which men 'became' lone fathers had some connections with the ways in which they performed and defined their roles as 'being' lone fathers.

It can be argued that in late 20th Century Britain to become a lone father is to take on what is generally perceived to be an unusual role. It seems clear that girls are socialised into their potential future roles of mothers in more powerful ways than boys are socialised into their potential future roles of fathers (Rapaport, Rapaport, and Strelitz, 1977). The relative distinctiveness of motherhood as opposed to fatherhood has been argued by, amongst others, Backett, whose research led her to conclude that:

> analysis of respondents accounts of family life indicated that the development of the mother role was much less problematic than that of the father. This does not mean that motherhood was regarded as 'easy', it most certainly was not. However, motherhood was described as having certain special features, and these defined its parameters and made it distinctively different from fatherhood. (p.77, Backett, 1987.)

The relative absence of these parameters for fathers means that there were 'double definition' problems for those who became lone fathers - they did not have either a clear model of fatherhood to orientate themselves towards, or of the form of fatherhood that lone fatherhood represents.

Before considering issues related to routes into lone fatherhood, it will be helpful to be briefly consider the ages of the sample at the time of the research.

The mean age of the sample as a whole was 41.6 years at the time of the interview, and the median age was 41 years (Haskey (1989) calculated the OPCS sample's median age for lone fathers for 1985-1986 at 44 years.) The mean age of the widowers amongst the sample was five years older than this, whilst the mean age of the divorced /separated amongst the sample was 3.4 years younger. Therefore on average the widowers were over 7 years older than the divorced/separated group.

There was also an interesting age distribution within these two sub-groups of the sample, in that amongst the widowers 75% of them were aged more than 36 years, whilst only 53.6% of the divorced / separated were aged over 36. The mean age for lone fathers with a pioneering orientation to gender roles was 43 years, and for those with a traditional patriarchal orientation to gender roles 41 years.

What were the other time boundaries within which lone fathers were operating?

The age distribution of the men in the sample at the point at which their partner died or departed ranged from 24 years to 54 years, and the length of time children had been resident with lone fathers at the point of interview ranged from 1 year (in fact, one year and three days) to 10 years.

What can clearly be seen from these figures is the diversity of the situations which confronted the lone fathers at the point of the disruption in their family lives which created the potential lone fathering family situation. For example, Jake BB, no. 28 at the point of disruption was 49 years of age, and had the responsibility of caring for, or arranging the care of, six children between the ages of 9 and 17 years and 2 adult children. Clearly, the challenges and responsibilities created in the domestic situation would be expected to be somewhat different from those which faced lone fathers such as Kev O, case number 14, who at the point of disruption was a 29 year old with the responsibility for newly born twins, or number 33, who was at that point a 24 year old with a 2 year old daughter to care for. The following table indicates the ages of the lone fathers and the number of years children had been resident in the lone father households.

Table 4.1
Age of father and length of residence
of children in lone father household

Age at time of disruption		Age at interview	Years children resident
1	54	59	5
2	47	57	10
3	32	35	2.5
4	37	43	6
5	32	34	1.5
6	47	51	4
7	40	45	5
8	35	42	7
9	52	54	1.5
10	44	47	3
11	35	39	4
12	36	41	4.5
13	38	41	3
14	29	34	4.5
15	47	53	6
16	32	35	3
17	32	35	2.5
18	39	42	3
19	31	36	5
20	27	36	9
21	37	40	3
22	45	50	5
23	41	46	5
24	34	38	4
25	37	45	8
26	30	33	3
27	25	29	3.5
28	49	55	6
29	43	49	6
30	26	31	4.5
31	34	36	2.5
32	43	52	9
33	24	26	2
34	36	41	5
35	34	35	1

Difference in the sample between the experiences of the divorced, and the experiences of the widowed, were apparent in relation to the length of time the relationship with the ex-partner(usually a marriage, and hereafter termed marriage) had endured.

Table 4.2
Length of previous marriage - years

	Mean	Minimum	Maximum
Total Sample (35)	13.9	4	27
Widowers (16)	17.3	5	26
Divorced (19)	11.6	4	27
Patriarchs(25)	12.8	4	26
Pioneers(10)	17.25	9	27

Whilst the shortest and the longest relationships had been experienced by those who subsequently were divorced, overall, the widowers became lone fathers after relationships that were on average almost 6 years longer than the marriage relationships of their divorced counterparts. With reference to relationships of 20 years duration or longer the difference is quite marked - 46.2 % of the sample of widowers had had a marriage that lasted more than 20 years in contrast to 5.3% of the divorced lone fathers with similar duration marriages. In terms of change, looked at purely in relation to number of years, the widowed men were therefore becoming lone fathers after a longer period in a relationship than the divorced men. The pioneers, as can be seen from the data, perhaps surprisingly tended to have been married for a longer period of time than the patriarchs. The fact that all had been married at least 9 years appears to indicate a possible relationship between length of marriage and attitudes towards gender roles.

The sample interviewed was characterised by differences related to the suddenness or otherwise of the ending of the relationship with the mother of the children. The category of lone father is one which some men can enter at one clear identifiable point in time. One example from the sample of this was Roy F.(no.6). He described how his wife, who had had chest trouble for years, had suddenly had difficulty breathing. An ambulance was called, but she died on the way to hospital. As he said:

> I never expected anything like that to happen, there'd been no previous warnings.

In this example then his situation changed at a clearly definable and distinct point in time from being a man with a wife to being a lone father.

The contrast to the situation such as Roy F.'s where there was a sudden, enforced, assumption of the role of lone father were cases where a couple separated and a long process of negotiation between the partners led to the child or children gradually coming to live with the father. One example of this type of situation from the sample was Albert P.(no.16). He described a long process during which the marriage gradually 'broke down'. He and his wife were legally separated for two years after seven years of marriage. They then lived together again for two years, following which

56

he worked abroad for a year, which he described as being a solution to financial difficulties, and also a 'test for the marriage.' On his return he and his wife agreed that the marriage was over, and they were divorced the same year. During his year abroad and the year following the divorce his wife had custody of the two children of the marriage, however relationship difficulties between the two boys and their new stepfather led to the boys asking to go to live with their natural father, which they did following discussions between their parents. Mr.P. reported that during this lengthy process he had known all along that the children would end up living with him, and that was what he had wanted, when he had been living with them prior to the marriage breaking down:

> I was the one who always tucked them in at night, they regarded me as security.

The following table represents the differences in the sample in relation to their perception of the forewarning that they had that their marriage was to be terminated by death or permanent separation.

Table 4.3
Forewarning of death or divorce

	No Warning	1-4 wks	1-12 mnths	1 yr plus
Total Sample(35)	11	9	10	5
Widowers(16)	5	4	5	2
Divorced(19)	6	5	5	3
	No Warning	1-4 wks	1-12 mnths	1 yr plus
Patriarchs(25)	8	4	10	3
Pioneers(10)	3	5	0	2

It can be seen that a large minority of the sample had no forewarning of the event that was to lead to them becoming lone fathers, and over half the total sample had less than 1 months forewarning. This contrasts with the position of a small minority of the sample - 14.3% of the widowers and 15.8% of the divorced - who had more than 12 months forewarning of the event. The figures for widowers relate to the period of time involved when the men perceived that their partner's illness or condition was terminal. 5 of the divorced men reported one or more periods of separation from their partner prior to the final split up. Patriarchs and pioneers differed in that pioneers either had little forewarning or greater forewarning, whereas a large subgroup of patriarchs fell within the middle range.

It could have been possibly expected that those men who became lone fathers as a result of divorce would have more forewarning of their future status than those who became lone fathers as a result of death. However, the impression from this sample is that this is not always the case, the widower had sometimes a longer indication of what was going to happen than the 'abandoned' lone father. A typical example of this was Dennis Q.,no.17, who had known that his wife had had an affair earlier in their marriage, but believed that it had ended. He described how he came home from work one evening and to his surprise found a note to say that:

she was leaving and would contact me sometime

the two children of the marriage having already arrived home from school and seen the note.

An example of the former category was Fergus W, case no. 23, whose wife died of cancer which had started 5 years prior to her death. Although Mr. W was only certain that his wife was going to die a week before her death, the possibility of her death, and of his becoming a lone father, had been for five years:

the nagging thing at the back of one's mind, she'd had surgery originally and was told that if she didn't have a reoccurence within three years she should be O.K.; however it reoccurred shortly before the three year period, so she had further surgery then radiotherapy.

What ways are there in which the route into lone fatherhood can be usefully conceptualised? Previous writers have suggested that the lone father may be categorised as 'active' or 'passive' or 'joint deciders.' (Hart, 1976, Burgoyne and Clark, 1984.) These categories have hitherto been used in relation to divorcing partners, thus:

Hart contrasts 'active' and 'passive' roles in the process of separation, and argues that those who portray themselves as 'acted against', just over half or her respondents, were less likely to be prepared for the process of demarriage which followed than their more active counterparts.(p.55, Burgoyne and Clark, 1984.)

In using these categories in their study of stepfamilies Burgoyne and Clark argue that Hart's third category, the 'joint deciders' in practice are not really participants in a joint decision:

It would appear from our findings that it is the rhetoric, rather than the realisation, of 'civilised divorce' which has pervaded recent experience of marital dissolution.(p.56, Burgoyne & Clark, 1984)

However, when the lone fathers who were divorcees were asked about their memory of their involvement in the decision to separate, there were a number who saw themselves as 'joint deciders.'

Table 4.4
Involvement in divorce decision

	L.F.major decider	Joint decision	Ex-Partner major decider
All divorcees(19)	6	8	5
Patriarchs(13)	5	6	2
Pioneers(6)	1	2	3

Therefore, the perception of nearly half of the lone fathers in this sample was that they had been involved in a joint decision about the divorce, and had felt very much that they had been 'joint deciders'. Whilst it might have been anticipated that possibly pioneers would have been more likely than patriarchs to have been the major decision makers with regard to the divorce decision, this is not shown to be the case on the basis of these figures. Therefore, it does not appear that men who were less active in the divorce decision were likely to 'fall back on' traditional patriarchal orientations to gender roles, and those who were more active were more likely to adopt more progressive attitudes towards gender roles. This suggests that some previous studies of lone fathers (Mendes, 1975, O'Brien, 1983) have overestimated the extent to which the involvement in the initial cause of lone fatherhood can have an impact on the lone father's subsequent 'career'.

Joint decision did not necessarily mean that the children would be cared for initially by the father. In a typical case such as Max DD, no.30, he described how he and his wife split up amicably following the gradual deterioration of their relationship and 'lots of arguments'. She kept the children as that seemed 'natural' but when she asked him a year later to have the children he agreed. Albert P, no.16, represents another similar case in the sample, although his perception was that he had a high expectation that his children, cared for with his consent initially by their mother, would come to live with him at some point in the future.

Ungerson in her work on 'carers', albeit of adults caring for other adults, suggests that males who become carers do so against the odds:

> Thus, as far as caring is concerned, I suggest that the male life-cycle contains definite 'start-up' and 'cut-off' points oriented around paid work. Full time paid work almost always acts as a buffer between the social and the family circumstances of a man and his availability for caring...only women are apparently the appropriate people to combine caring with paid work and child care. (p.65, Ungerson, 1987.)

Clearly, the process of becoming a lone father is what Ungerson would call a 'gendered' experience. If there is a strand in current perceptions that holds that it seems inappropriate for men to work and be involved in caring, this applies to child care as much as the care of adults. Thus lone fathers are always in the position of potentially having their child care activities defined as being inappropriate because of their gender.

What of those lone fathers who were widowers? They were likely to have had different experiences in respect of the ending of the marriage, and the process leading up to it. For some, this meant that if a partner was ill for some weeks/months /years then the opportunity to do what has been termed 'worry work' and preliminary mourning existed in a way that it did not for those whose partner died suddenly and unexpectedly. Contrast the position of Trevor A. and Frank. B. Trevor A.(no.1) described how his wife collapsed suddenly after mentioning that she had pains in her legs, was admitted to hospital, and apart from two days at home after five weeks, was in hospital for the rest of the time until she died six weeks later. Although his wife had been dead for five years Mr.A still found it very painful to talk about her and was moved to tears in the interview by the memory of her. He described how her death was not something that he had talked about with his daughter then (when she was 10 years old) or subsequently:

We never talk about it, although I think about her a lot.

Frank.B (no.2) in comparison told how 2 years before her death his wife had had to have a mastectomy for breast cancer, and that 6 months before her death the consultant had told him that her illness was terminal. He described how in the 6 months before her death he had had to assume responsibility for the housework and childcare as is wife was so ill:

It was like serving an apprenticeship.

Nevertheless during this period he was also very worried and did not see how he would be able to cope after her death. However, when he did become a widower he was surprised that:

Things seemed to drop into place

and he said that he and his children quite often reminisce about the good times they had had with Mrs.B when she was alive.

In the case of Frank B. then, in the time prior to the loss of his wife he was able to actively engage in the process of beginning to come to terms with a future with his children and without his wife. Clearly this was not an easy process, as he said, he did not see how he was going to be able to cope. However, when the time came for him to have to cope, he was able to do so; as he described it, he had 'served his apprenticeship' and 'things dropped into place.' He, like a number of other widowers, was able to use the the opportunity of the forewarning of the death of the partner to respond actively towards planning for the future.

In relation to the patriarchal relations of the household to become a lone father, whatever the reason, involves travelling a route which involves loss. In so doing, how far is it appropriate to see the route into lone fatherhood as a route involving mourning for the lost partner?

It has been suggested that there are four stages through which a bereaved person has to progress to satisfactorily resolve the personal issues that arise from bereavement. These stages and the tasks involved in them have been characterised as follows by Kubler Ross (1970) and Worden (1983) amongst others.

Task One - To accept the reality of the loss

As all those in the sample had dependent children, the need to provide in some way for those children appears to have acted to minimise the extent to which any of the lone fathers could totally deny the loss of the partner to a prolonged extent. However, interestingly this need to accept the reality of the loss, and the pain that it involved, was tangentially referred to by some fathers who said how 'good' and 'supportive' and 'undemanding' the children were in the first few months after the loss.

It needs to be remembered that in the case of the widowers the first few months refers to the period immediately after the death of the mother, in the case of the divorced men the first few months refers to the first time when they cared for them, which was not always immediately after the separation or divorce.

Task 2 - To experience the pain of the grief, to enable the bereaved to begin to come to terms with the loss

The bereaved can seek to not experience the pain, and suppression or avoidance of the pain of the mourning was what happened in the case particularly of some of the widowers in the sample. Here well meaning and sympathetic relatives so cushioned the lone father in an envelope of protectiveness and support that the widower appeared unable to do the grief work necessary to get through this stage to the next stage. Trevor A.(No.1) was typical of a man in this category, a man whose grief was still very near to the surface five years after the death of his wife that he could not talk about her in the interview without crying.

Task 3 - To adjust to an environment in which the deceased is missing

This is clearly related to the position described in relation to tasks one and two, and the impact of such factors as the needs of the children, and the support of significant others such as relatives, can apply at this stage. Kubler Ross, in writing of the terminally ill patient's family, argues that:

> A husband's sense of loss may be even greater, since he may be less flexible or at least less used to concerning himself with matters of children, school, after school activities, meals and clothing. This sense of loss may appear as soon as the wife is bedridden or limited in her functioning. There may be a reversal of roles which is more

difficult to accept for a man than it is for a woman. Instead of being served he may be expected to serve.(p.140, Kubler Ross, 1970.)

In writing this she is clearly perceiving sex roles in the family on traditional lines, and is pointing to the difficulties of a 'Father' taking over a 'Mothers' role. As this research shows, the position for lone fathers - widowers and non-widowers - is more complicated than that. However, Kubler Ross is correct in characterising the period as one of transition and change, men do not usually become lone fathers at any one instant, but experience a route into lone fatherhood which usually begins before the death or departure of the female partner.

Task four - to withdraw emotional energy and reinvest it in another relationship

In the case of lone fathers, particularly those who previously had had little contact with their children, this relationship could be not necessarily a relationship with another partner but a relationship with their children, and both these areas will be explored in later chapters.

Worden (1983) makes the point that the resolution of the tasks of grieving is an active rather than a passive process; it may be then that there is a link here with the notions of active and passive in relation to divorce. Just as some men involved in separation and divorce can be, it is argued, characterised as active and passive, it seems that not only will the circumstances of the death of the partner present greater or lesser opportunities for active involvement in the process of death; but the lone fathers involved may, for a mixture of reasons to be explored elsewhere, be more inclined to subsequently adopt an active or a passive orientation towards the grieving process and the grief tasks.

However, in relation to the different structures of patriarchy and forms of masculinities discussed earlier, it can be seen that general notions of activity and passivity are too crude descriptions of what is a complicated social reality. Clearly, some of the lone fathers in the sample went through active and passive phases. However, this activity and passivity can be seen to have differed in different areas of their lives. Thus, later chapters will show the different involvements - active or passive - of lone fathers in such areas as the domestic setting, the economic setting, the community, and relationships of sexuality.

How did non widowers perceive the processes by which their relationships with their female partners had ended? For some of them, such as Dennis Q, no 17 mentioned above, the other party had clearly been the initiator, and he was the recipient of the results of her actions. In this case,when he tried to contact his wife at work the next day he eventually discovered that unknown to him she had arranged a transfer to another office over 100 miles away. He was still unable to contact her until she phoned him two weeks later to say that:

She had gone off with another man and didn't want to come back and wanted a divorce..I went to see her taking one of the children; when I saw her I knew that the marriage was over and agreed to divorce proceedings.

With hindsight he felt that he had never been able to really trust his wife since her previous affair, she'd suddenly instigated the break-up but:

perhaps it had been coming a long time.

Others had been more active in seeking a route out of a relationship and family situation that they were finding unsatisfactory, although this was not being done as part of some conscious reframing of masculinities and gender roles, but as part of a process of trying to improve matters on the micro level.

Whilst for all lone fathers the early part of their lone fatherhood was potentially difficult, the amount of support and assistance they received and that they felt they needed differed. Some felt that there was no help or support that they lacked, others that there were particular kinds of help that would have been useful in the first phase of lone fatherhood. The following table summarises their perceptions of this area.

Table 4.5
Areas in which help would have been
appreciated in 1st 6 months

	Personal	Children	Financial	Legal	General	None
Total Sample	5	6	5	1	3	14
Widowers(16)	3	3	0	1	2	6
Divorcees(19)	2	3	5	0	1	8
Patriarchs(25)	2	5	3	1	1	13
Pioneers(10)	3	1	2	0	2	1

It can be seen that the largest sub category was of those who did not feel there was any particular area of help that they lacked in the first 6 months. For some, this was an expression of their perception that they were coping adequately, such as Frank.B (No.2) who, as already mentioned, found the period before his wife's death was the most stressful, and that after she died things 'just slipped into place.' For others, this was an expression of the fact that things were difficult and problems existed, but that no one could do anything to resolve them. Problems that came into this category included such issues as coping with feelings about bereavement as described by Trevor A.(No.1) or problems to do with the perceived impossibility of combining child care and paid employment, as described by Jack H.(No.8)

The proportion of the sample that perceived that there were no areas of help missing in the first six months was a very similar one for both widowed and separated/divorced lone fathers. However, patriarchs were much more likely to be represented in this category than pioneers. Why might this have been the case? Perhaps it implies that the presence of assistance is more likely to lead to the continuance of a traditional form of masculinity, as it was part of an environment in which the steady state of patriarchal masculinity with regard to gender roles was maintained.

The next largest category was those lone fathers who perceived that they would have appreciated help to do with self/personal issues, or to do with issues connected with their children - a combined total for these two categories of 40% for the widowed, and and a somewhat lower proportion of 26.3% for the divorced. Although the numbers were small, it can be seen that pioneers were more frequently represented in this category than patriarchs with regard to self issues, but under represented with regard to help with children, which implies that they felt that they met the demands of their children but were struggling to meet their own needs.

The difference between the two sub groups of widowers and divorcees is more marked still in relation to financial issues, but less marked with regard to analysis in respect of patriarchal and pioneering orientations. Assistance with this area did not prove to be an issue for any of the widowers in the first six months, but it did for over a quarter of the divorced/separated. This would seem to be largely related to issues connected with negotiations with the ex partner regarding financial matters - an area in which widowers inevitably were not involved. It was also the case that some widowers' financial positions as lone fathers were made more secure by investment and insurance policies maturing on the death of their spouse, so relative to their divorcing counterparts their financial position was more secure and less troublesome.

It was suggested earlier that the routes into lone fatherhood might be understandable as being similar to the stages of the bereavement process, even where the cause of lone fatherhood was not death. However, as this brief analysis has shown, the experiences of this sample of lone fathers could not all be readily accommodated by such a framework. There are some difficulties in generalising with respect to routes into lone fatherhood, as the pictures that emerges from the data is a complicated one which does not lend itself to the creation of a simple pattern or patterns.

What are the implications from this data with regard to different orientations to masculinities? It has been argued that these orientations can differ with regard to the different structures of patriarchal relations, and detailed considerations of these follow this chapter. At this point however, it is appropriate to sketch some of the themes with regard to orientations to masculinities and routes into lone fatherhood that will be explored in the later chapters.

A traditional patriarchal orientation can be seen to have led to lone fathers giving primacy to their positions in the economic setting, whilst seeking to retain care and control of 'their' children as a means of continuing to assert quasi-ownership rights over children as property. Their responsibilities in the domestic setting - particularly in terms of child care - were likely to have led them to seek to continue to have authority over their children, but to transfer tending responsibility for them to a delegated other - often a female relative. It might be that there is logically a paradoxical tension between a patriarchal orientation and lone fatherhood, resulting inevitably in patriarchs ceasing to become lone fathers by entering into new marital, or quasi marital, relationships with women partners. However, as will be shown later, this did not necessarily prove to be the case, many lone fathers with patriarchal orientations to gender roles were not contemplating, or seeking, such outcomes.

In relation to routes into lone fatherhood it can be seen that pioneering lone fathers tended to have been confronted with more changes than patriarchs, they had on average been previously married five years longer than patriarchs. Pioneers were also more likely to perceive that they lacked assistance in the early stages of lone fatherhood, which implies that those lone fathers who felt that they did not lack help were more likely to be in a 'steady state' position, where a traditionally patriarchal orientation to masculinities was less likely to be self - evaluated and reconsidered. This suggestion is also supported by the consideration of the areas of need suggested by lone fathers - pioneers tended to perceive need with regard to self issues, patriarchs with regard to children and child care issues. A picture thus begins to emerge of crisis and need being an influence in changing and reconstructing masculinity, with a lack of crisis and presence of assistance possibly being more associated with the continuance of traditional patriarchal orientations to masculinities.

The pioneering orientation can also be seen to have been more associated with lone fathers giving primacy to their involvement in the domestic setting, seeing domestic responsibilities as occupying a more central position in their lives. Whilst this did not necessarily mean that such men refused assistance with regard to the domestic sphere, they appeared to have reached a position where they derived more satisfaction from their involvement in the domestic domain. Where a traditional patriarchal orientation meant that some lone fathers were keen to return to or remain active in the economic setting, the logic of a pioneering orientation was that such lone fathers were less keen to do so unless it did not conflict with their responsibilities in the domestic setting, and were not keen to 'work at any price.'

In this chapter the similarities and differences experienced by the sample of men interviewed in relation to their becoming lone fathers have been considered. It has been argued that the experience of the initial process of becoming a lone father is of some significance in shaping the longer term role of being a lone father, but is not an overridingly deterministic factor in relation to later experiences of lone fatherhood. The processes involved in coming to terms with the losses involved in becoming a lone father have been considered. Following this there has been a brief discussion of orientations to masculinities and routes into lone fatherhood, and it has been suggested that change and crisis may have been associated with changing orientations to masculinities.

This chapter has been a brief introduction to some of the themes connected with the domestic setting, the economic setting, the community and neighbourhood, and the state, which will be explored in the later chapters. This study has found that the day to day child care and domestic experiences of the sample were of major importance in their lives, these areas will be considered in the next chapters.

5 Relationships with children

A key area for all fathers, but particularly lone fathers, is that of their interactions with their children. This chapter will therefore consider lone fathers experiences of involvement with their children, and will consider the meaning of the data from this study in relation to parenting, masculinities, and patriarchy.

How many children were there resident in lone father households?

Table 5.1
Children living with lone fathers

No. of children	at interview date	when mother left/died
1	15 families	7 families
2	14 families	18 families
3	4 families	6 families
4 or more	2 families	4 families

The above table indicates that the overwhelming majority of lone father households at the point of interview contained two or less children. However, if one looks at the position in relation to the number of children in the households at the point at which the households came into being as lone father households, a slightly different picture emerges, with a larger number of households containing three or more children, and a much smaller number of households with only a single child present.

Similarly, an examination of the number of adult children living in the lone father households at the point of interview, and at the point at which the household became a lone father household, presents two slightly different snapshots of family composition, although the numbers of lone father households with no, one, two or three adult children present is very similar at both points in time. In general, the typical lone father household in this sample consisted of the father, with one or two dependent children

67

and no adult children in the household, either at the time of the creation of the lone father household or the time of the research.

Table 5.2
Adult children living with lone fathers

Number	at interview date	when mother left/died
0	27 families	26 families
1	5 families	4 families
2	2 families	4 families
3	1 family	1 family

The age range of the children being cared for by the lone fathers was considerable, both in terms of the current ages of the children, and their ages at the time when the lone fathers assumed the care of them. A simplistic view of child care sees that the younger the children are, the harder they are to parent and the more demanding is the parental role, and conversely, the older the children are the easier they are to parent. Whilst it is true that the physical caring or tending functions are greater for younger children it seems more appropriate to see parenting as presenting different challenges at each stage of the childrens lives, and it is misleading to assume that these challenges a priori become fewer and easier to meet as the children grow older.

In relation to lone fathers, the age and relative dependency of the children would seem in this sample to have had different impacts, with the relative greater dependency of younger children becoming a positive aspect of the lone fathers lives for gender pioneering fathers, and a negative aspect for traditional patriarchs. To a lesser extent, the greater independence and relative self sufficiency of older children became a positive aspect of the lone fathers lives for patriarchal fathers, and a negative aspect for gender pioneers. This can be seen as a process whereby men who attached greater importance to their interactions in the economic sphere of patriarchal relations rather than the domestic sphere perceived their parenting roles differently from those who invested more in the domestic setting.

Clearly then, parenting is not a simple response to a matrix of 'objective needs' that children present at different ages and stages. A number of factors influence the social construction of the perception of childrens needs and parenting. For example, work such as that of Newson, Newson, and Lewis (1982) indicates that gender differences between children - as well as between adults - are an important variable. Having noted an increase in fathers participation with their respective one year old children between 1959 and 1979, they suggest that:

> the distinction between parental roles, involving the comparative distancing of the father from his family, occurs much earlier than at eleven years, and not necessarily because he is out all day....our

material suggests that fathers' perceptions of their status as subsidiary caregivers persists throughout childhood, and that they continue to see themselves and be seen as less skilled than their wives at understanding their children's needs.(p.186, Newson, Newson, and Lewis, 1982.)

Table 5.3
Age & gender distribution of children
at point of family disruption

Age and Gender of children				Age of Adult children
	Female	Male		
1	10			18,23,25
2	5	10,13		21
3	11	5,7		
4	13	9		
5	5,7			
6	5,16			18,20
7	3,13	2,6		
8	9	7		
9	10			18
10		12		21,24
11	12,13	10		
12	7,11,15			
13	16	13,15		
14	0	0		
15	15	7,12,	12	22
16		10,12		
17		9,11		
18	10	12,14		
19	5,6			
20	2	3		
21	0.5			
22	9	6		
23	6	4		
24		3		
25	6,10			
26		8,9		
27		1,2		
28	9,11,13 14,16,17			22,24
29		10,16		18
30	5	6		
31	2	9		
32	4,5	8,10		
33	2			
34	7			
35		8, 4.		

Table 5.3 shows the age and gender distribution of the children in the sample at the point of their mother's death or departure. It can be seen that the majority of households contained at least one child under the age of 10 at that point; 12 contained children of both genders, 12 female only, and 11 male only.

What were the experiences of the men in this sample before they became lone fathers in respect of their involvement in the households? Two examples drawn from the sample illustrate how different were the levels of participation in this area. Jeff S, no. 19, had been extensively involved in domestic work and to a lesser extent child care, before he became a lone father. Thus he assessed that in the pre-lone fatherhood period he had done 100% of the house cleaning, cooking, washing up and DIY, and 95% of the household shopping. In relation to child care, in the periods when his wife had 'gone missing' prior to their split up, he had stayed at home and fulfilled all the domestic duties, when his wife was at home he calculated that he had taken 100% responsibility for their physical care, and had done 50% of the buying/mending their clothes and discussing their problems; 30% of the playing with them and taking them out; and 20% of the feeding of them. On this basis then, Jeff S can be seen to have been actively involved in 'fathering' his children prior to his becoming a lone father, and clearly being a father for him at that point involved much more than simply being active in the economic sector.

An indicative example from the sample of a father who was much less actively involved in the domestic setting prior to becoming a lone father was Dave C, no. 3. In contrast to Jeff S who assessed that in relation to domestic work he did 100% of 3 activities, and 95% of a 4th, Dave C assessed pre-lone fatherhood his highest level of participation was 50% in 2 activities (household shopping and ironing), with his only other involvement in domestic activities being to do 20% of the washing up. In relation to child care the only activity he scored himself as being involved in was in taking the children out, his contribution to which he assessed at 20%. On this basis then, Dave C. can be seen to have been not particularly actively involved in 'fathering' his children prior to his becoming a lone father, and clearly being a father for him at that point involved a role closer to the classic functionalist role of the father in the family.

At the point at which those interviewed in this sample became lone fathers, there were different ways in which they responded to the responsibilities of child care and the management of the household. In some lone father households, such as No 2, Frank B, and No.6, Roy F, the families contained older children at the point of lone fatherhood - a 21 year old in the former, and an 18 and a 20 year old in the latter. The existence of these older children in part enabled each of these men to negotiate a realignment of the family circumstances to enable them to continue in paid employment when they became lone fathers. Thus, Frank B said that following the death of his wife, no external unpaid help with child care was forthcoming, but because of the children's ages, and his

70

being able to switch to nightwork, it had been possible to manage without live in help - his sister had assisted by doing the ironing each week.

Other lone fathers negotiated external help with child care, amongst numerous examples in the sample were No. 10, Cliff J, and No.11, Matt K. In both of these cases the availability of help from family living nearby yet outside the household was negotiated by them and enabled them to continue in paid employment. Thus, Matt K described how his mother did the (clothes) washing every Wednesday, gave his two youngest children their midday meal and evening meal every weekday, and looked after the children during the school holidays. In relation to his assessment of the domestic work he did before and after lone fatherhood, he described how pre lone fatherhood he did no cooking, washing up or ironing, and he does none of these post lone fatherhood (those jobs being shared between his mother and daughters.) The share of washing clothes he did declined from 25% of the household total pre lone fatherhood to 0%. Only 2 categories rated had increased, house cleaning from 0% to 50% (shared with daughters and mother) and household shopping from 25% to 100%; one category, DIY, had remained constant at 100%. The help from outside the family, he said 'just happened, it just started' and overall he said that he felt that he did not lack any kind of help or assistance.

Cliff J described a similarly intensive supportive relationship with his parents, particularly his mother. However in his case the help had built up following an initial post widowhood 11 months when:

> I wanted to do everything myself.. I used to have a set routine..Saturday used to be the main shopping day of the week, and for things I wanted every day such as bread I used to leave a note for the eldest laddy, and he would get it, or anything he thought we needed. I baked tarts and had a go, I sought a bit advice off me mother and I think this is how she drifted in to help me, which I appreciated very much.

At the point of interview, some 3 years after the death of his wife, he described how this process had gradually increased and now:

> my mother's over every day, and she does everything, I'd be lost without her.

He was however ambivalent about this help, reflecting that:

> She comes and goes when she likes, she's knocked the routine to hell.

This was reflected in his rating of the proportion of domestic work that Cliff J did; before he was widowed he assessed that he did 10% of the cooking, washing up, and washing, none of the shopping, house cleaning and ironing, and 100% of the DIY. As indicated earlier, in the early stages of lone fatherhood he did approaching 100% of the domestic jobs,

71

at the point of interview his mother's (and to a lesser extent his father's) involvement was such that he rated his contribution at 0% for cleaning, household shopping, cooking, washing up, washing, and ironing, only in the area of DIY had he retained a similar level of activity, still doing 100%.

Thus, where Matt K had had an unchangingly low involvement in domestic work pre and post lone fatherhood, Cliff J had had a perhaps not unusually low level of such activity pre lone fatherhood, a high initial level post lone fatherhood, and then had entered a stage of a low level of such involvement. Clearly he felt this later stage was both positive and negative:

> Mum and Dad wanted to do it, I've started to depend on them a bit too much now actually.

He perceived however that they derived meaning from their involvement, the ambivalences of the situation for him were illustrated when he said he:

> Wouldn't want to change it, there's times you feel like it and say, I've got to make a stand, to do things on my own, but when you're working full time as well it's rather hard, and you don't want to hurt their feelings, so you tread lightly.

There were other lone fathers who were in households where the demands of the household were greater than the care resources of the household, and the lone fathers concerned were unable or unwilling to negotiate external assistance to meet those demands. One such case drawn from the sample was No. 8, Jack H, who had felt that when his wife had left him he had had 'no choice' but to give up work as a miner to look after the children, then aged 5 and 3. His mother had been going to look after the children whilst he was at work, but the 3 shift system he had to work had made this too inconvenient, and whilst his parents had been supportive in offering him advice, this support had not extended to practical assistance with child care or domestic work. His pre lone fatherhood share of the domestic work of the cleaning, shopping, washing up, washing and ironing he rated at 0% and cooking at 5%, post lone fatherhood he rated himself as doing 100% of the washing and cooking, 95% of the house cleaning, 90% of the shopping, and 25% of the washing up - his children doing the remaining proportions of these tasks. The impression was left from Mr H's responses when he was describing the household setting that he had felt a passive actor in the process, and felt he was in the situation as a result of the impacts of other's decisions. A somewhat different orientation was that shown by other lone fathers who had given up paid employment outside the home as a result of their inability to negotiate assistance, but who had been much more active in trying to negotiate an outcome, such as case no. 21. This lone father, Ivan U, was geographically isolated from any relatives, but had initially post widowhood been able to negotiate a child minding arrangement to allow him to continue work. However, in the long term this had proved impossible to sustain, yet he was continuing to seek ways in which he could combine child care, domestic responsibilities, and paid employment.

How far were orientations to masculinity related to the existence of assistance with child care? The following table illustrates the lone fathers' assessments of the help that they had at the point of the research in caring for their children.

Table 5.4
Current help with child care

| | Source of help | | | |
	Ex-Partner	Relative	Other	None
Total sample(35)	2	10	12	11
Divorcees(19)	2	5	8	4
Widowers(16)	-	5	4	7
Patriarchs(25)	1	7	9	8
Pioneers(10)	1	3	3	3

It can be seen from this table that in relation to assistance with child care a mixed picture emerges, with divorced and separated lone fathers being more likely to have a mixture of kinds of assistance with their children than widowed lone fathers, and widowed lone fathers being more likely to have no assistance in caring for their children than divorced/separated lone fathers. For patriarchs and pioneers the data indicates a spread across the range of categories. Whilst it might have been felt that patriarchal orientations would be more likely to be found in cases where help with child care was present, and pioneering orientations where such help was absent, these figures do not indicate that this was necessarily the case. However, further analysis of the data shows that patriarchs who received help with child care received a greater level of assistance than pioneers, and those patriarchs who received no help were generally those with the care of older, more self sufficient children.

Children's experiences of the transition to lone father households

The members of the sample were asked about their perceptions of the extent of their children's awareness of the potential onset of lone fatherhood. This varied considerably - in some situations it was impossible for the children to be prepared for an event such as the death of their mother, either because of the age of the children or the unexpectedness of the event - for example in case no. 14 the children's mother died immediately after childbirth. Table 5.5 indicates the lone fathers' responses.

Table 5.5
Children's awareness of possible household changes

	Expected	Not expected/too young
Total sample(35)	4	31
Widowers(16)	1	15
Divorcees(19)	3	16
Patriarchs(25)	2	23
Pioneers(10)	2	8

What is striking from the above table is that in the overwhelming majority of cases the lone fathers' perceptions were that their children did not expect the family disruption. Why might there have been this lack of awareness about what was likely to happen on the part of children? Some of them were not told because the lone fathers themselves did not know of the impending disruption, fathers whose wives unexpectedly left them typically said of the event 'it came out of the blue' and 'it was a complete shock'. Thus, the children were not prepared because the father did not know, and as the mother's decision to leave was either very sudden or had been planned secretly she also was unable to tell the children of her plans. The suddenness of some deaths also prevented the option of telling the children - 'her death was totally unexpected.'

Other children were not told because they were too young, which applied to both separations - 'they were only 3 and 4 at the time, they didn't know what was happening' and deaths - 'they were too young.' The social construction of the age at which children were perceived old enough to know varied, in one case a widower felt that in relation to his wife's death his 10 year old daughter 'definitely didn't expect it, although she knew her mother was ill she was very young.'In other cases it was perceived by the lone father that the children were too young to be allowed to know, even if this meant denying the known facts to them. Thus, one widower said:

> They never expected that they'd lose their mother, they asked me if she was going to die, some children at school told them 'your mummy's going to die', I told them she would get better.(Len E, no. 5, at that point the children were aged 7 and 5.)

Although the majority of lone fathers said their children did not expect the impending disruption, in discussing this area further some of them acknowledged that they felt that perhaps the children had what one referred to as an 'inkling'; for example one divorced lone father said of his wife's departure 'it all happened too quickly' - for the children to expect it; but then went on to comment that 'perhaps our previous break up might have forewarned them.' In relation to terminally ill mothers, it was perceived that some children:

knew their mother was ill, but didn't expect it (her death) to happen, she'd been bedridden for 6 months so they might have had some idea. (Frank B, no.2.)

Another father felt that his children might have expected their mother to leave

I wouldn't be surprised if they did (expect it) on some level, the eldest one had known about his mother's previous affair.(Dennis V, no.17.)

This perception that children might have guessed what was happening even where they had not been told directly also applied in some of the minority of cases where lone fathers felt that their children had expected the family disruption. In all the 3 cases where children were in families where parents divorced and the children were felt to have expected the disruption, the children were perceived to have known that their mother had had a boyfriend.

In some cases, whilst children were not perceived to have expected the disruption, they were told in the immediate period prior to the disruption. Thus, one father said:

She told them she was going to leave, and I told them - they'd known for a month or so that she had a boyfriend. (Al L, no.12)

Another father said:

There was a lot of arguments and shouting in the home, so I think that when I told them I was going to have to leave to get a divorce they were upset, but in a way they were relieved..they saw some sort of calm when I left.(John Y, no.25)

There was one example of a formal joint family discussion involving the children regarding the decision to separate - Jake BB, no.28, described how the (older) children were involved in the decision:

Things had been bad for a long time, but it all came to a head quickly. One Friday evening she summoned a family conference of those who were still at home, and asked if they thought she had a part to play in the family. They said no, so the following Monday she moved (out).

In this family the father perceived that the marital relationship had broken down some time previously, but for a mixture of reasons - for the sake of the children, because of the family business, and for reasons of religious conscience - the couple stayed together.

Older - adult or near adult - children were in some cases treated differently from younger children. In 2 cases adult children were told that their mother was terminally ill, and in 1 case a father perceived that his eldest adult daughter had known of his mother's affair before he had, because mother and daughter had shared the same social activity which had led to the affair.

There are a number of possible explanations for the different processes and outcomes in relation to the awareness or non awareness of the children of the family disruption that led to the lone father family. Clearly, in some cases the explanation is that the children did not expect the disruption because no one expected it - the sudden death of the mother. In other cases, it was an event which was unexpected to the father, and was being kept secret or was spontaneous by the mother - her sudden departure. The expression 'it came out of the blue' was used by both widowers and divorcees to describe the death or departure of their spouses and their children's consequent gaining knowledge of the event.

In other cases there seems to have been a decision made not to tell the children. Two categories emerge here, firstly, where the outcome was uncertain the children were not involved in that uncertainty - either to 'protect ' them, or as means by which the adults could maintain some sort of denial of the process that was occurring. This was also clearly likely in some cases where the dying person was not aware that their condition was terminal. Thus, where mothers were terminally ill, it was sometimes not clear to the father what the speed of the death would be, and to protect younger children they seem to have not been told that the condition was terminal; to have had their questions avoided; or in one case at least, answered wrongly. Such an approach also had a positive pay off for the father, in that it allowed him more possibility of denying the nature of his wife's condition. It also, in presenting a picture to the children of normality, to some extent ensured that the children did not make the additional demands that they might have done had they been aware of their mother's condition. Related to this is the social construction of the knowledge of death and dying in late 20th Century Britain, where children are perceived to need protecting wherever possible from knowledge of mortality. Walvin (1985) has noted that in Victorian times the death of others, including parents, was a relatively common childhood experience, as the 20th Century has progressed the decline in mortality rates has coincided with an inversely proportional increase in taboos in relation to death.

The second category that emerged from the data was one where the creation of a lone father household appeared more certain, but the parent(s) felt it was inappropriate to tell the children, usually because they perceived that the children were too young to know, or too young to understand. In some cases this may have been appropriate protection of young children, but there appears to have been no general agreement about the age at which children could, and should, be exposed to 'bad news'. Although the numbers involved are small, it is interesting that there does not appear to have been any case in the sample where sub-adolescent children were told that their mother was dying, thus not

76

offering them the chance to begin to come to terms with their mother's death until after the event.

As indicated, a minority of children were perceived by their fathers as knowing that their mother was likely to leave the home, in each case the perception was that the children were aware of 'another man'. However, it is not clear how far this awareness of a boyfriend was perceived by the children as being likely to lead to the ending of the marriage, or whether that is a mistaken adult construction of the children's perceptions.

The tendency to have knowledge increased with the age of the children. This could have been for one or more of three reasons, firstly, because it was harder to hide things from older children (arguments, the existence of boyfriends, the seriousness of an illness.) Secondly, the fathers' appeared to perceive that it was more legitimate for older children be told details of what was happening, in saying that some of their children were too young to know, they were in one sense implying that older or adult children were 'old enough' to know. The third reason for the tendency to tell older children involved the father using the older child as a confidant, to share the information, but also to share the burden of the knowledge and possibly fear about the future - this would seem to have been more likely to have been the case in relation to diagnoses of terminal illness, particularly where - as in at least two of the cases - the terminally ill person was not told the diagnosis.

Whether the death or departure of the mother was expected or unexpected, in most of these households a time came when the children of the household were having to get used to changed living circumstances. The following table indicates the extent to which the lone fathers talked with their children about these changes after their mother had left or died.

Table 5.6
Extent to which the lone father
talked with his children when
their mother left/died

	A lot/some	Hardly/not at all
All sample(35)	23	12
Divorcees(19)	13	6
Widowers(16)	10	6
Patriarchs(25)	16	9
Pioneers(10)	7	3

This table indicates that whilst in the majority of cases some dialogue took place with the children, in approximately a third of the cases the death or marital breakdown was discussed hardly at all or not at all. Similar percentages of patriarchs (64%) and pioneers (70%) talked with their children post disruption about the event. Thus, where the evidence was that the majority of children were not prepared prior to the disruption by discussion, the majority had the disruption discussed subsequently.

In considering the cases where no talking took place, reasons advanced by the lone fathers included the age of the children, clearly some of the children were at a pre verbal stage and could thus have been legitimately seen as 'too young'. As with preparing children for their mother's death however, too young for some fathers had a high upper age range, one father saying that he didn't talk to his 10 year old daughter about her mother's death as:

I felt it was better as she was that young.(Trevor A, no.1)

Other fathers left it up to their children to make sense of what had happened, one father who felt that his daughter had known of her mother's boyfriend said:

We never talked about it, the boy was too young and the girl could see what had happened. (Keith G, no.7.)

At that time the boy was 3 years old and the girl 4 years old, which suggests that even her understanding of events would be less than complete. Another father, left with children aged 3 and 2 years, said he didn't talk about his wife's departure as 'they never asked for her.'

Those fathers who only briefly discussed what had happened with their children said such things as 'I told them the bare details' or 'I told them a bit, they were too young.'

In contrast, some fathers remembered how they had spent a great deal of time explaining events to their children. One widower (Fergus W, no.23) whose wife had been ill for some years, remembered the day of his wife's death:

That was probably the most difficult thing, because I had to go round to school and pick them up. I told them that they'd known that their mother had been ill, and God decides when somebody lives or they don't, and that she was no longer in any of the pain that she had had for a long time.(girl of 8 and boy of 6 at the time.)

Another widower told how he hadn't wanted to talk about it with his children but 'you've got to, it shouldn't have happened you've got to get over it.'

'God' and 'Heaven' were concepts that were used by three other widowers to explain the death of their mother to children - 'I told them she'd gone to heaven', 'I told him she was in heaven, to help him overcome his grief', and, in a reply which acknowledged the difficulty of understanding how children experience events ' I told her her mother was in heaven, it's a funny age 5, you can't really tell what they are thinking.'

78

Where parents were separating such explanations were not an available option. The possible future relationship with both parents was consciously discussed with some children:

> I told them that Mummy and Daddy don't get on any more, and that we'd decided to live apart, but they could go and see her anytime they liked.(Jeff S, no.19)

In other cases the future was more uncertain

> They wanted to know where she had gone and if she was coming back, questions I didn't know the answers to.(Dennis Q, no.17)

This theme of the suddenness of the event was reflected in a minority of other respondents answers, as with James CC, case 29:

> They came home from school ready to go on holiday, when they came home we had to sit down around the table and explain it.(That his wife had decided to leave that day.)

Finally, in several households the children continued to live with, or moved with their mother at the point of family disruption, consequently the explanations and discussions were handled by her, with the fathers being uncertain about what was actually said.

There are several possible explanations for the differing discussions with children about the disruption that led to the household becoming a lone father household. Those who did not discuss at all with their children what had happened appear to have not done so because of the age of the children, or in some cases because they found the subject a painful one either to discuss with a child, for fear of upsetting the child, or for perhaps for themselves, for fear of upsetting themselves. Parental power enabled some parents to define children either as being too young, when another parent might have felt they were old enough to have more explained to them, or, old enough to know for themselves, when another parent might have felt that a child might benefit from further explanation. In both of these types of situation it would seem possible that the needs of the parents were the determining factors in the handling of the children.

Some fathers appear to have offered a minimal explanation to their children, either because they feared 'upsetting' the children by telling them too much (and again, possibly upsetting themselves) or because, they did not know what information to give their children. For the widowers, the problem of explaining the unexplainable - the death of the mother - could be partially resolved by recourse to religious, neo-mystical explanations; some of the separating fathers, particularly those who had been unexpectedly deserted by their wives, either tried to avoid or struggled to give to their children an explanation for something that they did not understand themselves.

One factor which might have been felt to have been likely to have influenced the extent to which fathers talked with their children was the forewarning that the father had had of the death or possible separation, as such a 'lead in ' period would allow the father to consider and rehearse his response in hypothetical future circumstances. This seems to have applied in some cases, but not others, some fathers who had had more forewarning of the disruption event, appear to have talked fully with their children, but some fathers for whom the event was unexpected talked more fully than other fathers for whom the event could have been more readily predicted.

Some fathers appear to have had a more child centred approach to the crisis than others, actively seeking to engage with their children at what they perceived was a difficult time for the children, rather than being unaware of the children's needs, or occupied by their own needs. As can be seen by the data in table 5.6, pioneers were more likely to have actively engaged with their children than patriarchs. This active position in relation to their children does not appear to have been confined to either widowers or future divorcees. Thus, one widower who typified this child centred approach said of his children:

> I sat them all down and had a good talk, told them they weren't going to be split up, even if it meant selling everything and going somewhere else.(Andy R, no.18),

A separating father remembered that:

> I always encouraged them to talk about it because I believe it made it easier for them.(Roy F, no.5)

In some families there appears to have been ongoing discussion of the family's experiences in respect of parenting and changes. For some families where divorce had occurred, the continuing relationship of the children with their mother and the demands and routines of access visits meant that the subject was an ongoing focus. Thus, one divorcee said of his children:

> They talk about her and see her often, I try to keep it amicable mostly for the kids - it doesn't solve any problems not being amicable.(Al L, no.12)

Another father had developed a similar attitude to the subject of the ex-partner slightly more reluctantly:

> The children mentioned her in the beginning, when they mentioned her I didn't want to know, I just used to say I wasn't interested, which I'm not, but it wasn't fair to them, so they talk openly now, nothing specific just general. (Cary M, no.13.)

In relation to widowers' households, frequent conversations about the deceased tended to be concerned with either nurturing a happy memory or coming to terms with the loss. The father not wanting to forget the dead appeared to be the source of some discussions, sometimes related to wanting to keep alive with growing children a memory of what their mother had been like:

> I always like to bring her mother up, but I don't dwell on it - I don't harp on about it but I like to bring her mother into conversations. I hope that when she gets older she'll ask what her mother was like.(Roy F, no.6).

This theme was also one cited by widowers in families where the deceased was mentioned sometimes but not frequently. Fathers talked about 'reminiscing about the good times', and in one family there was occasional watching of videos of family holidays, as the father commented:

> I've dragged this video camera around on holidays, which at the time was a great nuisance, but now we can enjoy happy times together.(Fergus W, no.23.)

In some families the passage of time had reduced the extent to which the subject was focused on, one widower commented that such discussions were:

> Very rare,it's very rare we bring it up now - it just dropped off.(Rick O, no.15.)

This was 6 years after the death of the mother. Another said:

> We used to have tears, it doesn't come up as much as it used to.(Matthew HH, no.34.)

5 years after the death of the mother.

Where divorce had occurred, the passage of time, linked with the custody issue mentioned earlier, for some families meant that the subject was less mentioned than it had been previously:

> Initially we had a lot of discussions, but after that the subject was barely mentioned, particularly after custody was sorted out.(James CC, no.29)

Other fathers described how they felt that their children had accepted the position and rarely if ever mentioned it to them.

In some cases however it appeared that the subject of the ex partner was not mentioned because it had come to be a taboo area of discussion. This taboo for some was because the grief process was still alive; one father, five years after the death of his wife, said:

> I think about it a lot, but we never talk about it.(Trevor A, no.1, who then burst into tears.)

Another widower said:

> It's on my mind nine-tenths of the time, but, with the bairn, I let him bring the subject up instead of me.(Kev N, no.14.)

Another widower, appearing to be possibly blocked in the grieving process, said:

> They never mention her, they've been down to the grave and things like that. I've never visited the grave, I've bought a headstone - some people put flowers on a grave every anniversary, I've just tried to forget it.(Tony V, no.22, 5 years after the death.)

Feelings of anger were more prominent in relation to divorced fathers talking - or not talking - with their children about the children's mothers. Sometimes this was seen to be anger on the children's part, one father commented that:

> My daughter refuses to talk about her, my son doesn't talk about it, and I don't like to as I think it affects his nerves.(Alan D, no.4.)

At other times it was anger on the part of the father:

> Sometimes it comes out in arguments -'well, your mother didn't love you because she's left'...then I tell him that I'll never leave him.(David C, no.17.)

Other fathers seemed to have perhaps positively dissuaded their children from raising the subject, one divorcee felt that his children had been:

> Pretty good not asking questions.(Keith G, no.7).

For another father, who had said that his children had been too young to tell when their mother ran away and where there had been no subsequent access or contact, the only time he recalled discussing the subject was 7 years after her departure. Then, 2 years before the point of interview:

> The girl saw a photograph of herself as a baby with her mother - I told her she'd run away, they just took it, they probably knew anyway.(Roy F, no. 6.)

It can thus be seen then that a range of different adaptations had been adopted by lone fathers in relation to discussing the past and the absent mother. There are a number of different possible reasons for this, and a number of factors that appear to have influenced the different outcomes.

As discussed, the age of the children was an important variable, but as well as what might be seen to be appropriate behaviour in relation to sharing information with children with regard to their chronological age and stages of development there were indications that the circumstances some lone fathers were in led them to 'infantilise' or 'adultise' their children with regard to discussing, or not discussing the absent mother with them.

The reason for the absence of the mother was influential on how the father subsequently acted towards the children in relation to the mother. If the mother had died, some fathers were then influenced in their relations with their children by their own feelings of grief, and for some these feelings appear to have remained relatively unresolved. Some children were thus in the position of not having expected their mother's death, and not being afforded opportunities within the household to discuss the death and make sense of their mother's absence in the immediate aftermath of their loss or in the longer term. For these children, the impression is gained that their mother's absence, and the reasons for it, became almost a taboo subject. It also appears to have been a taboo subject in some families where the father felt hurt and deserted by the mother's actions in leaving the family.

Why then did some fathers and their children appear more able to discuss the absent mother? In the case of widowers, the impression is gained that those who were able at an appropriate early opportunity to share their sense of loss with their children, and seek to begin to make sense of events, were able to proceed through a more appropriate process, ending at a point where the mother could be remembered fondly but not necessarily painfully. Such fathers appeared to have, in the handling of the bereavement crisis in relation to their children, been able to use appropriate opportunities to allow the children - and possibly also themselves - to work through their feelings and make the events meaningful.

Divorcees were obviously in a different position; for example in those lone father families created by divorce where there was no contact for the children with their mother there was no significant indication that fathers were working to keep the memory of the absent mother alive. However, in some cases the need, or desire, to establish an appropriate platform for access appears to have been a positive force, and, as with the widowers, some divorcees appear to have been more able to be child centred in a proactive way than others.

The impression is gained from the data that some children were in the position, whilst not having expected their mother's death or departure, of being given opportunities to discuss, and make sense of, their mothers absence both in the immediate aftermath of their loss, and in the longer term. The time since the disruption of the household was an important variable in relation to the extent to which the mother was discussed and the meaning of her absence explored. However, whilst it could be argued that the passage of time was necessary for feelings to be worked through and appropriate adjustments made, time of itself did not simply mean that this process occurred. In some households the passage of time did not seem to have led to an increased enabling of the children and father to discuss this area. Thus, to know that in two households where the wife has been dead for 5 years she was hardly mentioned at the time of the research does not indicate that a similar process had occurred in those 5 years. This sample indicates that in one such extensive discussions and searching for explanations would have taken place to reach a point where, 'we talk about it at odd times'. In the other, the subject may never have been fully discussed and a situation may have developed where the father can tearfully say in relation to talking to his child about the loss of her mother 'I think about it a lot but we never talk.' As indicated, there was some evidence from the data that 'never talking' was only associated with a traditional patriarchal orientation to masculinities, with gender pioneering lone fathers as a minimum at least discussing the subject occasionally. In relation to coming to terms with and making sense of loss and grief, there is some evidence from studies such as Wallerstein and Kelly's (1980, 1990) and Mitchell's (1982) that discussing the marital disruption is more helpful than not talking for children and adults alike. 'Not talking' about emotional areas might be congruent with images of hegemonic masculinity, but perhaps those traditionally patriarchally orientated lone fathers who interpreted their gender roles in such a manner were consequently robbing both their children and themselves of the opportunity to appropriately make sense of the household formation changes they had experienced.

Lone fathers involvements with child care

Some studies of lone fathers (Bartz and Witcher, 1978, Pichinto, 1983) have suggested that lone fathers were men who had been highly involved in child care prior to becoming lone fathers, how far was this the case with this sample? To explore this the men were asked a questions about their involvement in child care pre- and post lone fatherhood.

The following tables lists the % involvement in each of these seven areas first pre lone fatherhood and then at the time of the research. (N=32)

Table 5.7
Lone fathers involvement in child care tasks.(%)

		0	1-24	25-49	50-74	75-99	100	Mean
Feeding	Pre	15	5	6	5	1	0	21.6
	Now	12	0	0	3	0	14	75.4
Supervise	Pre	9	6	7	7	2	1	32.7
	Now	7	0	0	4	5	16	85.1
Play	Pre	9	4	8	7	2	2	40.6
	Now	11	2	1	4	3	11	66.8
Take out	Pre	6	6	6	9	3	2	43.1
	Now	10	1	0	9	3	9	67.9
Physical	Pre	15	3	5	7	1	1	29.1
Care	Now	17	1	1	3	3	7	52.7
Buy/mend	Pre	22	3	4	3	0	0	10.9
Clothes	Now	12	2	2	4	4	8	56.2
Discuss	Pre	17	3	1	10	0	1	24.4
Problems	Now	7	0	1	7	4	13	76.2

Divorcees		0	1-24	25-49	50-74	75-99	100	Mean
Feeding	Pre	6	2	4	4	1	0	30.3
	Now	9	0	0	2	1	5	75.4
Supervise	Pre	3	2	4	5	2	1	47.5
	Now	5	0	0	3	2	7	78.8
Play	Pre	4	0	5	5	1	2	53.8
	Now	7	2	1	3	1	3	49.6
Take out	Pre	3	2	4	5	2	1	47.0
	Now	7	1	0	6	1	2	50.0
Physical	Pre	7	0	3	5	1	1	44.5
Care	Now	11	1	0	2	2	1	39.5
Buy/mend	Pre	11	1	3	2	0	0	13.5
Clothes	Now	7	2	1	3	2	2	43.0
Discuss	Pre	8	1	7	0	0	1	33.5
Problems	Now	5	0	1	4	3	4	70.0

Widowers		0	1-24	25-49	50-74	75-99	100	Mean
Feeding	Pre	9	3	2	1	0	0	12.3
	Now	3	0	0	1	2	9	86.1
Supervise	Pre	6	4	3	2	0	0	16.9
	Now	2	0	0	1	3	9	91.5
Play	Pre	5	4	3	2	1	0	26.2
	Now	4	0	0	1	2	8	84.1
Take out	Pre	3	4	2	4	1	1	38.8
	Now	3	0	0	3	2	7	85.8
Physical	Pre	8	3	2	2	0	0	14.8
Care	Now	6	0	1	1	1	6	63.7
Buy/mend	Pre	11	2	1	1	0	0	7.9
Clothes	Now	5	0	1	1	2	6	70.4
Discuss	Pre	9	2	6	0	0	0	14.6
Problems	Now	2	0	0	3	1	9	82.1

As can be seen, the areas considered ranged from practical 'tending' tasks - feeding the children, physically caring for them (the examples given here were brushing their hair, changing their nappies), buying/mending their clothes; through recreational activities (playing with them, taking them out); to discussing their problems with them. It was felt that this represented a broad range of activities which overall would represent a reasonable measure of the fathers different levels of involvement at different stages. 32 of the 35 fathers were able to rate their involvement in this way, 3 felt unable to assess their involvement via this method, and they were not pressed to do so. In the case of another father, no.14, he had become a lone father at a point immediately after the birth of his children, thus all his pre lone fatherhood categories in this rating are 0%.

The data indicate a general yet variable increase in child are activities by the members of the sample, with fewer fathers doing 0% in four of the seven categories, and more fathers doing 100% in all seven of the categories.

Looking in more detail at the differences between child care in widowers and divorcees families, an interesting difference emerges. In five of the seven categories there was an increased number of divorcees rating themselves at 0% post as opposed to pre-fatherhood, whereas in none of the seven categories was there an increase in the numbers of widowers rating themselves at 0%. At the other end of the continuum of involvement, whilst the numbers of fathers scoring their involvement at 100% increased, or was the same, for both widowers and divorcees, the increase was much greater amongst the sample of widowers than the sample of divorcees - the average increase in numbers in the 100% band in each category pre and post fatherhood is 7.67 for the widowers in comparison with 2.71 for the divorcees.

The three categories in which the greatest changes occurred were those of feeding children, supervising children, and discussing the children's problems with them. For feeding the children, there was a reduction in the number of fathers doing 0% from 15 to 12, and an increase in the number of fathers doing 100% from 0 to 14. This overall number masks a difference between widowers and divorcees, the numbers of divorcees in the 0% group increased from 6 to 9, whereas the numbers of widowers in this 0% group decreased from 9 to 3; both subcategories showed an increase in the 100% rating group.

In relation to supervising children, there was a reduction in the numbers of fathers doing 0% from 9 to 7, and an increase in the numbers of fathers doing 100% from 1 to 16 - this is the category with the highest 100% rating by the lone fathers. Again, this overall number masks a difference between widowers and divorcees, the numbers of divorcees in the 0% group increased from 3 to 5, whereas the numbers of widowers in this 0% group decreased from 6 to 2; both subcategories showed an increase in the 100% rating group.

In relation to discussing the children's problems with them, there was a reduction in the numbers of fathers doing 0% from 17 to 7 - the biggest drop in the 0% rating in any of the categories - and an increase in the numbers of fathers doing 100% from 1 to 13. In this category there was not the difference noted between widowers and divorcees described above.

The category in which there appear to have been least changes is that of taking the children out, although there was an increase in the 100% rating group from 2 to 9, and an increase in the 0% group from 6 to 10, generally for the whole sample the changes appear to have been less than for other categories. Analysis of the mean % scores indicates interesting differences between the subsamples of divorcees and widowers, in every category the average percentage involvement of the widowers was lower pre lone fatherhood, and higher at the time of interview than was that of divorcees.

Generally change was greater for widowers than for divorcees. In five of the seven areas explored the widowers rated their contribution to the task as being at least 75% at the time of the interview, whereas in none of the seven areas involved was there such a high average rating for the divorcees. This contrasts with the pre lone fathering situations, where in five of the areas examined the widowers rated their average involvement as being less than 20%, in only one of the areas was there a similarly low rating on the part of the divorcees prior to the family disruption.

Interestingly, the two areas where this change was on average smallest for the widowers: taking the children out, and playing with the children, were also the two areas in which the involvement of the divorced fathers decreased post lone fatherhood. These are areas of interaction with children that are often seen to be the proper province of the father in 'typical' families, and the usual way in which a man 'helps' his wife in relation the care of the children. It thus seems that in some lone father households, the absence of a second partner does not mean that the father expands his previous role behaviour, but is forced to seek to curtail aspects of his previous fathering role to enable him to take on what could be termed the more essential 'mothering' tasks.

What picture emerges if the data regarding child care is analysed for the two groups of patriarchs and pioneers?

Table 5.8
Patriarchs involvement in child care tasks - % (n = 22)

		0	1-24	25-49	50-74	75-99	100	Mean
Feeding	Pre	10	3	5	3	1	0	20.2
	Now	8	0	0	3	2	9	72.7
Supervise	Pre	5	5	5	5	2	1	35.0
	Now	3	0	0	4	3	11	81.0
Play	Pre	4	4	6	6	0	2	38.9
	Now	7	2	0	3	2	8	66.7
Take out	Pre	3	5	2	8	2	2	44.3
	Now	6	1	0	6	2	7	70.5
Physical Care	Pre	10	3	4	4	1	0	23.7
	Now	8	2	2	2	2	6	50.9
Buy/mend Clothes	Pre	13	3	4	2	0	0	12.3
	Now	10	1	1	2	3	6	54.4
Discuss Problems	Pre	12	3	0	6	0	1	22.9
	Now	5	1	0	5	2	9	72.6

Table 5.9
Pioneers involvement in child care tasks - % (n = 10)

		0	1-24	25-49	50-74	75-99	100	Mean
Feeding	Pre	5	2	1	2	0	0	25.7
	Now	2	0	1	1	1	5	83.3
Supervise	Pre	5	1	2	2	0	0	26.4
	Now	3	0	0	0	2	5	96.4
Play	Pre	4	0	2	2	2	0	49.2
	Now	4	0	1	1	1	3	67.1
Take out	Pre	4	0	4	1	1	0	39.7
	Now	4	0	0	3	1	2	61.4
Physical Care	Pre	5	0	1	3	0	1	42.8
	Now	6	0	0	1	1	2	57.5
Buy/mend Clothes	Pre	9	0	0	1	0	0	7.1
	Now	3	1	1	2	1	2	60.7
Discuss Problems	Pre	5	0	1	4	0	0	28.1
	Now	1	0	2	1	2	4	85.0

It can be seen from these figures that the largest increases in mean scores for patriarchs were in the areas of feeding the children, and discussing their children's problems with them. The lowest mean increase was in the area of physical care of the children. For pioneers, during the lone father period there was a higher mean rating in every area of activity (in comparison with patriarchs) except for that of taking the children out, with the areas of most increase being those of supervising the children, and of discussing their problems with them. These figures appear to indicate that whilst for both groups the average level of involvement with their children increased, pioneers recorded a higher level of activity than patriarchs. Both groups increased their involvement in the area of discussing their children's problems with them, patriarchs involvement had increased considerably in the more traditionally paternal area of 'taking the children out', pioneers in the more traditionally maternal area of supervising the children.

The figures in relation to child care tasks are complicated, and represent adult child relationships in a variety of settings. Thus, the meanings of the figures cannot be conclusively established, but it is possible to consider some reasons for them.

There is evidence to support the hypothesis that in general lone fathers interactions and involvement with their children were greater than they had been in the pre-lone fathering state. The men in the sample were not intensively involved with their children prior to the family disruptions that led to the single parent households being established, thus the data from this sample tends to contradict the findings of Bartz and Witcher, 1978, and Pichinto, 1983, that they would have been. The data indicates that lone fathers were on average more involved with their children at the time of the research than they had been prior to becoming lone fathers, which supports the similar finding of George and Wilding, 1972. The biggest changes in involvement appear to have taken place for widowers rather than for divorcees. A possible explanation for this is to do with the transitions into the disruption of the family. In some families the worsening of the marital relationship led to the mother spending less time in the family home, thus drawing the father into more of the child care tasks, and in some cases the absences of the mother or the unavailability of employment for males led to the father not being at work or taking time off paid work to care for the children. In at least one case (no.19) where a wife went missing a lone father took time off work and took over the child care roles, and chose not to seek help from available relatives, because he wanted to keep his wife's absence hidden from family and friends. Thus, pride or machismo - a perception that his position was not congruent with images of hegemonic masculinity - rather than an active wish to provide child care led to his increased involvement with his children in the early stages of his marriages breakdown.

By contrast, the lesser involvement of widowers and of patriarchs is a reflection of their locating themselves within the paradigm of minimalist fathering, compounded for those men whose wives were terminally ill for some time prior to their death by a need or desire to focus on their wives needs, consequently having less time or energy to be involved with their children. Thus, in a divorcing family there is a sense in which at times the adults are seeking to 'deinvest' in each other, whereas in a family where a partner is dying the level of investment in the dying partner is likely to be increased rather than decreased by the other partner.

An alternative explanation for the lower rating of widowers than divorcees in relation to child care pre disruption is that whereas the actual involvement of the two groups might not have been in reality substantially different, with hindsight the widowers are viewing their ex wives' involvement as being even larger than it was, and/or the divorcees are viewing their ex wives' involvement as being even smaller than it was. Thus, widowers might be harking back to a 'golden age' prior to their wives deaths, and idealising the contribution of their wives, whereas for divorcees if there ever was a golden age then the process of separation and divorce for many of them would have led to the assessment that the metal was fool's gold.

However, in relation to child care the mother was still potentially available for her children in situations where divorce had occurred. This availability post disruption - in some cases - of the children's mother in divorced families is one explanation for some of the lower involvements in child care tasks on the part of the divorced lone fathers, with the mother fulfilling parts of the child care tasks.

The increasing age of the children is one explanation for some of the changes. Thus, as children grew older, they were generally perceived to be able to do more for themselves in relation to physical care, and were often seen to be able to entertain themselves. However, widowers appear to have on average defined their roles with their children in relation to child care tasks as demanding more time from them than do divorcees despite the increasing age of the children. Could a possible explanation be that widowers had responsibilities for different ages of children than divorcees, and were thus drawn into a different kind of involvement in child care tasks because of the consequent different needs of their children? Such an explanation presents certain problems however as it rests on a view of childrens needs as being biologically determined, rather than at least in large part socially negotiated and constructed. In this particular case the explanation also seems to be less likely to be plausible as if one examines the age of the youngest child in the households at the point of the creation of the lone father household and at the point of the research it can be seen that there were not in fact major differences between the widowers and the divorcees households in relation to age of the youngest child.

It can be seen that in all categories at the time of the creation of the lone father families there was a majority of households in which the youngest child was in the 5-10 years age range, and at the time of the research there was a majority of households in which the youngest child was in the 11-16 age range. This similarity in the sample in relation to the ages of the youngest child would seem to indicate that the apparent differences in involvement in relation to child care tasks of widowers and divorcees cannot be explained by the ages of the children alone.

Table 5.10

Table 5.10
Age in years of youngest child in households

	Widowers			Divorcees		
	0-4	5-10	11-16	0-4	5-10	11-16
Then	3	10	3	5	13	1
Now	3	5	9	1	6	12

	Patriarchs			Pioneers		
	0-4	5-10	11-16	0-4	5-10	11-16
Then	9	16	0	2	6	2
Now	3	8	14	1	2	7

Gender differences of children do not appear to be the cause of the differences in the changes charted in relation to child care tasks. It might - stereotypically - for example be felt that in families containing female children the girls would be able to be more self reliant in relation to child care. However, three quarters of the widowers families contained female children as opposed to slightly over half of the divorcees families.

Lone fathers' perceptions of their children's needs

How far were different levels of lone fathers' involvement in child care related to differences amongst the children? In relation to disabilities, four of the widowers were caring for children who had some form of disability compared with only one divorcee. In some cases the disability could be described as moderate, thus one father (Frank B, no 2), described how his child, who had diabetes, 'leads a full life apart from the injections', having six monthly hospital checkups. In other cases the disability was more serious, thus Dave C, no 3, described how his son, 10 at the time of the research, had become blind following an operation shortly after Mrs B's death. During this period Mr C had thus perceived himself as having two reasons for becoming intensively involved with his children:

> I took everything on myself, it was the only thing I could do to cope with the situation, if they'd gone to live with relatives I'd have never found my own feet and been dependent all the time,

and through what he now perceived as having inappropriate feelings towards his son

> I used to be very overprotective, but now I let him go out to play with the other kids.

Other children, whilst not having major disabilities, had received other than minor medical treatment whilst being cared for by the lone fathers. Again however this was only a minority of children - three in divorcees families and four in widowers families. For the widowers' children this treatment was for physical conditions, whereas in two of the divorcees families a child had been seen by the child guidance services, one for 'general nerves', another because of excessive nocturnal enuresis. In another family the children, whilst being cared for by their mother following the separation were seen regularly by an educational psychologist because of worries about their progress (John Y, no.25), which worries had disappeared when the children had begun to be cared for by their father.

As indicated in the previous chapter, the sample were asked about any kinds of difficulties they had experienced in relation to child care in the first few months of the lone father households, their responses are summarised below. ('Troublesome' and 'upset' and 'good' and 'no problem' were separate categories which have been merged for this table):

Table 5.11
Children's behaviour in first
three months of lone father's care

	Troublesome/upset	Good/no problem	As usual
Total sample(35)	12	15	8
Divorcees(19)	8	7	4
Widowers(16)	4	8	4
Patriarchs(25)	7	14	4
Pioneers(10)	5	1	4

The most common assessment of children during this first three months stage was that they were 'no problem' or 'good'. However, patriarchally orientated lone fathers were much more likely to have formed the 'no problem' or 'good' assessment than lone fathers with pioneering orientations. 5 men rated their children as 'upset', where men rated the children's behaviour as troublesome both ratings were given by traditional patriarchs. This appears to indicate that some patriarchally orientated lone fathers were less aware of the complexities of the demands of child care in the domestic setting than were pioneers.

Based upon studies done by Rutter (1967) on common childhood problems, the children in the sample were rated by their fathers in relation to the existence at a moderate or serious level of problems in 14 areas,(with the option of them designating additional problem areas):

1   Bedwetting
2   Poor concentration
3   Sleep difficulties
4   Restless activities
5   Shyness
6   Nervous habits
7   Aggression
8   Clinging behaviour
9   Poor speech
10   Insistent demands for attention
11   Lying
12   Stealing from home
13   Stealing outside home
14   Temper tantrums.

Fathers were given a card in respect of each of their children, and asked to tick the relevant rating for each category area, based on their definition of none, moderate or serious.

Table 5.12
Fathers perceptions of childrens problems
- all children, N=59

	None	Moderate	Severe
14	32	0	0
13-12	22	0	0
11- 6	20	4	0
5- 2	1	29	5
1	2	9	2
0	1	11	35

The lone fathers were asked to indicate problems that they perceived at any point during their care of the children. These figures indicate the majority of children were seen to have none of the problems suggested, or only a small number of moderate problems. It might have been anticipated that more problems would have been defined by the lone fathers, because the children they were caring for had all experienced the trauma of a breakdown in their parents marriage due to death or divorce, and one might have expected that this would show itself via an increase in such behaviour as, for example, temper tantrums or bedwetting. As George and Wilding (1972) indicate, it might be that men in lone father families are inclined to minimise their children's difficulties to reduce the possibility of their parenting skills being doubted. However, in this research the questions about children's behaviours were introduced some way into the interviews, at a point by which some rapport in the interviews could be perceived to have developed, and also at a point by which it had been signalled to the interviewees that a non-judgemental approach was being adopted for the interviews. Also, it was indicated in introducing the list of problems that these were indicative of the kinds of problems that it was normal for children to sometimes experience, thus seeking to give the respondents permission to acknowledge problems they perceived their children having without it being felt by them that acknowledgement of such problems was an indicator of their inadequacy.

In a minority of cases children were rated as having severe problems in some areas, and some children were experienced as being particularly problematic to care for by their fathers. Thus, Keith G, no 7, rated his son as having moderate problems in 8 of the categories, including stealing from outside the home, temper tantrums, lying, and clinging behaviour, and his daughter 3 moderate problems (aggression, clinging behaviour, and lying) and a serious rating for bedwetting. In this case, as in the case of number 20, social services were monitoring the family, the father was still having difficulty coping with the children and care was an option. No.20, Arthur T, rated his daughter in the none category for all 14 problem areas, but rated his son as having one moderate problem (stealing outside the home) and 4 serious (restless activities, aggression, clinging behaviour, and lying.) It is worth noting also that in both these cases the fathers' recollected that there had been professional concern via the SSD about the standard of child care in the home prior to the lone fathers assuming sole care.

In analysing the kinds of behaviour that were seen to be problematic, the gender of the children involved appears to have had an impact, both on the nature and the extent of the problem. Overall only 2 ratings for girls were in the serious problems category - one bedwetting, and one clinging behaviour - whereas 16 ratings for boys were in the serious problem category, with four ratings in the temper tantrums category and three ratings in the aggression category being the highest scored categories.

In the moderate category, the gender difference continues, with boys on average receiving 2.6 ratings in the moderate problem category as opposed to an average for girls of 1.5 ratings in the moderate problem category. The form of problem behaviour varied, thus, the highest rated moderate problem area for boys was that of poor concentration, which was rated as such for 37% of boys. Next rated for boys was temper tantrums, which was rated as being a moderate problem area for 26.6% - although it was rated as being a moderate problem area for nearly half boys in divorced families, and no boys in widowed families. Equally highly rated for boys, with exactly the same variation between divorced and widowed families, was lying. At the other end of the continuum, the area most likely to receive a nil problem rating for boys was stealing from the home, in which only one rating (moderate) for boys was not in the nil category (although four boys in divorced families were rated by their fathers as presenting moderate difficulties in relation to stealing from outside the home.)

As indicated, girls were rated as having virtually no serious problems, and many fewer moderate problems. The highest rated moderate categories for girls were clinging behaviour (26.6%), temper tantrums

(23.3%), and insistent demands for attention, shyness, and aggression (all 20%).Girls in divorced families were far less likely to be rated as having moderate problems, on average receiving only one such rating as opposed to girls in widowed families who on average received nearly two moderate problem ratings. Three behaviour categories received nil ratings for all girls - restless activities, stealing from home, and stealing from outside the home; and shyness and nervous habits received only one moderate rating each for girls in the sample.

For all children, the figures were analysed to show the ratings of problem categories, combining moderate and serious ratings. The most frequently rated problem was temper tantrums, with 31% of the children rated assessed by their parents as having problems in this area. Next were poor concentration and lying, both involving 25% of children, followed by clinging behaviour and aggression, which was perceived as being problematic in relation to 21% of children. Restless activities and shyness were present for 18% of children, nervous habits for 10% of children, poor speech, bedwetting and sleep difficulties 8% of children, stealing outside the home 6% of children, and stealing from the home 3% of children.

Some children were rated as having none of the problems listed - a clear gender difference emerged again here with 44% of girls receiving a 100% nil problem rating in relation to the 14 categories assessed, compared with only 6% of boys receiving such a rating.

What do these figures mean? Firstly, it should not be felt that a situation in which children were rated by their father as having no problems would be a priori 'better' or preferable to a situation in which children were rated by their fathers as having some problems. Childhood is a difficult process, and it is 'normal' for children to exhibit problems at some point, particularly if a stressful experience has occurred or is occurring. (Erikson, 1977, Kahan, 1989, Morgan and Righton, 1989, Rutter, 1975.) Thus, if the rating of the 10 year old son of Dave C (no.3 case) is examined, we see that he is rated as having moderate problems in 3 areas (restless activities, shyness, and poor speech) and serious problems in 3 areas (aggression, insistent demands for attention, and temper tantrums.) However, this is the child who following the death of his mother became blind after surgery; if he had been rated as having no problematic behaviour it would have been surprising, and the 3 areas of serious problems can be seen to be likely to be related to his experience of death and disability. It is not simply the extent of the problematic behaviour that has to be considered, but the meaning of the behaviour in relation to the personal histories and social contexts of the families.

Related to the extent of problems assessed, what do the differences in ratings for girls and boys mean? It is popularly assumed that single parents find it easier to care for children of the same gender. Greater difficulties were reported by single mothers with regard to their sons than their daughters in a number of studies.(Biller, 1974, Hetherington, Cox and Cox, 1976, Wallerstein and Kelly, 1980). However, there is little evidence that the reverse is necessarily the case for single fathers and their daughters, and the evidence of this study does not significantly support the popular assumption that it would be so. Why then might the lone fathers in general have found their sons to have more difficulties than their daughters? One explanation is that the girls in the sample were better behaved and better adjusted than the boys, and found it easier to cope with the family disruption that had occurred. Gender socialisation and gender stereotyping could however mean that girls were more likely to internalise difficulties that they were having, and were thus less likely to be seen as having problems that warranted consideration, than were boys, who were more likely to 'act out' problems and have them noticed and acknowledged. As metaphors for gender differences, it is interesting to note that the only incidences of girls being rated as having serious problems were for bedwetting and clinging behaviour, with more incidences for boys in the serious problems category for aggression and temper tantrums.

An alternative, speculative, explanation is that the girls in the sample were better able to work through their feelings in relation to the family disruption, and were thus 'better adjusted' to the situation in the lone father families than the boys. The high rating for poor concentration for the boys could indicate that the boys were possibly preoccupied with matters related to their mother's absence and its consequences, with the high ratings for girls in relation to clinging behaviour and insistent demands for attention being a reflection of this working through process for girls.

A third possibility is that lone fathers were more inclined to empathise with and be more sensitive to the difficulties being experienced by their male children, and be less aware of, or minimise, the problems experienced by children of the opposite gender. Possibly a father who has been hurt by the accidental or intentional departure of a female partner would be more likely to identify with a son who has been similarly hurt, and less likely to identify with a daughter who could provide an unconscious reminder of the absent female partner. Thus, the children's problems could have been more equally distributed between the genders than the fathers assessed, the differences in the outcomes being due to the fathers social constructions of reality rather than the ontological positions. This would seem to be particularly the case with fathers who were seeking to adopt the traditional paradigm of minimalist fathering, who would thus be inclined to see girls as being more able to care for themselves.

Fathers were asked a series of questions about their relationships with their children in relation to how they perceived their disciplinary role, and difficulties they particularly experienced in parenting.

Table 5.13
Discipline of children problems

	A lot/some	Hardly ever	No
Total sample(35)	11	4	20
Divorcees(19)	7	2	10
Widowers(16)	4	2	10
Patriarchs(25)	10	2	13
Pioneers(10)	1	2	7

The above figures indicate that whilst discipline of children was perceived as being a problem for a minority, the overwhelming majority of men who reported disciplinary problems were from those who had adopted patriarchal rather than pioneering orientations. Disciplining of children is a particularly interesting area, as it is one of the few child focused functions seen to be legitimately discharged within classic nuclear family households by fathers adopting a traditional fathering role. As such, the move to a lone fathering household could be seen to have a number of possible consequences in relation to discipline. It could be that fathers would continue to be the source of discipline, and would experience no greater difficulties than they previously had in discharging this function. Alternatively, it could be that the transition to a single parent household for some lone fathers would lead to disciplining difficulties, as the previous disciplining of children had depended on a two partner division of labour in this area. Perhaps therefore in the domain of domestic relations traditional patriarchal authority is crucially dependent on a mothers presence, and those lone fathers who were unable to adapt their parenting styles to accommodate the absence of a female accordingly experienced difficulties in this area.

Some fathers did report that the transition had presented problems. Thus, Len E, no 5, recalled how when his wife was alive she was the source of the main day to day control and discipline, with him being the final sanction - the classic 'wait till your father gets home role.' However, as a lone father he found that in relation to disciplining his two young daughters:

> It's harder for me to chastise them, they really feel it, I'm their chief provider and playmate, but when they do something wrong I have to chastise them, and that they find very hard to take - how can I be nice one minute and nasty the next; and I found that really hard.

This merging of roles was also taking place in a situation which was influenced by the route into and causes of the lone fathering. Thus, Len E recalled that he had tended to spoil his children after their mother died, which had had consequences for discipline:

I'd say no to little things and then change my mind, so when it came to saying no to big things they wouldn't accept it, my fiancee noticed and pointed it out, since then I've had to work hard to be stricter, I've had to go over the top and then come back down.

This striking a balance between caring and controlling, between being tough and tender, was a theme that was explored further.

Table 5.14
How does the LF strike a balance
between being tough and tender compared
with when in 2 parent household?

	No change	Tougher	More tender	Difficult to do both
Total sample(35)	15	4	8	8
Divorcees(19)	8	3	4	6
Widowers(16)	7	1	4	3
Patriarchs(25)	10	3	4	8
Pioneers(10)	5	1	4	0

Some fathers felt that they had not had to change their behaviour in this area, and that they were able to be the same as they had always been. Other felt that they were tougher, or more tender, and some felt, as Hipgrave (1978, 1981, 1982) has suggested they might, that striking the balance was difficult. The figures for the subsamples of widowers and divorcees were very similar, with a slight tendency for more divorcees to have become tougher than widowers. It can be seen that clearer differences emerged in relation to the pioneering sub - group; half felt that they had become more tender, and none felt that they had difficulties in striking a balance in combining toughness and tenderness. Only one pioneer felt that he had had to become tougher - because his mother who assisted in child care was 'softer' with them than his partner had been, so he felt that he had to compensate for her influence. Therefore a gender pioneering orientation was associated with adopting a 'softer' approach towards children, and a more traditional patriarchal orientation was more likely to be associated with difficulties in defining a parenting role which effectively merged and mediated toughness and tenderness.

Those who felt they had not changed in this area spoke of 'Just acting normal,' or 'being myself'. No change did not necessarily indicate that the father had not thought about the area carefully, perhaps the best example of this was Jake BB, no 28, (pioneering orientation) who said that:

I've been very fortunate in that they're all (the children) thoroughly sensible and we have a very easy sort of relationship, for sensible reasons there are certain rules - when the girls are out I need to know

98

where they are, who they're with, and when they're going to get home; or I'll tell them to put on a coat if it's cold and they'll tell me to stop being an old granny. Because of my wife's behaviour I did try to compensate and keep the temperature at an even level, I was the one who went to parents evenings and it devolved over quite a long period that they looked on me as father and possibly mother as well, I was 1½ parents really.

A small number of fathers felt that they had to behave in a tougher way than previously, with a tendency for the divorcees to relate this toughness to a need to assert control where the children might be treated differently by the ex partner, or by a part time carer for the children. An example of this was in the case of Chris Z, no 26, (the single pioneeringly orientated lone father who felt he had adopted a somewhat tougher approach) whose mother did some of the caring for the children whilst he was at work:

Their Grandma is a lot softer than their mother ever would be, sometimes I have to check them.

Others felt that they had to be tougher because the children were at a particular point in their development where they needed a 'firm hand.' The needs of developmental phases had to be mediated by the absences of the mother in the minds of some fathers, and an oft expressed need to fill that gap. Thus, Al M, case 12, (patriarchal orientation) started off by saying that he:

Had to be tough, as they go through this teenage thing.......I tend to give in more, be a bit softer, you try to be both mother and father, try to play both parts and be softer like a mother would.

Other fathers felt that they had softened their behaviour towards the children, (a theme which also emerged in Hipgrave's, 1982, study.) Thus Cliff J, no 10, (pioneering orientation) said:

I had to mellow that little bit and talk, discuss it more, to talk things out about who should do what and see if everybody was happy.

Cary M, no 13, (pioneering orientation) felt that being a lone father allowed him to be:

a lot less tough now, previously she (ex wife) had used me as a threat or a disciplinarian

and Rick O, no 15 felt that:

You've got to be a bit softer sometimes, that's the line she would have taken with them.(she being his ex wife and them being the children.)

Other fathers - all from the traditional patriarchs subgroup - experienced striking a balance between being tough and tender as at times problematic. Fergus W, no 23, felt that when his wife was alive and he was often working away:

> She was a probation officer so she thought out other people's behaviour reasons more than I did, and if I was tired and (the children) were jumping about I'd shout at them, although you can't blame them if they haven't seen you for 3 days.

Subsequent to becoming a widower he felt that he'd had to make efforts to:

> Soften my approach considerably to the children, but it's difficult to think as a businessman and act as a woman and a mother.

Aidan FF, no 32, highlighted another gender dimension in this area when he said:

> Although I can be tender when I feel they need it, the boys would cuddle up to a woman whereas they won't cuddle up to me.

Cliff J, no 10 also elaborated eloquently on this theme in talking about his children:

> I often used to wonder if I was giving them the right kind of love, you say to yourself 'I wonder which way (his dead wife) would have done it', knowing that it would be done in a different way. With them being laddies you couldn't put your arms around them and cuddle them, you would just sit and talk to them and try and show it that way - I found that was hard, you would try to show your affections, and with them being lads you couldn't show it like a woman would - which I did at times, I'd say 'come here, what's a matter with you son,' and put my arms around them, but not in the way a woman would. It's hard to explain, and yet when you think about it it's not, it's easy to explain, you can't go around kissing them and things like that that she would do. I found that very hard, trying to come to a happy medium how you could express yourself to them - if they'd been younger you could have said 'come her' and got them to sit on your knee.

Earlier in this chapter an analysis was made of the lone fathers responses to a list of common childhood problems via which they assessed their children. In the research interviews, having asked the lone fathers questions about discipline, they were also asked without the prompt list which of their childrens' behaviour caused them most difficulties. The table below indicates their responses.

Table 5.15
Children's behaviour which causes most difficulty

Most difficult
behaviour

	Total sample(35)	Widowers(16)	Divorcees(19)
None	13	7	6
Untidiness	8	3	5
Bedtimes/late nights	5	2	3
Behavioural problems	5	1	4
Sibling squabbling	2	1	1
Wanting money	2	2	0
Problems with female advice	6	4	2

	Total sample(35)	Patriarchs(25)	Pioneers(10)
None	13	8	5
Untidiness	8	4	4
Bedtimes/late nights	5	4	1
Behavioural problems	5	5	0
Sibling squabbling	2	2	0
Wanting money	2	2	0
Problems with female advice	6	6	0

One third of the sample reported no problems, some felt this was unremarkable, while others were slightly apologetic almost about it - You might think its impossible but he's great. The extent of non problematic behaviour reported in response to this question triangulates with the large sub group of children who were seen to be non problematic in relation to the check list discussed earlier in this chapter.

Untidiness, particularly in relation to the children's bedrooms, was a common source of complaint as indicated above. This was not seen to be a major problem, interestingly it is perhaps the kind of problem that a father who has to shoulder the major burden of child care and domestic responsibility is likely to notice, whereas a father who leaves such duties to someone else - for example a wife - is perhaps more likely not to notice such untidinesses.

Getting the children to come in on time, and getting them to bed, was a difficulty expressed by a small subgroup consisting largely of divorcees. Several fathers saw this as being an irritant 'Whatever time I say it's always ½ an hour later', in at least one other case it hinted at insecurity on the part of a child:

getting him to bed's a problem, if I'm out he won't go until I'm in.(Rick O, no.15.)

101

The gendered dimension of difficulties with children emerged in that 6 fathers - all patriarchs - raised the difficulties they had, or expected to have, in relation to their daughters. For some, this was to do with specifics - physical development and puberty; for others it was more general and undifferentiated - the fact that they were seeming to 'miss female company' or 'a womans touch' as it was variously described. None of the fathers raised these issues as the first or only difficulty that they had, thus commonly another difficulty - typically untidiness - would be mentioned, with the subsequent rider that, for example:

> I can show them about joinery and gardening and cooking and washing, but there's certain things that they need to learn off women.(Tony V no. 22.)

Some fathers, such as the one quoted, had female relatives or girlfriends who could talk with daughters about these 'certain things', as for example did Wally I, no 9, who remembered, having complained that his daughter would:

> Nag and nag for something until she gets her own way, and then she doesn't know the value of anything....she'd asked me about a talk that they'd had at school about puberty, I couldn't deal with it so I sent her to talk with one of my nieces, which was no problem.

The data indicates that most of the lone fathers felt that they were doing a reasonably good job of caring for their children, at least on the basis of there being a relative absence of difficulties. It does seem however that in relation to their children for the most part the horizons of the lone fathers concerns and expectations were immediate or short term rather than long term. Thus, difficulties were experienced in relation to their impinging on daily routines, such as untidiness, rather than on longer term issues such as a child failing to achieve its potential in terms of social or educational development. This could be perhaps because the single parents in this sample were concerned to chart their way through what were often the demanding social processes of child care, domestic labour, and paid work by focusing on the job(s) in hand, and not having too long a time perspective. It could also be because for many of the men, 'not having a wife to depend on' meant that an untidy childs bedroom - which pre lone fatherhood would have gone unnoticed, assumed greater importance in the single parenthood state.

However, some men in the sample did consider the longer term future and the position of their children. It is commonly perceived that mothers often do not want or are ambivalent about their children growing up and leaving home, how far was this an issue for the lone fathers surveyed? To find out, the question put to them was 'Some people dread the day their children will be all grown up and left home because of the loss. Does that apply to you at all or not?' The responses are summarised below:

102

Table 5.16
Dread loss when children will be grown up and left home

	No	Yes	Don't know
All sample	24	8	3
Widowers(16)	11	2	3
Divorcees(19	13	6	0
Patriarchs(25)	21	4	0
Pioneers(10)	3	4	3

The largest category was of those who said no, some of these had already experienced children leaving home, and related that to answering this question. Thus, Jake BB, no 28 said of the children who had already left:

> I haven't lost them, what I always wanted was a situation when they didn't need me any more but still wanted me, and so far that's what seems to be happening.

Other fathers echoed the theme 'I'm a firm believer in everyone leading their own lives', others felt that departure would mark a success point. Thus, Kev N, no 14, felt that when it happened:

> It would be an achievement,

and Arthur T, no 20 said that:

> If they want to leave when they get to that age they can, that's one point on my behalf, I'll have fetched them up.

Other fathers felt that they would be pleased to have demanding responsibilities lessened:

> I'm looking forward to it more than worrying.(John DD, no 25.)

> I'll be glad, I'll be relieved.(Al L, no 12)

or that they would by that point have invested in other relationships:

> Before I had a girlfriend it bothered me, but not now. (Dennis Q, no 17)

> It'll be right for them, and I'll be married. (Andy R, no 18)

Some fathers then saw their children's leaving as being inevitable and natural, the not unwelcome end of child rearing responsibilities, a proof of their parenting success, or a chance to invest in or develop adult relationships. Others viewed their children's departure with more

103

ambivalent feelings. Thus, when asked if he dreaded the day, Alan D, no 4, replied:

Oh yes, ain't I going to be a lonely guy when they leave home

and Dick X, no 24 said:

Yes - unless things improve for me - but if anything happened before then my whole world would collapse.

James CC, no 29, described how:

I think that that's true, I certainly miss the other 2, and now Jack's getting to the age when he's hardly ever in, yes I do feel that that period of my life has slipped away, I'll have to start finding other interests now, soon I'll have to think of ways of filling all my spare time when Jack's away.

The data presented in this chapter has indicated that the extent to which the lone fathers were traditionally patriarchal or gender pioneering with regard to relationships with children in the domestic setting impacted on their attitudes to their children.

What might be the explanation for these different attitudes? There is some indication that a patriarchal orientation was associated with less investment in children as a source of meaning and purpose in life than a pioneering orientation, thus patriarchally oriented lone fathers in the main did not dread the day when their children would leave because their children were a responsibility they would happily relinquish. They appear to have seen their children's future departure as a chance for themselves to have greater freedom to be active in the other patriarchal structures of relations - for example, in relation to sexual relationships - or as a form of 'proof' that the difficulties of lone parenting had been overcome. The minority who feared the day, did so because they saw it as creating a gap in their lives to be filled, they did not expect that they would be able to become more active in the other patriarchal structures of society and thus with the departure of the children they would become 'lonely guys.'

The gender pioneering fathers appear to have had a more varied response in this area. Pioneeringly orientated lone fathers as a group reflected more diverse and ambivalent feelings, illustrating that child care can be both a responsibility and a source of meaning. With regard to this point, in an eloquent testimony to the meaning he derived from his lone parenting experiences in the domestic setting, Jeff S, no.19, felt that:

I don't think I'll ever be this happy again - they'll grow up and they'll go away and I'm not looking forward to that at all. Some people in this situation would probably be sitting here looking for the light at the end of the tunnel, well, I'm not, I just want things to remain as they are, I bet not many people could say that.

The extent to which pioneering lone fathers child care roles represented a change from traditional parenting roles is illustrated by the following table.

Table 5.17
Major influence on child care role

	Own parent	Ex-partner/other	None
Total sample(35)	10	10	15
Divorcees(19)	7	4	8
Widowers(16)	3	6	7
Patriarchs(25)	10	6	9
Pioneers(10)	0	4	6

This shows that a number of patriarchally orientated lone fathers were influenced by the ways their parents had pursued their parental roles, none of the pioneering lone fathers listed their parents as the major influence; which indicates how, with regard to daily child care practice in the domestic setting, some lone fathers were constructing and living a model of parenting and masculinity which marked a form of break from past practices.

Other data shows that in thinking about their lives gender pioneering lone fathers were much more likely to think about the impact of changes on the domestic child care setting than on other settings. This was illustrated in their responses when they were asked an open ended question about what they felt the main difference would have been if the children were living with their mother rather than their father.

Table 5.18
Differences if children were
living with mother rather than lone father.

	Focus of answer	
	Self/mother	Children
Total sample(35)	24	9
Divorcees(19)	15	4
Widowers(16)	11	5
Patriarchs(25)	20	5
Pioneers(10)	4	6

The above table illustrates that the attitudes in relation to gender roles that formed the basis of the patriarchal/pioneering categorisation for this study were substantially congruent with attitudes towards the importance of children, lone fathers categorised as pioneers on the basis of their

105

responses to gender role questions were three times more likely to think of changed circumstances in relation to the impacts on their children than were lone fathers categorised as patriarchs.

The situations in which lone fathers were rearing their children, their attitudes to the past, and their fears and aspirations in relation to their and their childrens futures, were complicated and complex, and this chapter has mirrored these complications and complexities. It is clear that lone fathers as a group did not have one single orientation towards, or way of relating to, their children, there were forms of masculinities and parenting rather than a single form of masculinity and parenting with regard to fathering experiences in the patriarchal relations of the domestic setting. It is clear however that in the overwhelming majority of cases lone fathers were more involved with their children than they had been in the periods prior to their becoming lone fathers. Thus sociological theories which argue that men are not involved substantially in the daily practices of child care in the household setting are not valid in relation to the experiences of the majority of lone fathers, and, the evidence from this sample is that many lone fathers were involved in a greater level of child care activity than has been found to be the case for other groups of men. (Morris, 1990.)

The demands and rewards of child care appear to have been more central to the lives of some lone fathers than of others. Two different forms of masculinity can be seen to have been adopted by lone fathers with regard to child related issues in the domestic setting. A gender pioneering form was associated with according children and their needs a central position, with taking major responsibility for child care and child tending, and with developing a role with regard to child care and fathering that marked a form of discontinuity from past parenting influences. Such an orientation was also frequently related to adopting a more 'caring', softer approach to child care than in the pre lone fatherhood period. A traditional patriarchal form was associated not with a neglect of child care and children's needs, but with a perspective that was at times less child centred, which gave equal or greater primacy to social interactions and obligations in the other patriarchal structures of social relations. This form of masculinity was more associated with sharing child care responsibilities with others. Traditional patriarchs experienced more difficulties with child care discipline problems than did pioneers, and were more likely to be worried about parenting girls than pioneers. A traditional patriarchal orientation was more likely to involve the pursuance of a fathering role influenced by the lone fathers' own parental models.

Fathering, particularly lone fathering, is not solely about child care however, it is also concerned with the fulfilling of a variety of domestic management tasks and functions. Whilst these are often related to child care, it is necessary that the primary focus of the next chapter is to consider and explore the domestic management roles of the sample interviewed.

6 Lone fathers and the domestic setting

This chapter explores lone fathers' domestic work roles, particularly focusing on what is commonly known as housework. It begins with a consideration of why the area of lone fathers and housework is of significance for this study; then examines briefly different sociological theories of the family in relation to housework. Following this, the chapter explores the members of the sample's involvement in housework. It concludes with a discussion of the significance of the findings in relation to the nature of gender roles, masculinities, and parenting.

The importance of housework

Men do work, women do housework: such is the implicit assumption around which much family life is organised. The fact that housework is work has however increasingly come to be accepted, not least because of the work of such sociologists as Oakley. The blurb of first edition of her book 'The Sociology of Housework'(1974) states that:

> The importance of the book lies in the correction of the traditional view that women 'work' outside the home but not inside it.(Back cover, Oakley, 1974.)

This chapter focuses on an area which challenges a different traditional view, that men do not 'work' inside the home. In large part, the significance of this chapter is simply that; to examine the ways in which men who were not living in a marriage or a similar intimate relationship, who had the care of dependant children, got housework done. However, as well as the interest and significance of exploring housework in the lone father families at a micro level, the findings of this chapter also have a significance for more macro theories of gender and parenting, of masculinities and fathering.

There is a sense in which images of masculinities, and images of fathering, do not include other than males engaging in at most peripheral, supportive involvement in housework. Biological determinists such as

Tiger and Fox (1974) have argued that this is based on genetic patterns evolved over time, linked to men's 'natural' hunting roles and women's 'natural' homemaking and child rearing and nurturing roles. Anthropological evidence from a range of cultures develops this argument and supports the notion that such gender divisions are widespread. Stockard and Johnson (1980) have noted that hunting and warfare are usually men's occupations, and argue that men's general greater authority is related to their activities in these areas and women's activities in domestic areas. The crudity of such historical biological determinism has been criticised (Bleier, 1984) and such explanations rest on unfounded assumptions that domestic activities are inevitably more highly valued than extra - domestic activities. However, it can be argued that whilst such theories are bankrupt in terms of considered explanations of past and present gender social processes and relations, their place in much popular thinking means that their power to influence gender perceptions and expectations should not be underestimated.

What has been termed the public:private dichotomy (Gamarnikow and Purvis, 1983) in social life is also of major significance in relation to gender and power, domination and exploitation. The history of sociology has been until recently a history which has examined the public face of society, but in a way which has been in a sense gender blind. Thus, gender differences have been taken for granted attributes not considered worthy of unpacking at other than the most superficial level. As a reflection of this process, it is interesting, and ironic, to note that whilst sociology has been preoccupied until very recently with the (often implicit) study of men, it has not in the process developed a substantial or impressive body of literature about masculinity. Thus, Carrigan's comment on the literature on masculinity that:

> Its empirical content turns out to be slight. Though most social science is indeed about men, good quality research that brings *masculinity* into focus is rare. (p.64, Carrigan, 1987.)

This research is one small part of the process of creating empirical studies in social science which seek to bring masculinity more into focus.

A range of research studies, (e.g. Balding and Glendenning, 1983, Horna and Lupri, 1987, Oakley, 1974) indicate that the majority of housework is done by women, sometimes with the 'help' of men. Certainly, media images of gender roles show the range of functions that can be termed housework as not lying easily within the boundaries of norms of masculinity. Whilst it can clearly be seen that the technical ability and physical effort involved in performing housework do not inevitably mean that women are more innately suited to the activity than are men, socialisation, ideologies of gender, and expectations combine to perpetuate the linking of women, rather than men, with housework. Morris's survey of the research studies in the UK led her to conclude that:

Even in employment women continue to bear the main burden of domestic work. Men have increased their participation, but not in amounts sufficient to offset women's increased market work. (p.90, Morris, 1990.)

In relation to gender images developed through childhood, Harris has pointed out:

Even if the woman works, the role which will be most visible will be her domestic role. As a result the expectations that the children will acquire through being socialised in such a family will be that the family role of the wife is the dominant one. (p.73, Harris, 1983.)

There is evidence to show (Delamont, 1980) that girls through childhood are expected to do more housework, than boys. Evidence of gender differentiation also can be seen in children's toys (Delamont, 1980, Goodman, 1974,) although attempts are made by some parents - and fewer toy manufacturers - to challenge gender stereotypes. So girls are more frequently than boys the recipients of toys that are related to housework (and child care), be they scaled down versions of adult appliances - e.g. brushes, ironing boards, cookers - or miniature versions to assist them in their care of My Little Pony or Barbie and Ken.

In contrast, boys do not expect, and are not expected, to engage to nearly as great an extent in housework (or child care) in reality or playfully during childhood. Thus, the impression is that for most boys Action Man is the nearest they get to playing at such activities, and the accessories of Action Man are related not to domestic activities but the world of warfare - there do not appear to be plans for any manufacturer to develop a more home and child centred Action New Man.

Therefore in general boys do not play at housework. As men there is the likelihood that they will not expect to do it as a major part of their lives, (and when they do do it they will be less likely to have developed competencies, partly because of their juvenile recreation.) Such a gender role differentiation pattern has been illustrated in a number of studies. For example, the 'classic' 1950s study of working class life 'Coal is our Life'(1956) painted a picture of family life in which:

A man's centres of activities are outside his home; ..the wife's position is very different. In a very consciously accepted division of labour, she must keep in good order the household.(p.180-181, Dennis, Henriques, and Slaughter, 1956.)

Subsequently, it has been argued (Frankenberg,1976) that this rigid gender division of labour was the consequence of miners' being in a system of oppressive and exploitative relationships which they 'passed on' to 'their women' rather than fighting back as a class. Such an analysis would thus in part explain why, in the major coal strike of the 1980s, when the miners did 'fight back', women in mining communities were able to become massively involved in the struggle in the community. However, the media images of changes in gender roles during that period have possibly been exaggerated, Shaw (1994) argues that striking miners perceived picket duty and other similar activities as being their 'work' during the strike. Consequently, women during that period were still seen to be responsible for servicing and supporting their menfolk, and when the strike was finished and the men returned to work, the women in the majority of cases returned to their household functions.

The relationships of production have of course changed since the 1950s, and partly as a result of these changes, writers such as Willmott and Young (1973) have argued that families are moving towards greater equality between the adult partners, and that roles are becoming more symmetrical. Their conclusions have been criticised for being overoptimistic about the extent of the movement towards greater gender equality in marriage. Thus, the picture painted by Whitehead is seen to be more typical:

> The domestic roles of men also include doing a number of jobs around the house. Bringing in firewood, carpentry, and electrical work are men's jobs. Decorating is mainly done by women. Being the provider goes with a quite natural organisation of the home around a man's daily routine. The husband expects a meal to be ready when he gets home and for his wife to have finished her work. Her work is to wash, cook, washup, clean the house, wash and iron the clothes, and take primary responsibility for children. (P.101, Whitehead, 1976)

The ideological and social construction of the family thus assigns men to a minor, peripheral role in relation to housework. Such macro views do not however give a great deal of information about the 'actual experiences' of men and women in relation to housework. Studies such as Oakley's (1973) have provided valuable data on women's relationships to housework and wider issues such as gender roles. Oakley goes on to assert that 'the housewife role (is) specifically a feminine role'. How then do single parent fathers perform this 'specifically feminine role', the logic of Oakley's argument is that they cannot, nevertheless the men involved in this sample were having to chart a path through the kinds of demands and obligations that parenting, managing a house, and (often) engaging in paid employment dictate.

Studies of men, including other studies of lone fathers, have not focused on this area to any great extent. For example, George and Wilding's study (1972), although mentioning it in passing, only devotes slightly more than a page to the area, and does not engage significantly with the meaning or significance of household tasks for the fathers. Russell's study (1983) in Australia on 'the changing role of fathers' looks most intensively at the two areas of child care and playing with children, and housework or domestic work are not seen to be sufficiently significant areas to warrant indexation, although again these areas are touched on in scattered

110

references throughout the text. Greif's study (1985) of US lone fathers examines the area in a little more detail, relating the area directly to the responsibilities of childcare, and noting that the common assumption of the father who has to run a household is that he will do it inadequately. Before looking in detail at this sample's experiences in this area, it will be helpful to consider in more detail the nature and meaning of housework.

One simple way of defining housework would be to argue that housework is what housewives do. Using this argument, whilst there is no male equivalent for the word 'housewife' (although the term 'housemen' has been recently suggested) for the vast majority of men in the sample, the domestic responsibilities and childcare roles they performed would, if performed by women, qualify them for the label 'housewife'. Oakley puts forward Hunt's argument that:

> The definition of who is, and who is not, a housewife is phrased in terms of *responsibility*: thus a housewife is the person, other than a domestic servant, who is responsible for most of the household duties (or for supervising a domestic servant who carries out these duties). (p.29, Hunt, 1974.)

Davidoff (1976) concludes that housework can be viewed as work, as part of the overall economic system, or as part of the culture of society. Focusing on housework as work, for any household to function the needs of its members have to be serviced, and housework in part consists of the meeting of basic human needs, (e.g. food, warmth, shelter.) Thus housework in these terms consists of the taking of responsibility for, and fulfilling, certain tasks related to these human needs of the household.

Over time, the extent and nature of these tasks has not been static. For example, if one considers the area of food, in some households at some times the household would be largely self sufficient in relation to obtaining food. In other societies, such as the UK in the late 20th Century, very few households are self sufficient in relation to food, thus the task of 'shopping' is one which has to be performed to obtain food. Shopping is work in that it involves focused activity, and some people are paid to shop, for example, part of many (paid) local authority home helps roles is to do shopping for their clients.

Housework then consists of activities which have practical, social, and economic meanings, and the gender dimension is interrelated with these meanings. These meanings of housework has been explored particularly by feminist writers, thus Davidoff (1976) has argued that much (female) housework is concerned with 'boundary maintenance' between chaos and control via such mechanisms as dirt control and tidiness, and particularly in the 20th century, the increasing value placed on child rearing has increased the tensions between being a good child rearer and being a good houseworker. It is not least because of these tensions that Oakley (1973) concluded that housewives are not a leisured class, and that in her sample of housewives dissatisfaction with housework predominated.

The studies of lone fathers cited above almost imply that lone fathers were not usually involved in running households prior to becoming lone fathers; how true was this for the sample studied, what proportions of household tasks were the lone fathers involved in pre lone fatherhood, and what proportions were they involved in at the time of the research?

Lone fathers involvement in domestic work

The men in the sample were asked to rate their percentage involvement pre lone fatherhood and at the time of the research in 7 areas:

1   Cleaning house
2   Household shopping
3   Cooking
4   Washing up
5   Washing clothes
6   Ironing
7   DIY.

The first six areas represent what Oakley called the 'core tasks' of housework, and as such contain activities which can be seen as being potentially creative, such as cooking, and potentially more routinised and mundane, such as cleaning. Whilst the desirability to replicate aspects of previous studies is a powerful argument for using these same six categories, on reflection it might have been useful to have subdivided cleaning into 'clean cleaning', that is dusting, tidying up,   and vacuuming; and 'dirty cleaning', such as cleaning the bathroom and toilet. Such a division might have given interesting insights into the more detailed aspects of the kind of boundary maintenance to which Davidoff (1976) referred.

DIY was included as it was felt it was likely to be a particularly 'male' area of household involvement. This 'maleness' of DIY applies both in terms of its ideological and media image, and in terms of its practice, and it is thus particularly interesting to compare mens' involvement in this area in relation to the other areas.

Whereas a small minority of men had felt themselves unable do the similar rating exercise in relation to the child care tasks described previously, all the sample felt able to rate their involvement in the 7 areas of household activity described.

It is important to note at this point that the data generated and analysed, like much of the other data in this research, is based not upon observation and external measurement, but on the recollections and retrospective analyses of the men who were the subject of this study.

Table 6.1
Fathers proportional involvement in domestic work
pre and post lone fatherhood   n=35

		0	1-25	26-50	51-75	76-99	100	Mean
Cleaning	pre	16	12	5	1	1	1	15.1
	now	3	3	7	4	6	12	67.2
Shopping	pre	8	12	11	1	2	1	28.6
	now	3	3	4	0	5	20	76.4
Cooking	pre	15	11	4	1	1	3	20.6
	now	3	6	3	1	4	18	70.6
Washup	pre	9	18	5	0	1	2	21.3
	now	3	8	9	1	4	10	56.8
Washclthes	pre	21	7	3	1	1	2	16.6
	now	7	3	4	2	4	15	65.5
Iron	pre	25	8	2	0	0	0	5.4
	now	13	5	4	1	2	10	42.5
DIY	pre	2	1	1	2	4	25	87.1
	now	2	1	1	0	1	30	89.7

For the sample as a whole, the category in which the men were most heavily involved during both periods was, as expected, DIY, with 29 fathers doing at least 75% of the DIY pre disruption, and 31 doing at least 75% of the DIY postdisruption. (with the mean of involvement being 87.1% pre and 89.1% post lone fatherhood.)

Regarding changes in the categories with 100% ratings, shopping represents the category which shows the greatest change, with an increase from 1 to 20 fathers in this 100% band. In relation to the mean ratings, this represents a change from 28.6% to 76.4% - the latter being the highest mean score of the categories other than DIY.

Similar increases in mean scores of approximately 50% are found pre and post disruption for three of the other categories - cleaning (15.1% to 67.2%), cooking (20.6% to 70.6%) and washing clothes (16.6% to 65.5%), with cooking showing the second biggest increase, after shopping, in the 100% ratings.

The ratings for ironing also indicate a major change in behaviour pre and post lone fatherhood, with no men in the sample doing more than 50% of the ironing pre lone fatherhood, and 13 doing more than 50% post lone fatherhood - with 10 rating themselves as doing 100% latterly. However, the mean score for ironing post lone fatherhood was only 42.5%, the lowest for any category by some 13%.

For the pre lone fatherhood period, ironing also received the lowest score, on average only 5.4% of the ironing was done by the men in the predisruption period, with 25 in the sample assessing their contribution then as nil for this category - a figure which had decreased only to 13 in relation to the assessments at the time of the research.

Clothes washing had the next highest 0% rating for the pre lone fatherhood period, with 21 out of the total sample thus rating their involvement. However, the mean for washing clothes during this phase was slightly higher, at 16.6%, than was the mean for cleaning at 15.1%. The other categories, as indicated, all had relatively low pre lone fatherhood mean ratings.

To summarise then, for the sample as a whole, DIY was the household activity in which there were least changes for the periods assessed, with a continuing high level of activity of fathers in this traditionally masculine area. The image of this area as being a particularly masculine one is borne out by these figures. The next fewest changes were in the categories of washing up, where fathers tended to move from a low level of activity to a medium level, and ironing, where fathers moved from a very low level of activity to a medium level. In both these areas the approximate average increases in involvement were 35%, although the scores for ironing were at the lower end of the ratings. All the other categories recorded average increases of approximately 50%, with lone fathers on average doing at least 60% of each of these household duties in the lone fathering period.

Widowers and divorcees involvements in domestic work

Given this analysis of the sample as a whole, how far were the experiences of widowers and divorcees similar or different for the two periods analysed? The following two tables show the figures for these two subsamples.

Table 6.2
Divorced fathers % involvement in domestic work n = 19

		0	1-25	26-50	51-75	76-99	100	Mean
Cleaning	pre	5	9	3	0	1	1	20.7
	now	2	2	3	3	4	5	65.2
Shopping	pre	3	6	6	1	2	1	37.0
	now	2	1	2	0	3	10	77.1
Cooking	pre	6	6	4	1	0	2	25.2
	now	2	3	3	0	3	8	65.7
Washup	pre	6	6	5	0	1	1	25.3
	now	2	6	6	1	2	2	43.4
Washclothes	pre	12	3	2	1	0	1	14.5
	now	5	0	4	1	3	6	57.8
Iron	pre	13	5	1	0	0	0	4.7
	now	8	3	3	0	1	4	34.7
DIY	pre	1	0	1	2	3	12	86.0
	now	1	0	0	0	1	17	93.6

Table 6.3
Widowers % involvement in domestic work n = 16

		0	1-25	26-50	51-75	76-99	100	Mean
Cleaning	pre	11	3	2	1	0	0	8.4
	now	1	1	4	1	2	7	69.8
Shopping	pre	5	6	5	0	0	0	18.7
	now	1	2	2	0	2	10	75.6
Cooking	pre	9	5	0	0	1	1	14.7
	now	1	3	0	1	1	10	76.5
Washup	pre	3	12	0	0	0	1	16.5
	now	1	2	3	0	2	8	72.4
Washclothes	pre	9	4	1	0	1	1	19.3
	now	2	3	0	1	1	9	75.2
Iron	pre	12	3	1	0	0	0	6.2
	now	5	2	1	1	1	6	51.8
DIY	pre	1	1	0	0	1	13	87.5
	now	1	1	1	0	0	13	85.0

It can be seen that on average widowers experienced greater changes in their performances, having a lower involvement pre lone fatherhood, and a higher involvement post lone fatherhood.

With respect to domestic duties, DIY involvement for both groups was similar for both pre and post lone fatherhood, albeit there was a slight mean decrease from 87.5% to 85% for widowers (the only category in which there was a mean decrease), and an increase from 86% to 93.6% for divorcees - the highest mean rating for any household or childcare task.

Leaving aside DIY, a trend emerges similar to the one found in respect of childcare involvement. Thus, the tendency was for widowers as a group to have a lower mean proportional involvement in domestic duties whilst they were still married, and a higher mean proportional involvement at the time of the research. In all activities except washing clothes, the widowers had a lower average involvement pre disruption, in all areas except shopping the widowers had a higher average involvement at the time of the research. Excluding ironing, the mean involvement of widowers whilst married was in all categories less than 20%, only in the category of washing clothes was the mean involvement of divorcees less than 20% whilst they were married, and at 37% for shopping it was almost twice as high as the 18.7% mean rating of widowers for this category. Widowers involvement in cleaning was particularly low with a mean rating of 8.4%, increasing by an average of 61% by the time of the research.

Ironing for both groups was clearly a little engaged in - and to be avoided if possible - domestic activity, having the lowest mean involvements of all categories for both groups pre disruption and at the point of the research. It can also be seen that ironing received the highest ratings in the 0% categories for both groups predisruption and at the time of the research, and the lowest number of ratings in the 100% category for both groups pre and post disruption. The exceptions were shopping by widowers when they were married, which received a similar 0 in the 100% category, and washing up post disruption for divorcees, which received 2 as opposed to 4 ratings in the 100% category at the time of the research. At the other end of the continuum, DIY received the highest number of ratings in the 100% category for both groups predisruption and at the time of the research. In four categories - shopping, cooking, washing up, and washing clothes - 50% or more of the widowers rated themselves in the 100% involvement category, whereas shopping was the only category in which 50% or more of divorcees rated themselves in the 100% band.

To summarise, an analysis of the assessed proportional involvement of the lone fathers in relation to the domestic duties explored shows a very high involvement in DIY activities pre disruption and at the point of interview, and a low involvement in ironing for the same periods. Mean proportional involvement in domestic activities showed a general tendency to increase. Examination of the differences between widowers and divorcees shows a tendency for widowers to have lower proportional involvements whilst they were married, and higher proportional involvements at the time of the research. The converse applies to divorcees, with the exception of the area of clothes washing, divorcees assessed that they had higher proportional involvements whilst they were married, and lower proportional involvements at the time of the study. The mean proportional increase in all domestic activities between the pre lone fatherhood period and the time of the study was 32.8% for divorcees, and 54.3% for widowers. What of patriarchs and pioneers?

Table 6.4
Pioneers % involvement in domestic work n=10

		0	1-25	26-50	51-75	76-99	100	Mean
Cleaning	pre	3	5	1	1	0	0	19.5
	now	1	1	1	2	2	3	67.5
Shopping	pre	4	2	1	1	2	0	30.2
	now	1	0	0	0	2	7	87.5
Cooking	pre	2	5	1	0	0	2	26.5
	now	1	2	0	0	1	6	71.0
Washup	pre	2	6	0	0	0	2	26.7
	now	1	1	2	1	1	4	66.5
Washclothes	pre	7	1	1	1	0	0	9.0
	now	1	0	2	1	1	5	74.0
Iron	pre	6	4	0	0	0	0	3.6
	now	5	0	2	0	0	3	38.0
DIY	pre	0	0	0	1	1	8	95.9
	now	0	0	0	0	0	10	100.0

Patriarchs % involvement in domestic work n=25

		0	1-25	26-50	51-75	76-99	100	Mean
Cleaning	pre	13	7	4	0	1	0	13.4
	now	2	2	6	2	4	9	67.2
Shopping	pre	4	10	10	0	0	1	28.0
	now	2	3	4	0	3	13	72.0
Cooking	pre	13	6	3	1	1	1	18.2
	now	2	4	3	1	3	12	70.5
Washup	pre	7	11	5	0	1	0	19.2
	now	2	6	7	0	3	6	52.7
Washclothes	pre	14	6	1	1	1	2	19.8
	now	6	3	2	1	3	10	62.0
Iron	pre	19	4	2	0	0	0	6.2
	now	8	5	2	1	2	7	44.4
DIY	pre	2	1	1	1	1	17	83.6
	now	2	1	1	0	1	20	85.6

It can be seen that those who adopted gender pioneering orientations in general had more involvement in domestic work during the pre - and in the lone fathering periods. This applied to every category of domestic work except ironing, where patriarchal lone fathers had slightly higher ratings. However, there is little evidence from this data that the prelone fatherhood relationships had been ones marked by symmetrical domestic roles. Clothes washing and ironing were areas of little activity by either sub group prior to their becoming lone fathers, and the latter remained an area which lone fathers sought to sub contract out or avoid in the majority of cases. DIY was an area which pioneering lone fathers had moved from almost total responsibility for to total responsibility. The mean of the changed involvement in all seven areas was 42% for pioneers, and 34.1% for patriarchs. Therefore, in general, pioneers having started lone fatherhood from a baseline of greater involvement in domestic work than patriarchs had increased their involvement in domestic work during lone fatherhood more than patriarchs.

What possible explanations are there for these figures in relation to involvement in domestic activities pre and post lone fatherhood? The picture painted by most men is that, prior to their becoming lone fathers, they were living in marriages in which there was little sense of equality in relation to the respective domestic work roles of the male and female partners, what Bott (1957, 1971) has termed 'segregated conjugal role relationships.' Three different forms of orientations to housework can be seen to have been adopted by the men in the sample during their marriages:

Firstly, those who left all, or all but a tiny proportion, of the household tasks to their partner, feeling that it was the woman's legitimate role (although even these men had a high involvement in DIY because that was seen to be legitimately the man's work.) Thus Keith G, no 7, typified this orientation, with an assessed involvement of 100% in DIY, 5% in cleaning the house, 1% in household shopping, and 0% in cooking, washing up, washing and ironing. This low level of involvement reflected an orientation to family life and the distribution of work between the adult partners in the family which was expressed by Keith G as that 'the woman should stay at home, she's the one that got to look after the house.' Fathers who at the time of the study were located in the traditional patriarchal category had frequently adopted this approach to housework prior to becoming lone fathers.

Secondly, those who left the majority of domestic work to their partner, but had a higher level of activity in one or two areas of domestic tasks as a way of 'doing their bit.' A typical example of this type of involvement can be seen in the case of Roy F, no.6, who did 100% of the DIY, 100% of the washing up, 50% of the house cleaning, and 0% of the household shopping, washing, cooking, and ironing. Thus Roy F did exactly the same as Keith G in having a 100% rating for DIY, and four 0% ratings, but differed in additionally having a high involvement in the remaining two categories. Roy F was not untypical in seeing that domestic gender roles were not God given:

> women have got to have a choice, but it would be difficult for both (mothers and fathers) to have full time jobs, we worked it that I worked during the day and my wife worked at evenings...I think men are a bit dominant in the North East, which is a pity, what's sauce for the goose is sauce for the gander.

Lone fathers who were patriarchs or pioneers were both represented in the subgroup who had adopted this approach to housework pre-lone fatherhood.

Thirdly, those - the minority - who had had a high level of involvement in a range of domestic activities - fathers who as lone fathers had adopted pioneering orientations were more likely to have exhibited this approach to domestic work in their pre-lone fatherhood period. Such involvement did not appear to have occurred because the men felt it was 'ideologically sound', but rather because they were not hostilely resistant to it; because they were open to change; and circumstances - their unemployment, or the absences of their partner for other reasons, such as illness or marital difficulties - created the conditions in which it was more likely to happen. The latter reasons applied in a typical example, that of Jeff S, no. 19. He rated his pre divorce involvement as being 100% for child care, house cleaning, cooking, and washing up, 95% for household shopping, and 0% for washing and washing up. He explained how his involvement in domestic work had increased as his marriage had deteriorated and his wife had spent increasing periods of time out of the home, so that when his wife and he finally split up it was easy for him to do the cooking:

> it was no problem because it didn't change, I'd had to do all the cooking when I was married.

However, he had not gone into his marriage with the idea of establishing a 'symmetrical relationship'. Thus, he said of becoming a lone father:

> It's certainly given me a great awareness of the allocation of sex roles - I never used to think about it at all, but I would never have dreamt that I would end up dusting and polishing and cooking and everything else. Before I got married I'd always assumed that when I got married it would be the traditional stereotyped roles within the family, but I've come to think that there's nothing wrong with men doing the housework, also, I think there's nothing wrong with women going out to work, it's up to them.

Oakley (1974) felt that patterns of husbands participation in domestic work were class related. In this sample it appeared that the labour market conditions that applied to particular occupations, which occupations are themselves typically seen to be the definers of social class membership, played a part in setting the boundaries of potential involvement, not least in relation to the amount of time and energy potentially available for domestic work.

Did members of the sample have any preferences in relation to areas of housework? The domestic tasks were also rated by the sample in terms of most liked through to least liked.

Table 6.5
Rating of household tasks most liked (1)
through to least liked (7)

All sample (35)	Widowers (16)	Divorcees (19)	Patriarchs (25)	Pioneers (10)
Rating	Rating	Rating	Rating	Rating
1. Cook	Cook	Shop	Cook	Shop
2. Shop	Shop	D.I.Y.	Shop	D.I.Y.
3. D.I.Y.	Washclothes	Cook	D.I.Y.	Cook
4. Washup	Clean	Washup	Washup	Washup
5. Clean	Washup	Clean	Clean	Clean
6. Washclths	D.I.Y.	Washclths	Washclths	Washclths
7. Iron	Iron	Iron	Iron	Iron

The most liked activities for the sample were cooking and shopping, whilst ironing was by a wide margin the least liked category for the sample as a whole, and for all the subsamples. Widowers differed from divorcees in rating DIY activities much lower, and washing clothes much higher. Patriarchs and pioneers ratings were similar, with a slightly smaller range of mean scores for pioneers than for patriarchs. These figures imply that the sample preferred to engage in tasks that can be seen to be either creative - such as cooking, and shopping, or clearly 'masculine', such as DIY. Washing up is also a major 'traditional' arena in which men can do housework and remain 'real men', which may explain its relative popularity; and possibly household tasks involving boundary maintenance between dirt and cleanliness, are seen to be more the province of females rather than males, thus explaining their lower rating.

The management of housework

The daily management of housework, interrelated to childcare, was, for the sample, a gendered experience. To an extent, the common expectations of men in relation to housework are that they cannot do it, or if they can do it they will be at best barely competent. Men's worth as people and as representatives of their gender is not measured in relation to the performance of housework in the same way that women's worth often is. Thus, the private world of housework is one in which women can be publicly accountable if social norms of performance are transgressed. Writing of research into households where child care deficiencies had led to state intervention, Packman noted that in relation to children coming into care:

> for over a quarter of the children the mother's standards of physical care were thought to be inconsistent or poor. (p.45, Packman, 1986)

Yet, men are not normally held to be accountable publicly for their performance in this private world. Packman again:

> Information about the fathers' standards was harder to come by, partly because so many were absent, and partly because, even when present, the social workers rarely saw the fathers in action as parents. (p.45, Packman, 1986.)

Lone fathers are by definition present in their households, and thus have to engage directly or indirectly with housework. What then were the strategies that the men employed to do housework at the levels of performing, and making sense of, the activities?

Some men had been involved in housework in a minor way prior to the household disruption; and post disruption they continued to be involved in a minor way. Such men could be seen to be adopting a traditional masculine approach to housework, and their roles as men, and their roles as fathers, could be seen to be largely congruent. However, as it has been argued that ultimately these two roles are not congruent in principle or practice, they did not necessarily experience the two as being satisfyingly congruent.

Other men had to assume greater, if not all, responsibility for housework post disruption, and did so whilst seeking to perform housework tasks at the minimum possible level (for example, never ironing any clothes). For such men, ideologies of masculinity were perhaps stronger than ideals of parenting, and they were likely to experience their situations as being more satisfying as men than as parents.

Other men had to assume greater, if not all, responsibility for housework post disruption, and did so, in a positive rather than a grudging way, seeking to perform housework tasks fully, effectively and efficiently. Such men were in some ways according more closely to ideological ideals of parenting than ideological ideals of masculinity. However, such performances would not necessarily lead to the denial by them of their masculinity, as they were often able to see housework as being not so much an affective activity as an instrumental activity; to see housework as being 'a job', technical, routinised, and standardisable.

These ways of managing housework in everyday life were not unchanging, and there were examples of some men becoming more active in the sphere of housework over time, and others becoming less active, often related to the availability or desires of others - usually female relatives or girlfriends - to get involved in the area of housework.

As indicated, one way in which lone fathers asserted a form of power and control over housework was by creating a routine.

Table 6.6
Set routine for doing housework?

	Yes	Do things as necessary	No
Total sample(35)	17	7	11
Divorcees(19)	10	4	5
Widowers(16)	7	3	6
Patriarchs(25)	10	4	11
Pioneers(10)	7	3	0

This table indicates the sample was almost equally divided into those who had a routine and those who did not. 'Having a routine' varied from having a detailed, systematic way of doing housework to having general pattern of activities. A typical example of this former group was Trevor A, no. 1, who said:

> I tidy up everyday, I do that job before I do anything else. Mondays is washing day, and cleaning; Tuesdays I do my shopping, I do general housework every other morning - housework's the first priority before I do other things

Another example of this very organised approach to housework was no 33, Kevin GG, who said:

> I do the upstairs Tuesday, the downstairs Wednesday, the washing on Friday, and shop every day - I've got a regular routine; if you'd come tomorrow I'd have done the downstairs.(the room we were in, which looked immaculate)

Others were less systematic, but nevertheless had developed a form of routine. Typical of such an approach was Len E, no 5, who in describing how he did housework said:

> I do housework every Saturday morning and one night per week, the rest of the time, I just keep the place tidy, I do (clothes) washing most nights, but that's easy with the automatic.

Amongst those who did not have a routine, two sub categories emerged. Firstly, there were those who did not have a routine from choice, feeling that they did not need one, typical comments from members of this subcategory were:

> I don't have a routine, I just go shopping regularly, otherwise I do things as they need doing (Rick O, no 15) and

> I just do things as they arise, I just take them in my stride. (Arthur T, no 20).

Others reported that they did not have a routine and experienced it as problematic, typical comments were:

> I just do things when they pile up, I never do any ironing, I don't have a routine (Keith G, no 7) and

> No, its very haphazard, catch as catch can (Wally I, no 9) and

> I just do it (housework) when I can fit it in, but I don't seem to have time for anything (Ivan U, no 21.)

Analysis of the data on housework routines regarding patriarchal or pioneering masculinities illustrated clear differences between these two groups; a greater proportion of pioneers than patriarchs had a developed routine in relation to domestic management. Whilst smaller subgroupings of each group had a routine in the sense that they did things as they were necessary, none of those with a pioneering orientation felt that they did not have a routine, in contrast to nearly half of the patriarchs who assessed themselves as being in this category. Perhaps this indicates that pioneers felt that housework was a legitimate and necessary area of masculine practice, whereas some patriarchs did not and resisted systematically intervening in the area.

This latter position would accord with stereotypes of masculinities which lead to the expectation that men would not derive any satisfaction from doing housework, or, if they did, it would be likely to be from the more 'gender neutral' tasks, such as cooking, and less likely to be from doing more 'female specific' pollution control and boundary maintenance tasks, such as cleaning.

Table 6.7
Anything about doing housework satisfying?

	Yes	No
Total sample(35)	15	20
Divorcees(19)	8	11
Widowers(16)	7	9
Patriarchs(25)	10	15
Pioneers(10)	5	5

Slightly under half the sample found something satisfying about doing housework, with similar proportions of widowers and divorcees being represented in both categories. There was a tendency for pioneers to be more likely to experience some aspect of housework as satisfying than patriarchs, which perhaps indicates more satisfaction in the domestic role. Cooking was the most frequently described satisfying activity (6 specific mentions.) However, it was not described by any of the men as being satisfying because of the intrinsic acts of creation involved (although one man did express satisfaction at being able to buy 'better, more wholefood' than his wife had done.) Rather, cooking was seen to be satisfying as a symbolic and actual 'gift' to the children of the household, and as a means by which the fathers had their success as parents validated by their children.

Cary M's (no. 13) and Tony V's (no 22) comments typify this duality of cooking functions as experienced by some of the sample:

> It's nice when you've made a meal, and it's really nice, and they're all happy with it

> Just feeding them, and seeing that they eat it, they're the best critics in the world kids, they'll tell you if they don't like it.

The comments of Cliff J, no 10, also indicate a similar duality:

> To see them eat a meal that I've made, and when I'd done anything, the washing or the ironing, for them not to complain, and say that's not right, I found that very rewarding.

This latter quote illustrates another point, namely that some lone fathers found satisfaction in doing housework tasks that were not 'gender neutral', tasks which, such as washing, ironing, dusting, are traditionally seen as being more feminine. The above comment was however untypical in that whilst the satisfactions derived from cooking can be seen to have been related to positive, or a lack of negative, feedback from the children, generally, cleaning tasks were seen to be satisfying in themselves. Cooking was an 'other directed' activity, cleaning was a 'self directed' activity. The following two responses are typical illustrations of this:

> Getting the house up to scratch and looking nice on a Saturday, it's nice when I've done it. (Albert P, no.16)

> It's nice to polish, hoover, and dust, and then sit down with a cup of coffee and look around and say - all really clean, that's my work - housework doesn't bother me at all, I don't mind doing it. (Len E, no.5)

Such responses, typical of a fifth of the men in the sample, the majority of them representatives of the pioneers rather than the patriarchs, indicate that housework was satisfying because it afforded an end product, and a sense of completeness. In terms of labour, housework was framed as an activity over which these men felt they had control, they were not alienated from the process of their labour, and they felt satisfaction in achieving a product.

The sense of completeness was perhaps not simply on the level of having completed a job, although the satisfaction that can be derived from being able to perceive the achievement of an 'end' in such a potentially endless activity as housework should not be underestimated. On a more symbolic level, perhaps feeling incomplete is something that men in a lone fathering situation can be often likely to feel. The very terms lone fathers and single fathers imply a certain incompleteness, and lone father households inevitably derive from disrupted family situations. Also, whilst 'mothering' as an image and ideological construct involves a grouping of certain activities and functions about the boundaries of which there is a broad social consensus; the boundaries of 'fathering' as an image and ideological construct is much less clear - is more incomplete. Also, it can be argued that under capitalism all men are likely to feel incomplete, (Kimmell,1987) and are thus seeking to either avoid this sense of incompleteness or find ways of life becoming more meaningful.

On all these three levels, deriving satisfaction from housework can possibly be seen to have wider and deeper symbolical meanings than simply finishing the job - to give meaning to the experience of being lone fathers, to the experience of being fathers, and to the experience of being men. Housework became a vehicle for the generation of such meaning because it was there, because it needed doing, and because it represented a channel for a physical statement of competence and caring.

However, more than half the sample did not feel there was anything satisfying in doing housework, for the majority, it appeared that housework was not satisfying at all. It was something that had to be done, but as quickly as possible, in as limited a way as possible, and, ideally, getting someone else to do as much as possible. Most men in this category simply said housework wasn't satisfying, of the few who did elaborate they said such things as:

It isn't a barrel of fun, I just plod on. (Arthur T, no. 20)

I don't like it, I'm doing what I have to do. (Wally I, no.9)

I don't like housework, I have to keep the house clean so I just do the best I can. (Trevor A, no.1)

How far was the presence or absence of a routine for doing housework related to a presence or absence of any satisfying aspects of housework?

Table 6.8
Relationship of 'having a routine'
with 'expressed satisfaction with
any aspect of housework.'

		Satisfaction	
		Yes	No
	Yes	10	7
Routine			
	No	4	14

125

Whilst having a routine did not necessarily lead to a feeling of satisfaction with any aspect of housework, an absence of a routine was more likely to coexist with an absence of any satisfaction with housework - those without a routine were less likely to express satisfaction, and more likely not to express satisfaction, than those with a routine in relation to housework.

The largest subcategory in the sample were the men who had not got a routine in relation to housework and did not feel that any element of housework was satisfying, indicating that an absence in an area of 'doing' was related to an absence in an area of 'meaning.' A typical example of the linking of these two areas was Wally I, no.9, who said in relation to whether he had a routine:

No, it's very haphazard, catch as catch can;

and in relation to whether any aspect of housework was satisfying

Nothing - I don't like it, I'm doing what I have to do.

The next largest subgroup were men who felt that they had a routine and reported some aspect of housework as satisfying, indicating that activity in the area of 'doing' was related to the existence of an area of meaning. The comments quoted above of Len E typify this subcategory.

A minority of the sample (20%) comprised the third category, those who had a routine but did not feel any aspects of housework were satisfying. As such, they were perhaps not totally dissimilar from what is often seen to be the position in relation to 'typical housewives'. Representative of this category was Trevor A, described earlier.

Oakley (1974) argued that the creation of routines and the specification of standards in relation to housework were ways in which women were able to create rewards in relation the tasks involved. She also indicated that routines, rather than reducing the time subsequently spent in housework, had a tendency to increase the amount of time spent in this area of activity. Why then were some men who developed routines able to feel some satisfaction in doing housework and others not? The evidence from this study is inconclusive, but it points to the possibility that if doing housework is a supplementary activity to other activities - holding down a paid job, looking after children - if the individual concerned can devote sufficient time and energy to achieve limited self specified goals, housework can have intrinsic satisfactions. Housework holds no intrinsic satisfactions, even if routinised, if one of two other conditions applies. Firstly, if the individual concerned is trying to do housework in a situation where there is not sufficient time, or labour power, available to achieve even limited specified goals. Secondly, if almost limitless time, or labour power, is available, the potential goals become much greater, and as such become gaols which imprison the domestic worker not goals which can be readily and satisfyingly achieved.

What then of the smallest group, the men who did not have a routine and yet found some elements of housework satisfying? It was typical of this group to indicate that they had previously had a routine for housework, but changed circumstances - their ceasing paid work, or the increasing assumption of responsibility by their growing children, had meant that they had had more time to do housework or less need to do housework. Typical was James CC, no. 29, who said in relation to the questions on routine and housework satisfaction:

> I used to have a routine, now, with the children left home or older, I do it (housework) when I can, nothing routine...I've generally found it all satisfying.

Before concluding the examination of the area of lone fathers and housework, it is important to consider the extent to which the men in the sample received assistance in doing housework. Children were a potential, and in many cases an actual, source of housework assistance. Whilst many of the children helped their parents to do housework, in the case of approximately a third of the sample the children did no housework - in some cases because the children were, or were perceived to be, too young.

In the cases where children did contribute, their contribution varied from an estimated 1% of two activities (shopping and washing up) to doing 100% of some activities. Thus, John Y, no.25, estimated that his teenage daughters did 100% of the cleaning, washing and ironing, 85% of the washing up, and 75% of the cooking - with him doing 100% of the shopping and DIY, 25% of the cooking, and 15% of the washing up. Daughters were twice as likely to be involved in housework than sons, the comments men made about this indicated that they felt that their daughters were keen to be involved in this area. It could be considered that fathers were overestimating their daughters willingness to be involved - it could be that such a perspective made it easier for the fathers - as when John Y referred to above said 'the girls have it all organised'. It also needs to be noted that daughters involvement was not always simply as labourers, they also, in at least one case, acted as quality controllers - Al L, no. 12, said that he would:

> Hoover every morning, if she doesn't think I've done it properly my daughter does it again when she comes home from school.

Obviously, such a response from a female child is likely to have multiple causes and meanings - for example, offering assistance, implicit standard setting, veiled criticism of standards attained. It also can be seen to be a possible assertion of gender rights, a statement of a perception of femininity's 'rights' to certain functions in the domain of domesticity over masculinity's 'rights' in that area.

In relation to the type of household activities which were done by children, gender had an impact. Washing up is generally seen to be the household chore which is most commonly done by husbands to 'help' their wives, and washing up was the most commonly done chore by children to 'help' their lone fathers - some washing up was done by children in over a third (13) of the households. Cleaning - often of their own bedrooms - was done by children in 12 households. Both these activities were performed by children of either gender. In contrast, washing clothes was done by children in 9 households, but in only 1 of these was it done by a male child: clearly clothes washing was framed and performed as a feminine activity. Cooking, done by children in 8 households, was done by both genders, as was shopping which was done by children in 6 households. In contrast, ironing, done by children in 7 households, was done by girls in 6 of the 7 households. DIY was not reported as an activity children engaged in in any households. Thus, there were three forms of child assistance: gender neutral, gender specific, and age specific.

Assistance with housework from non household members was totally absent for some fathers, and massively present for others. To give two typical examples, Cliff J, no. 10, reported that his mother and father did 100% of all housework tasks (including DIY), and Andy W, no 18, reported that, with the exception of DIY which he did himself, his fiancee did between 70 and 100% of the other housework tasks. Fifteen lone fathers had assistance in housework from non household members (therefore twenty did not). Who were these external domestic labourers? The following list indicates who they were

Mother and/or Father	4 households
Girlfriend/fiancee	3 households
Mother in law	2 households
Paid female cleaner	2 households
Married daughter	1 household
Aunt(ex wifes)	1 household
Ex wife's sister	1 household
Sister	1 household

Again, as with assistance from children, this list indicates that such help with housework was not gender neutral, but came largely from women.

Housework, masculinities, and fathering

This chapter has indicated that there were a variety of different forms of participation of lone fathers in housework. Some did almost all the housework, others virtually no housework at all. Some had no assistance, others the assistance of external household members, or their own children. Some had developed routines, some had high expectations of housework standards; others had no routines, others had less clear expectations of housework standards. Some found some satisfaction in doing housework, some found housework problematic. The superficial lack of common themes is however deceptive. Clearly, as has been shown, housework was an area in which gender had a range of different impacts. It is not simply gender - although gender is rarely simple - which has to be considered in relation to lone fathers and housework. Related issues to do with masculinities, and parenting have also to be considered.

It has been argued that images of masculinities did not equate effectively or exactly with images of parenting and fathering, thus, each individual sought to define himself as a lone father within the domestic setting with unclear role models at the level of cultural relations for what to do and what not to do; what to like and what to dislike doing.

For some men then, the process of doing housework became an assertion of their masculinity, for others, it was more of a process of searching for and defining an effective and meaningful parenting role which accorded with their perceptions of masculinity.

What is clear from this study is that virtually all the lone fathers took more responsibility for housework than they had done prior to their lone fathering periods, and the impression is that there were not such high levels of dissatisfaction with housework as found by Oakley (1974) in her study of housewives. This would appear to be possibly for reasons related to forms of masculinities. Patriarchs tended to have had a low level of involvement in housework and were less likely to be dissatisfied by it because others took some responsibility. Pioneers tended to have experienced greater change and had a higher level of involvement in housework, but the meaning of housework for them appears to have been part of a process of being 'good fathers', part of a process of self validation. It was not the case that the absence of assistance with housework automatically led to a pioneering orientation being adopted, nor was the presence of actual or potential assistance inevitably associated with a traditional patriarchal orientation.

It also needs to be noted that the evidence appears to be from this study that lone fathers, whether they were solely in paid employment or not, generally felt respected by others because they were lone fathers, thus the fact that they managed to do housework might be seen to have been for them a mark of their credibility.

Housework then is an interesting area for understanding more about the nature of lone father households, and more about the nature of parenting and masculinities. As indicated, housework is traditionally seen to be 'women's work'. The next chapter will explore the positions of lone fathers in relation to what is traditionally seen to be 'men's work' - paid employment.

7 Employment, unemployment, and lone fathers

This chapter examines the paid employment and unemployment histories of the lone fathers in the research sample. It begins with a consideration of why the area of paid employment is of significance for this study. It then examines briefly different sociological theories of the family and of gender roles in relation to paid employment. The chapter then explores the members of the sample's involvement in employment, and concludes with a discussion of the significance of the findings in relation to the nature of gender roles.

Capitalist society rests on the expectation that people between certain ages 'work', or if they are unemployed, aspire to work, (and, as will be discussed later in this chapter, 'people' in this context invariably means 'men.') Thus, questions are commonly asked of individuals such as 'what do you do', meaning 'what employment do you do' or 'what are you', meaning 'what is your occupation.'

For lone fathers it is important to consider the nature and meaning of paid employment because the sample are men, and because they are single parents. In capitalist society, being a man is directly related to being a worker; therefore to understand one it is necessary to consider the other, and to consider one it is necessary to understand the other. Tolson makes this point when he argues that:

> the extent to which definitions of gender interpenetrate attitudes to 'work' is not fully understood. For it is not simply that sexuality enters into the division of labour, differentiating 'men's' and 'women's' jobs. Nor is it a matter merely for legislation, to be reformed by 'equal pay' and 'opportunity'. For men, definitions of masculinity enter into the way work is personally experienced, as a life long commitment and responsibility.(p.48, Tolson, 1977.)

It is also important to consider this area because the form of work that has been developed in industrial capitalist societies leads to a situation in which there is likely conflict between commitment to paid work and commitment to parenting. This tension is more commonly experienced by women, but is also likely to be keenly felt by lone fathers.

In industrial society work activities are instrumental activities directed either towards meeting one's own needs or those of one's family, household, or community, and/or towards securing the means by which such needs can be met. Work, in our society, involves providing goods or services for which others are willing to *pay*. (p.103, Brown,1987.)

'Work' then is paid employment; an instrumental activity; a means by which individuals are able to obtain the resources to continue their lives, and the lives of their families and households. Work is also a gendered experience, and cannot be fully understood without consideration of the extent to which it is part of patriarchal relations in society. Nor can it be considered as being an individual activity separate from the wider economic form of society, and the social relations that have a relationship with that economic form.

Work can have a variety of meanings for individuals in capitalist society, it is a means by which individuals seek to obtain resources which enables them to negotiate and attain a position in social life. The ownership and control of resources to enable life to continue is a basic human need, such resources are either inherited or earned. It is clear that there are great inequalities of wealth in Britain, and the rise of the so called 'affluent workers' who were seen to herald the 'classless society' has not reduced these inequalities. Within the paid labour force, non manual working males on average earn 50% more than male manual worker, and women earn on average only 60% of their male counterparts.

Therefore the resources generated by such work vary considerably and affluence and abject poverty coexist within the same system. For the purposes of analysis, the subject of the economic positions of lone father households will be explored in the next chapter.

Work is also a means by which individuals seek to obtain resources which enables them to negotiate and attain a position in social life. The resources that individuals can command do not simply fulfil their biological needs, to a major or a minor extent they also have an impact on their relative positions and involvement in social life. As Townsend has noted:

> Different types and amounts of resources provide a foundation for different styles of living..there exists a hierarchy of styles of living which reflect differential command over resources. (p.921, Townsend, 1979)

He suggests that there are three major modifying factors on the differentiation of the earnings system and its impacts:

1   The varied number of dependants that 'earners' have - which has a particularly significant impact in the UK, where a high proportion of resources are distributed through the conduit of individual earnings rather than via social security or state controlled income maintenance or creation schemes.

2   The proportionally large sector of the population who are not earners, who are retired, or unemployed through disability or sickness, or through lack of demand for their labour, or because domestic commitments - such as are experienced by many women, and by some of the men in this sample - make paid employment unavailable for them.

3   Those who have access to resources other than via earnings. At the wealthy end of the spectrum, a recent survey noted that 182 of the 400 richest individuals in the UK had inherited their wealth.(p.20, Sunday Times Magazine, 4.4.1993.) Inheriting wealth does not simply have an impact on the super rich, it also has an impact in increasingly wider sections of society.

Work can also be a means by which individuals assess and affirm their 'success' in life, in relation to positions both within and between occupations. Not 'working', not being engaged in paid employment, particularly if it is without 'socially acceptable' reasons, is often seen to be a major indicator of an individuals lack of success, both by themselves, and by others.

Related to this, work can also be a means by which individuals give meaning to their lives. Individuals do not simply work to live, they can also be seen to live to work, and also, to live *through* work. Work is not simply a neutral sale of labour power, there are a variety of 'orientations to work' (Brown, R.K., 1973; Daniel,W.W.,1973), including the quest for meaning and satisfaction, for validation by self and validation by significant others. If the example of coalmining is taken, doing such a dirty, dangerous job does not only bring material rewards; Dennis, Henriques and Slaughter write:

It is clear then that the work a miner does and the wages he receives both express concretely his status as a man and a member of his profession (p.74, Dennis, Henriques, and Slaughter, 1956.)

and Williamson notes that whilst his grandfather:

experienced his work as a matter of routine..he went to the pit because he had to (p.101, Williamson, 1982.)

he also suggests that:

My grandfather, like many others, was proud of his skills as a hewer. He enjoyed the company of other men. He liked the

132

conversation - 'the crack' as he called it. He took great care in his work and enjoyed seeing jobs done properly, with precision. And he valued his autonomy.(p.85, Williamson, 1982.)

It can be seen that what Burns (1967), has argued in relation to leisure, namely that leisure structures are a source of meaning and satisfaction in everyday life can also be said to apply in (an often gendered way) in relation to work:

The breadwinner's role (in theory) gives men a sense of identity, of structural location. (p.189, Brittan, 1989.)

So, if paid work can be any and all of these things to the individual, in what ways do different sociological theories analyse the significance and importance of work for the individual, the family, and the society?

Different sociological explanations for men's engagement in paid work

Prior to industrialisation production and consumption were largely, although not exclusively, centred on the same households. The pace and place of industrialisation and its effects varied, Mitterauer and Sieder note that amongst the influences on the changing structure of European families was:

The separation of the dwelling place and the place of work, which brought about a separation of the professional and the private sphere of life. This took place everywhere, though at different times and in different social milieux. (p.7, Mitterauer and Sieder, 1982.)

Since the separation into the professional and private spheres brought about by industrialisation men have become and remain dominant in the public sphere and women in the private sphere. What sociological explanations are there for this gender differentiation?

Functionalist analyses of the significance of work and gender are related to this public : private division. Implicit in the functionalist explanations in the earlier chapter in relation to housework is an explanation of why men engage in paid work. Thus, there are advantages in households developing a specialist division of labour, with one partner concentrating on domestic tasks and the other on obtaining material benefits from outside the household. Given the capitalist form of industrial societies does not encourage collective child care and domestic management, then these functions have to be fulfilled from within the household. What then could be more natural, and more socially convenient, than that the adult who biologically produces the children should remain at home and care for them and manage the household, leaving the other adult free to pursue and engage in paid employment? Therefore, men work and women do housework.

133

However, as was explored in the previous chapter, the complexities of social life in this area are not so easily or simplistically explained. Thus, as Harris has pointed out, the combination of low marriage age, small family size, long life expectation, and schooling for children all contribute to create a position where:

> The wife, even if she plays the family orientated role, will be able to work for a large part of her married life. However, her career will be interrupted by child-bearing (p.72, Harris, 1983.)

Consequently, rationality would seem to dictate that the sensible choice individually is that men go out to work; the sum total of these individual decisions is a form of society in which men dominate in the public sector and women in the private sector. The impact of historical and social forces has to be added to these individual decisions, in that women's low activity rate - and by implication men's high activity rate - in paid employment can also be related to Harris's proposal that:

> All known industrial societies have developed from societies where economic activity was controlled by men and where the superiority of men was taken for granted. (p.73, Harris, 1983.)

Therefore functionalism argues for a certain rationality in men going out to work. The logic of this position is that single parent families headed by men are dysfunctional - for the household and for the society - if they prevent or impede the man's involvement in the world of work.

Marxist analysis of work has tended to focus on the relations of production rather than the relations of gender. Marx argued that social relationships were conditional on the relationships of production, and on the relationships of capital. Harris has argued that:

> Marxism provides us with an elaborate theory of capitalist society, but tells us very little about the family (p.179, Harris, 1983.)

The logic of this position is that marxism has subsequently continued to have an essentially materialist perspective allocating primacy to the mode of production.

Most marxist perspectives would see the logic of humans selling their labour power in the market as constituting men selling their labour in the market, with women being engaged in the biological means of production (what has been called the production of reproduction, Hearn, 1987.) The fluctuating needs of capital and of the economy therefore largely allocates men to the primary labour market, and women to the secondary labour market or a position in the 'reserve army of labour.' It is almost as if Marx's dichotomous differentiation into capitalists and workers is echoed by a dichotomous differentiation of the latter grouping into male (paid, public) workers and female (unpaid, private) workers. It could also be argued that excluding most women from a primary role in the paid

134

economic sector of society allows the alienated men to feel superior to the women, allows them to be unselfconscious of the reality of their alienated positions and feel that they are benefiting from capitalist economic and social relationships, rather as poor whites felt they benefited from apartheid in South Africa.

Consequently, the needs of the economy dictate that the man services the economy, and the needs of the man dictates that the woman services the man. The presence of the man in the public sector is functional for capital, the presence of the woman in the private sector is functional for the man, and consequently for capital. Under this system, both genders lose out, marxists would differ in their analysis of whether women would always tend to lose out more than men, or whether class was a more dominant social division than gender.

Most feminists however would argue that under capitalism women lose out more than men, and would explain men's dominance in the public sphere of work not as a result of the functionalist needs of society, not as a result of the needs of capital, but as a consequence of patriarchal power and oppression. Howell has suggested that the roots of this can be found in in late medieval Europe where the changes wrought by capitalism provided opportunities for men to assert and exert their patriarchal power:

> When high-status work was removed from the family production unit and became inaccessible to married women, women surrendered an important source of authority to men. Men gained more than women lost, because the identical work now acquired greater economic, political, and cultural importance than when it had been contained within the family production unit. In this way men's authority inside and outside the household was increased at the expense of women's. (p.181, Howell, 1986.)

Gamarnikow and Purvis have commented critically on the tendency for functionalism and marxism to concur that:

> Society is defined by the public sphere of male activities, institutions, hierarchies and conflicts. (p.3, Gamarnikow and Purvis, 1983.)

Feminism questions the patriarchal sexism that flows from these positions, and, as Morgan (1985) has discussed, feminism challenges taken for granted assumptions that relate to social and family life and gender roles. To oversimplify somewhat, feminists differ in their analysis of the root of the problem of women's oppression, for some the problem of patriarchy is men, for others the problem of patriarchy is the patriarchal relations that flow from the particular economic form. (Oakley, 1981). Specifically in relation to the critique of the institution of the family, Morgan (1985) argues that feminism's contribution has been twofold. Firstly, to challenge the assumptions that underpin daily practices, such as the assumption of a conventional division of labour and the separation of home and work. Secondly, to concentrate on gender differentiation within families, particularly resource division within the household and its relationship to the sexual division of labour.

As such, feminist scholarship (Bradley, 1989, Walby, 1989) has charted and challenged a range of assumptions about the relationship of women to paid and domestic work, noting how gender divisions lead to the position where:

> The key feature of patriarchal relations in paid work is that of closure of access by men against women. This involves the exclusion of women from paid work or the segregation of women within it. This leads to the devaluation of women's work and low wages for women, which itself becomes a social fact with determinate effects, not only on women's paid work, but in other areas including the domestic sphere and other aspects of gender relations. (p.222-3, Walby, 1989.)

If these are the implications and consequences of the world of work for women, what are the implications and consequences of the world of work for men? It could be argued that as most sociology until recently has been implicitly about men, then to know what sociology has to say about the relationship of 'men' to 'work' it is only necessary to read standard sociological texts. However, with respect to relationships to, and relationships in, work, there has until recently been an absence of an appreciation of the impact of gender divisions. Brown was one of the earliest to make this point when he argued, in relation to industrial sociology, that he was not wishing to say that:

> Men and women are so different that no generalizations, no accounts of generic social processes in industrial situations can possibly be true for both sexes; rather that the possible significance of the different social situations which men and women are, by virtue of their gender, both within and outside the factory (and these can change) must always be considered in evaluating any research which it is argued has general implications. (p.26, Brown, 1976.)

With this in mind what then were the social processes in paid employment situations in which the men in this sample were involved?

Paid employment, unemployment, and lone fathers

All the men in the sample were of employable age, that is, they were over the age of 16 and under the age of 65. However, they were not all in employment at the time of the study, the following table indicates their employment positions then.

136

Table 7.1
Employment position of sample at time of study

	Emp.full time	Emp.part time	Unwaged
Total sample(35)	18	1	16
Divorcees(19)	9	0	10
Widowers(16)	9	1	6
Patriarchs(25)	14	1	10
Pioneers(10)	4	0	6

This table indicates that there was almost exactly a 50:50 split between those who were in paid employment and those who were not. Therefore, even having regard to the notorious tendency for 'official' figures to underestimate unemployment, the proportion of those in paid employment is much lower than for males in the wider population (at that time nationally approximately 13% of the whole labour force was registered as being unemployed.) There was a tendency for patriarchs to be in employment, and pioneers to not be in employment, at the time of the study.

At face value it appears that more of the sample were not engaged in paid employment than might have been expected on the basis of evidence from some previous studies. These studies (Ferri,1973; Hunt,1973) have indicated a tendency for lone fathers to be more likely to be unemployed than fathers in two parent families, but to a lesser extent than is found in this study. Thus, George and Wilding (1972) noted that at the time of their research 23.3% of their sample were unemployed; and they felt that unemployed lone fathers were overrepresented in their study as the Supplementary Benefit Commission had been a major source of their sample. In the wider population at the time of their study the official unemployment rate was 5.9%.

Writing in the USA, Greif's (1985) study of single fathers illustrates the impact of a different benefit system and different social and cultural norms and expectations. In a sample of 1,136 he records of their employment experiences in the lone fathering period that only one gave up work completely. He gives no figures for the extent of unemployment at the time of his study. (although he indicates that approximately 9% of his sample had been fired from or quit a job during the time they were single parents.) Moving back across the Atlantic, a recent British study in the south of England (O'Brien, 1984) gives a total figure of approximately 16% of her sample of lone fathers as unemployed at the time of her research.

Although the number of lone fathers in this sample who were not employed was higher than in other studies of lone fathers, in comparison with single mothers, the 56% of lone fathers in employment (all but one full time employment) represents a larger proportion of lone parents in employment than tends to be the experience of single mothers; Martin and Roberts research (1984) indicated that 34% of lone mothers were in paid employment, 21% part time, 13% full time.

The wider social context of employment and unemployment

Any discussion of the employment and unemployment experiences of the sample has to take place within an understanding of the wider economic context in which the experiences occurred. For the post war UK, the following are the measured unemployment rates, leading up to the period of the research:

	Mean	Maximum
1947 - 50	1.5%	1.6%
1951 - 54	1.7%	2.1%
1955 - 60	1.5%	2.0%
1961 - 65	1.4%	1.9%
1966 - 73	2.7%	4.0%
1974 - 78	5.0%	6.1%
1979 - 84	9.8%	13.0%

(Sinclair, 1987)

These figures show that national unemployment rates were rising during this post-war period, and, other things being equal, one would have anticipated that single parent men would be more likely therefore to be or become unemployed in the 1980s than in the 1950s. However, other things are not equal, in that this study took place in a region of the UK which experienced greater levels of unemployment during this period than other regions. As Sinclair notes:

> In the UK in November 1985 there were 7 English counties and 3 Scottish regions where unemployment fell below 10%, the former were all in the south of England, quite close, but not too close, to London...1 of the Scottish regions was an agricultural area..and 2 were regions strongly affected by the oil industry..There were 8 English counties where unemployment exceeded 16%..1 was a remote coastal county, Cornwall (19.2%), the other 7 were urbanised industrial areas in the northern half of England: Cleveland 22.2%, Durham 18.7%, Tyne and Wear 19.9%, Humberside 16.9%, Merseyside 21%, South Yorkshire 18.0%, West Midlands 16.5%. All were suffering from the declining traditional industries such as coal mining, the docks, motor assembling, shipbuilding, and textiles. (p.99, Sinclair, 1987.)

Therefore, three of the seven counties with the highest UK unemployment rates formed the substantial part of the region from which the men in this sample were drawn, 32 of the 35 men in the sample were resident in Cleveland, County Durham, or Tyne and Wear. As these figures also indicate, the research took place in a period in which the region the men and their families were living in was declining industrially and economically more than many other regions of the United Kingdom (Hudson, 1986.)

Byrne (1989) has noted how in the period between 1981 and 1984 the Northern region of England lost 53,000 jobs in manufacturing industry and 8,000 jobs in mining; between 1976 and 1984 a total of 191,000 jobs were lost in the region. Alongside this, the actual numbers of full time jobs available for men declined even further with employers switching from using male full time workers to female part time workers. Clearly, the individual employment experiences of the men in the sample can only be completely understood in relation to this regional economic position.

The nature of the sample's employment

For those who were in employment their occupations included self employed businessmen, engineers, joiners, members of the professions, and manual labourers. Table 7.2 indicates the proportions of the sample, by current, or if unemployed, previous occupation, engaged in manual and non-manual paid work (for the purposes of this analysis manual work is defined as including semi-skilled work)

Table 7.2.
Employment and unemployment of sample
in manual/non manual work.

	Manual work(n=23)	Non-manual work(n=12)
Employed	10	8
Unemployed	13	4

This data indicates that the majority of the sample were, or had been, engaged in manual work of one kind or another, which probably reflects the fact that the northern region of England from which this sample was drawn has a higher proportion of manual workers than many other parts of the United Kingdom.

The table also indicates that, whilst equal numbers of the lone fathers were employed in manual and non-manual work at the time of the study, lone fathers engaged in non-manual occupations were proportionally much more likely to be in paid employment than unemployed in comparison with lone fathers in manual occupations. The proportions were similar but reversed: for every lone father in manual occupations who was employed there were approximately 1½ lone fathers in manual occupations who were unemployed; for every lone father in a non-manual occupation who was unemployed there were approximately 2 lone fathers in non-manual occupations who were employed.

139

These differences in employment would appear to be related to at least three variables: the demands of being a lone father; the greater power of men in non-manual occupations to negotiate flexible working arrangements (such as the use of flexitime, and taking work home); and changes at a structural level in the employment of labour during the 1980s.

At the point at which they became lone fathers, only two men in the sample were not employed. One of these was unemployed because of redundancy following the liquidation of the company for which he had worked as a machine operator. As a married father his wife worked and as he said:

> I was unemployed and looked after our daughter before the marriage broke up, so I just carried on.(Kevin GG, no 33.)

The other unemployed member of the sample at the point of becoming a lone father had been a plater in the shipyards, when the yard decided to cut back on labour as he said

> I took redundancy when it was offered because of my wife's illness. Rick. O, no. 15.

Thus the majority of the sample were classifiable as employed immediately prior to their becoming lone fathers, 31 in paid employment and 2 as mature undergraduate students in receipt of grants. Therefore, for these men the experience of being a lone father in relation to employment was one of either becoming a lone father and continuing in paid employment, or becoming a lone father and ceasing to be in paid employment.

Table 7.3
Effects on paid employment
of being a lone father

	None	Employment affected	Took redundancy
Total sample(35)	12	18	5
Widowers(16)	4	8	4
Divorcees(19)	8	10	1
Patriarchs(25)	9	13	3
Pioneers(10)	3	5	2

Lone fathers whose employment was not affected

These figures indicate that amongst those who continued to be in paid employment, there was a group of men who perceived that their employment was not affected by their change in parental status. Invariably, this was because they were able to continue in work with the assistance of others (usually female relatives) for child care. When asked how being a lone father had affected their employment, the following were typical responses of this group:

> It hasn't really affected the number of hours, or the number of shifts, but probably people are a little bit more flexible if I need to be off for a particular reason.(Chris Z, no.26, Electrician in a public utility)

> It's not affected it at all, I like going to work, I like getting out of the house. We've always managed on basic time, there was always somebody needing a door hanging or something on a Saturday morning, that was my pocket money (Tony V, no.22, Joiner for a local authority.)

> Not at all, because of the assistance of my mother-in-law to look after the kids.(Joe II, no 35, Bus driver)

> Not at all, if I need any time off for any problem (my employers) have told me I can take it, they've been very helpful - I do slightly more work at home which previously I would have done at the office. (Dennis Q, no. 17,Office Manager.)

> Not at all, but I work shifts at the moment, I'm doing a lot of overtime to save for a new house..if it wasn't for my mother I wouldn't even be able to work at all, she's done the main job of looking after the kids lately. (Danny AA, no. 27, civil servant.)

These men then were able to so arrange their child care responsibilities as to enable them to continue working as before, and the figure most often referred to as being of assistance in relation to child care was the mother in law, or mother, with sister in law or sister also being mentioned as sources of assistance.

Two things are striking about this. Firstly, it is interesting to note how a gender division of labour in relation to child care and paid employment was often created (or recreated) for such lone father households, with the man going out to work with the assistance of a caring woman. Secondly, it is also interesting to note how the existence of available female relatives increased the chances of a man being able to continue in paid employment. This was not so in every case, there were examples of men who had to give up paid employment despite living near potential female supporters, for example Jack H, no. 8, was unable to continue in paid work despite living in the same village as his extended family, including his parents living in the next street. (His parent's need to continue in their paid employment meant that they were unavailable to care for their grandchildren.)

There were also instances of men who had no relatives available who nevertheless were able to continue in paid employment to largely the same extent, Dennis Q, cited above, had neighbours who 'kept an eye on his children' after school, and looked after them during the school holidays. Nevertheless the impression from this sample is that the availability of relatives - usually female - increases the possibility of lone fathers being able to pursue paid employment. The following table illustrates the relationships between employment and child care assistance.

Table 7.4
Employment and assistance with child care

		Lone fathers employed	
		Yes(19)	No(16)
Help with child care	Yes(21)	16	5
	No(14)	3	11

Thus the majority of lone fathers in employment were doing so with assistance with child care, and the majority of lone fathers not in employment were receiving no assistance with child care. The evidence from the sample's comments was that the availability of assistance led to employment continuing, rather than lone fathers deciding to continue work and then seeking assistance with child care. It would also seem from some of the comments that the longer a man continues in paid employment as a lone father, the easier it becomes to continue as children get older and more able to look after themselves.

Lone fathers who negotiated employment changes

Not all the men in the study either continued working as they had before or became unemployed; as the figures indicate a subgroup modified their working arrangements. The typical strategy employed was to create a situation in which the demands of paid work were less likely to come into conflict with the demands of unpaid (domestic) work. Some men found this easier to achieve than others, for example Fergus W, no. 23, a self employed businessman, who explained:

> I'd always worked from home, until recently I used to travel a great deal, I've changed my work role, partly to be away less, and also because one area of work was becoming more limited and I wanted to move into another area. Therefore, one thing has pushed me into changes which have then led me into doing another thing - it's working well.

Another illustration of the ways in which lone fatherhood presented challenges which had become opportunities was recounted by Jake BB, no. 28, a self employed professional:

> Before I worked 7 days a week, 52 weeks a year; now that I've got a full time partner I can take time off, and I'm not having to work

142

against the clock all the time, so I'm enjoying work more than I've ever done.

Another group, whilst remaining in paid employment, had to change jobs because of becoming or being lone fathers. The example of Wally I, no. 9, was typical of this group. Prior to his wife's death, her assumption of the child care and household responsibilities had meant that he could work unfettered by domestic demands, which, in his case, meant that he could work in the construction industry in various parts of the UK and the rest of the world. Following his wife's death however, as he said:

> I had to take a job locally, it's meant a 50% drop in my money, with no overtime or living away expenses.

Another lone father, Kev N, no. 14, moved from permanent full time employment to more casual self employment as a jobbing builder to enable him to share the care of his infant children with relatives following the death of his wife:

> I had to leave paid work to look after the kids, I used to have a steady job with a guaranteed income, now it depends on the flow of the work.

The above examples reinforce the impression given by the figures presented that those engaged in manual occupations were more likely to be unable to combine the demands of full time paid employment with the demands of child care in comparison with those engaged in non-manual occupations. However, with regard to the non-manual workers, several men reported experiences of feeling that they had been passed over for promotion at least partly because of their being single parent fathers (e.g. cases 5, 29, 34.)

Lone fathers who ceased paid employment

A group of men in the sample ceased paid employment as a result of becoming single parent fathers. For some, this was immediately upon assuming their new parental status; others did not lose their jobs so quickly, but eventually the pressures of their domestic demands meant that they had to terminate their employment. Thus Al L, no 12, recounted how:

> Six months after I started looking after the kids I gave up work because I couldn't manage the shifts - it was the biggest mistake I ever made, at the time you never think of the future, you never think the kids are growing up.

The evidence from the comments of other fathers was also that those who ceased employment did so because their domestic responsibilities sooner or later made them unavailable for work. The extent to which these men 'chose' to 'give up' work should not be overestimated, in that having assumed responsibility for their children, they were faced - as they perceived it - with no choice if they wished to continue fulfilling those caring responsibilities. As child carers this was not an unusual process, given the paucity of facilities to assist parents with child care in the UK. However, as men experiencing this process they were more unusual - Marshall, Rose, Newby and Vogler (1988) estimate that only 1% of men in any social class leave paid employment because of domestic responsibilities, compared with between 36% and 47% of women in different social classes who do so.

Employment, unemployment, and social class

This study has as its focus an exploration of the social divisions of gender, rather than the social divisions of class. What however, is the position if the figures on employment are analysed by social class membership? The categorisation of individuals into social class groupings is a potentially complex area. It was decided, not least but not only because of the relatively small numbers in this sample, to adopt a two fold classification, which places in class one (hereafter called middle class) those who were currently or previously engaged in higher, intermediate or junior management, administrative and professional roles; and in class two (hereafter called working class) those who were currently or previously engaged in skilled, semi-skilled, or unskilled manual work.

This neo Goldthorpian classification by market and work situation has been defended by Marshall, Rose, Newby, and Vogler (1988) who note the impact of gender in social class classification when they argue that Goldthorpe's class categories present difficulties with regard to the analysis of women's occupations. On the basis of this classification into social class categories, closer analysis of the data indicates that the tendency for working class members of the sample to find it harder to continue in paid employment in comparison with their middle class counterparts should not be overstated, as the following analysis of the subsamples of the study indicates.

Table 7.5
Social class and changes in employment status

	Remained in f.t. employment	Left f.t. employment
Middle Class	10	7
Working Class	9	9

Morris (1990) has described relationships between unemployment, stress, and a sense of well being. How far were the sample members stressed by their employment experiences?

144

Table 7.6
Employment and experience of life stress

		Employed	
		Yes(19)	No(16)
Life stressful as l.f.	Yes(22)	10	12
	No(13)	9	4

The above table indicates almost equal numbers of employed lone fathers experiencing life as stressful or not stressful. For those not in employment, the tendency was much stronger for them to experience life as stressful, only a minority of those not employed did not report stress, in 3 of the 4 cases in this category the men concerned had accepted or negotiated redundancy.

Did being employed appear to have any direct relationship with lone fathers' experiences of health? Members of the sample were questioned about their health, and of any changes they perceived compared with their health prior to their becoming lone fathers.

Table 7.7
Lone fathers experiences of employment
and health pre lone fatherhood
and at time of study

	Employed	
	Yes(19)	No(16)
Health same or better(24)	14	10
Health worse(11)	5	6

The data indicates that the majority of lone fathers rated their health as being at least as good at the time of the research as it had been prior to their becoming lone fathers. Whilst the largest subgroup was those who were employed whose health was the same or better, and the smallest those who were employed whose health was worse, there was no clear relationship between unemployment and worse health. On the basis of these figures therefore it does not appear to be the case that lone fathers who were unemployed experienced the same negative effects on their health as those suggested by the studies Morris (1990) reports on unemployed men in two parent families. To consider why this might be it will be helpful to reflect on the relationship of employment and unemployment to patriarchal and pioneering forms of masculinities.

Employment, unemployment, and masculinities

What were the possible relationships between orientations to masculinities and experiences of employment and unemployment? The data indicates that the majority of those who had expressed a patriarchal orientation were in paid employment and the majority who had expressed a pioneering orientation were not.

The position of the patriarchs in employment was congruent with traditional, hegemonic masculinity - they were in a position in which they were able to have responsibility for their children and households as lone fathers, and continue in paid employment. As indicated in the earlier discussion, for some this involved a certain amount of stress meeting the different demands of work and home, and some felt that their careers had been damaged by the process.

There was a group of patriarchs who were not employed, and who were keen to be involved in paid employment but were unable to reconcile the demands of work with the demands of household and childcare:

> It's very hard, you can't start at 9 and finish at 3; I can't get a job that fits in with the (school) hours. Dick X, no. 24.

> After my wife died I carried on working on the oilrigs for 15 months, one of my wife's friends looked after my daughter. When she had to give up looking after her I had to give up work, I'm not free to get around and look for jobs. Ivan U, no.21.

These men could be seen to be in the position of being imprisoned by their traditional patriarchal form of masculinity, forced by circumstances to be confined to a private / affective role, yet wishing that they could adopt a more traditional public / instrumental masculine role. For them, the possibilities that their situations afforded them of greater involvement in, and satisfactions from, parenting and fathering were tainted by their perceptions that they were not fulfilling an appropriate masculine role within the boundaries prescribed, and perceived by them, of 'hegemonic masculinity.' (Connell, 1987.)

However, there was a group of men, who appeared to some degree to have negotiated a pathway through single fatherhood which did not involve paid employment; and who subsequently did not appear to experience not being involved in paid employment with a sense of loss and regret. Sometimes, generally associated with a patriarchal orientation, such men had been able to negotiate or accept redundancy payments for themselves, as applied with cases 1, 2, 6, and 15, all of whom were widowers. Thus, typical of this subcategory, Roy F, an ex shipyard worker, case number 6 said:

> When I was working I found it hard to concentrate at work worrying about my daughter, and I couldn't do any overtime. I found the hour

before and after school very hard to cover, therefore I was glad to take the chance when I was offered redundancy.

Ironically, for men such as this, the national increase in unemployment rates throughout the period of their single fatherhood in the 1980s, and the decline in the heavy industries of Northern England during this period presented them with redundancy possibilities that they could use positively. Thus, for them, redundancy was not so much a personal tragedy as an opportunity to resolve conflicting demands and desires.

What of the men with pioneering orientations to masculinities? In some cases, they had not been in circumstances where redundancy was an option, but at the time of the research were unemployed, not actively seeking work, and relatively content with their domestic roles. This applied to three men in particular, in all cases divorcees, they had not been in permanent, settled full time employment at the time of obtaining their divorces or custody of their children. What did they have to say about their experiences:

> When I finished college I applied for over 80 jobs, because I thought it was expected, but I knew I wouldn't take it if I got one. So, I just gave up as I became convinced that because of the children I couldn't take a job anyway.(Jeff S, no.19,)

> I used to work on big building sites, I can't travel to them and look after the boys - I think I'll have to retrain but I'm not worried about that.(Albert P, no.16.)

> I was unemployed and looked after our daughter when the marriage broke up, so I just carried on.(Kevin GG, no. 33.)

In each of the above three cases, the men concerned expressed satisfaction and contentment with their fathering and domestic roles. Such an orientation should not however be perceived as 'skiving' or 'scrounging' or having an easy time. It was perhaps realistic for them not to expect or want full time employment, the demands of the job market in this region at the time of the research were such that many men and women were surplus to the requirements of the market. Therefore, their acceptance of their unemployed state was realistic. Interestingly, it seemed that they were able to perceive that their unemployed state did not diminish them as men, they were able to see their roles as legitimate despite the potential conflicts such roles carried in terms of their incongruency with hegemonic masculinity. The explanation for this may lie in the fact that unemployment for them did not mark a drastic change from their previous states.

To an extent then, the men in this third category, in relation to paid employment, could be seen to be pioneers of a new gender role, they experienced and lived a form of masculinity which did not have as its foundation employment/instrumental work, but domestic/affective work.

However, in relation to paid employment, these men had not turned their backs on paid work as spontaneous acts of will motivated by radical ideological positions in relation to gender roles: the domestic and wider structural positions they were in had enabled them to see unemployment as an opportunity rather than a crisis.

Gender, masculinities, and employment

It is clear from the data presented, and the analysis of this data, that issues of gender and masculinities are intertwined and interconnected with issues of employment and unemployment at the level of day to day practicalities and practices; and at the higher level of ideologies, images and myths. There are different expectations in relation to the genders about employment - masculinities are connected with 'being employed', and employment policy, practices, and realities are shaped by, and shape, notions of gender differences and masculinities.

Evidence of the ways in which women are disadvantaged in the area of paid employment are well documented (Bradley, 1989), and such disadvantages and the inequalities that arise from and are reinforced and maintained via the labour market should not be underestimated or dismissed. What is less articulated in the literature are the details of the relations between paid employment and masculinities, the ways in which the one shapes and is shaped, reinforces and is reinforced, by the other.

The above data has illustrated how some lone fathers appear to have been relatively content with a situation in which they were unemployed and doing domestic work, whilst others appear to have felt more stressed and diminished in experiencing what were objectively very similar situations. For some their perceptions of the importance of paid employment had diminished, whereas for others the reality or the idea of paid employment still had a central significance in their lives. This latter position consists of a perception of a masculine role close to the concept of hegemonic masculinity, Alan D, case no 4, was describing such a position when he said:

A man out of work's a fish out of water, a woman out of work isn't - a man's a better man if he works, if a woman works it doesn't matter so long as one of them's home for the kids; it's better for a man with his wife if he works, he gets skits *(is teased)* if he's out of work that he has to put up with.

This comment is a clear indication of how patriarchal structures within society are interconnected, and yet different masculinities can operate within different structures. Alan D was speaking somewhat traditionally about the patriarchal relations of employment, and yet in his comments about gender roles later in the interview with him he expressed a perspection which was congruent with a gender pioneering form of masculinity. This illustrates how individual men can pursue different

148

masculinities within the relations of the different patriarchal structures of society.

Clearly it a mistake to assume that there were no orientations to employment other than the dominant model of the traditional patriarchal form of masculinity, and clearly some lone fathers had developed an orientation to employment which, implicitly rather than explicitly, in its daily practice challenged the dominant, yet narrow, concepts of masculinity.

In doing so, some of them were employed, some were unemployed. It has been argued (Brittan, 1989, Ingham, 1984.) that most men in capitalist societies derive their primary focus of identity from their paid employment roles. What this chapter has shown is that this was true for some lone fathers; they could so organise their employment experiences to ensure that being a lone father did not appear to cause them particular stress, and was congruent with hegemonic masculinity. Other lone fathers however had their orientations to employment roles challenged or changed, with subsequent consequences for some with respect to their involvement in the domestic sphere of patriarchal relations. The objective experiences of the men in the sample cannot be divorced from their subjective experiences to understand these processes. Paradoxically, as has been argued earlier, to be a 'good man' in terms of paid employment is not in many ways congruent with being, or even being available to be, a father.

Also, related to, interwoven into, but not necessarily causal of, the different experiences of the men in the sample were the different economic positions of the lone fathers and their households, which is the subject of the next chapter.

8 Lone fathers and the economic setting

To understand the position of lone fathers and their households it is necessary to consider their economic circumstances, both past and present. The economic situations of different single parent households define boundaries within which the lives of the household members are pursued. This chapter begins with a consideration of the economic positions of single parent households in general. Following this, the chapter focuses on the particular economic situations of the single fathers in this sample; and concludes with a discussion of the relationships between the areas of money, parenting, and masculinities.

The economic position of single parent households

There is a body of evidence to indicate that single parent households are more likely to be households that suffer economic disadvantage than two parent households.

Writing in 1969, Marsden's survey of 'fatherless families' - the majority of lone parent families - showed the widespread extent of poverty and lack of resources available to such families, arguing that such deprivations stretch back throughout four centuries of poor law arrangements. This existence of poverty in many one parent households should not be seen to be the result of the feckless or spendthrift habits of lone parents, rather it is in many cases due to low income levels.

What then are the sources of income of lone parent families? The implicit assumption of much state policy in the past century has been that the norm is families which are financially supported by the male adult's wages, and other family types are deviations from this norm (e.g. see Land, 1985). Thus, Thane has written that policy makers in the last century:

> Took for granted the universality of the stable two-parent family, primarily dependent upon the father's wage, and the primacy of the family as a source of welfare. (p.29, Thane, 1978.)

150

Sources of income therefore can be seen to have a gender dimension - lone fathers could be assumed to continue in paid employment and therefore derive an income and have potential difficulties in child care; lone mothers could be assumed to continue in (unpaid) child care but have difficulties in pursuing paid employment from which to derive an income.

The post Beveridge system implicitly divided lone parents into the 'innocents' and the 'guilty' or 'non-innocents.' Thus, Millar writes, these two groups consisted of:

> On the one hand, widows and separated and divorced women who could prove they were not at fault and, on the other hand, all the rest - unmarried mothers, widowers, separated and divorced women unable to prove they were not at fault. (p.27, Millar, 1989.)

Following the replacement of national assistance by supplementary benefit, lone parents were entitled to receive benefits and were not forced to pursue paid employment. Nevertheless there is some indication that lone fathers were at times encouraged to do 'proper man's work'. George and Wilding reported that 9.6% of men on supplementary benefit felt pressured to come off benefit and take up paid employment. However, even George and Wilding, at least at the time of writing up their research, were clearly not unsympathetic to the view that lone fathers should be 'proper patriarchs' and do paid work. They write:

> This last point about pressure to return to work is one which it is difficult to evaluate. There comes a time when it will be in the father's and children's interests that he should return to work. A little judicious encouragement from the Supplementary Benefit officer may reasonably be seen as part of the welfare officer's function. What would be quite intolerable is that pressure should be brought to bear on a father to return to work where he has pre-school children and little possibility of making adequate arrangements to provide for their care. (p.81-82, George and Wilding, 1972.)

The recommendations of the 1974 Finer Report in relation to lone parents' financial positions were that all lone parents should be eligible to a 'guaranteed maintenance allowance'; that this benefit should be non-contributory; and that the state should administer, and take over responsibility for collecting maintenance payments.

Despite the fact that the Finer proposals were never fully implemented, some changes were made so that lone parents were, from 1975, entitled to receive increased child benefit as a result of their status, and were entitled to earn slightly more than other categories of adult claimants before their supplementary benefit income was affected.

At the time of the fieldwork for this study the Supplementary Benefits system was still in operation, it has been gradually replaced throughout the latter part of the 1980s by the income support system. Clearly those

151

who administered the SB system were likely to be influenced by the hegemonic gender perceptions that, other things being equal men should go out to work and women should stay at home and look after children. However, the increase in, and incidence of, unemployment prior to and during the course of this study appears to have had an impact - the lack of paid employment vacancies seems to have been likely to have reduced the pressures on those lone parents in this sample who were not working in paid employment to seek such employment.

An area of income that is generally of more significance for single parent mothers than single parent fathers is that of maintenance payments from former partners. Only one of the men in this sample received any maintenance from his ex partner,(Dick X, no.24), the remaining 18 divorcees were thus totally dependant on their earnings and/or benefit or similar payments. In contrast, 61% (433,000) of single mothers were due to receive such payments in 1989, although only 13.1% of the money due was actually paid by the men concerned, with the balance remaining unpaid or coming from the DSS (The Guardian, p.20, 28.12.1989)

In part because of this perceived 'drain' on the state's resources there has, parallel and subsequent to these findings, been an increasingly vociferous argument from many political quarters that such men should be held more responsible for the financial support of their children. (e.g. Margaret Thatcher's NCH speech of 17th January 1990, reported in 'The Guardian' on 18:1:1990). Consequent on this the Child Support Act, which became operational in April 1993, seeks to ensure that absent fathers (and mothers) are more financially responsible for their children than has been seen to be the case in the past. The methods of the Child Support Agency have proved extremely controversial in the first months of its life; indicating the tensions that exist in respect of decisions about the ongoing maintenance of children by absent parents.

One recent survey of the financial position of lone parents argues that, despite the differences within the heterogeneous group termed 'lone parents':

> It is important to note also the similarities in the circumstances of these families. Chief amongst these is the very high degree of dependency on supplementary benefit...8 out of 10 mothers were on benefit..only 17% of the lone mothers in the sample were never on benefit during the period of the study. (p.165, Millar, 1989.)

Millar goes on to show that in contrast to two parent families, lone parent families were more likely to be in poverty, and to remain in poverty. She argues that lone mothers are more likely to be living in poverty than lone fathers, because of the inadequacy of state benefits, and the difficulties of escaping from dependence on state benefits if one is a lone parent.

152

However, Millar notes that the sample of lone parents her data derives from - 1890 lone parents - contains only 41 lone fathers and states that:

> lone fathers are less likely to be poor than lone mothers ... The focus of this study is therefore on lone mothers rather than lone fathers. The lone fathers are included where possible, but the sample numbers means that they cannot be included in any detailed analysis.(p.41, Millar, 1989.)

Therefore, Millar's social policy focused macro study of lone parents financial positions' is less than adequate in relation to describing and analysing the economic experiences of lone fathers.

The economic experiences of lone fathers

What then are the experiences of lone father families? Writing of 'motherless families', one study said that:

> the majority of our sample felt themselves in some measure worse off financially than they had been before the family became motherless... A lot of the evidence we gathered is of course subjective. It is the fathers feelings about the situation uncorroborated by hard factual data...Whatever the objective reality the fathers' subjective feelings have a reality and validity of their own. (p.107, George and Wilding, 1972.)

A number of studies of lone fathers in the USA have touched on the issues of finances, some reporting financial difficulties as being common amongst their sample, others either reporting no financial difficulties or ignoring the subject completely. For example, Barry (1979) found that the most frequently voiced complaint amongst the sample she studied was of 'financial pressures,' whereas in a study by Smith and Smith (1981) the majority of lone fathers felt able to continue in paid employment and consequently did not report a 'significant' loss of income. Greif's study of divorced single fathers illustrates the heterogeneity of lone fathers positions, in that the incomes of the members of his sample ranged from under $10,000 to over $100,000. He records that:

> What many of the fathers cannot escape - and what does not feel good - is that they are not earning as much money as they used to, and that they are not able to concentrate on advancement. They had always believed they would be able to get ahead, to achieve status in the world through success at work and earning a decent income. Instead they are achieving a different kind of status - that of being seen as being a good father. (p.70, Greif, 1985.)

Greif raises the important point that the subjective meaning of the economic circumstances prevailing for different lone fathers is likely to be at least as important as the 'objective reality.' George and Wilding's earlier quote also focuses on the link between the subjective and the objective in relation to economic factors.

The data collected during this study also suggests the importance of subjective feelings in relation to the economic positions and lives of the lone fathers and their households. As has been described throughout this study, there were different orientations by lone fathers to masculinities. It could be argued that these positions were essentially interactionist, the product of the personalities of the men involved and their social relationships, and not related to wider structural factors. The questions thus need to be asked, how far were orientations related to different economic positions; how far can men in similar economic positions develop, adopt or hold different orientations, or how far are orientations to masculinities economically determined?

What factors has it been suggested are of significance in relation to the economic position of lone father households? A number are relevant; Townsend has argued that:

> poverty is the lack of resources necessary to permit participation in the activities, customs, and diets commonly approved by society. (p.88, Townsend, 1979)

As will be shown, not all the lone father households were 'in poverty', and some were relatively 'comfortably well off.' It was decided as part of the research design that data about the general economic positions of the households, rather than the exact income details, would provide the most meaningful picture. Thus, the source of the households income was established, and a description of the assets, the debts, and the economic experiences of the households in relation to day to day items and larger items and demands was obtained. Information was also obtained about the perceived cause of any economic problems suffered by the households, and about the relative economic positions of the lone father households compared with the period prior to the establishment of the lone father households. The lone fathers were also asked about their perceptions of their futures, which generated further data for some households as they related their future prospects (positive or negative) to their perceived economic situations.

Prior to becoming lone fathers the overwhelming majority of the sample had earned their income via work, during the course of being lone fathers a number had become dependent for their income on some form of benefit, redundancy payments, or pension.

154

Table 8.1
Main source of income of lone fathers
at time of study

	Earnings	Benefits
Total sample(35)	18	17
Divorcees(19)	9	10
Widowers(16)	9	7
Patriarchs(25)	14	11
Pioneers(10)	4	6

The sample was almost equally split between those who were in full time paid employment and those who were not. The distribution between those who derived their main source of income from earnings, and those who derived their main source of income from benefits was relatively even between widowers and divorcees, pioneers were more likely to be on benefit than patriarchs. In general then, the period of lone fatherhood had for the sample as a whole led to an increase in the proportion of men non-waged, but this change seemed to be relatively similar for widowers and divorcees.

Given this position, what were the experiences of the men in the sample in relation to the adequacy of their incomes? They were asked to rate how adequate their present income was, in general, and in relation to day to day living, expenditure on larger items, and savings.

Table 8.2
Adequacy of income

	V.adequate/adequate	Barely adequate/inadequate
Total sample(35)	22	13
Divorcees(19)	10	9
Widowers(16)	12	4
Patriarchs(25)	14	11
Pioneers(10)	8	2

It can be seen that the majority of the sample rated their income as being very adequate or adequate. This is perhaps surprising, in that the evidence from other studies might have led to the expectation that more lone fathers would be likely to have rated their incomes as inadequate. The above data appears to indicate that those lone fathers who had a patriarchal orientation to masculinities were more likely to rate their income as inadequate than were those with a gender pioneering orientation. This difference seems to accord with Greif's suggestion that some lone fathers are able to make the shift from prioritising rewards in the economic sphere of relations to prioritising rewards in the domestic sphere of relations.

There were also differences between the subgroupings of widowers and divorcees, nearly one in two divorcees rated their income as being barely adequate or inadequate compared with one in four widowers giving a similar rating. The explanations for these differences can be at least partly related to the different processes involved in becoming single fathers; the process of divorce often involves a division of assets between partners, leaving the lone father in a poorer situation at the end of this process. Only one of the lone father divorcees received any form of maintenance payments from their ex-wives, several of them had had to make cash payments to their ex-wives to 'buy out' their ex-partners property rights, or were committed to making such a payment at some point in the future.

What were the lone fathers ratings of their health in comparison with the pre-lone fatherhood period?

Table 8.3
Perceived adequacy of income
and rating of health

		Health	
		Better/same(24)	Worse(11)
Income	Adequate(22)	15	7
	Barely /Inadequate(13)	9	4

Here the data appears to indicate that a barely adequate or inadequate income had the same impact on the overall distribution of the sample into categories in respect of health as it did in respect of feelings of stress, with fewer lone fathers feeling that their health had deteriorated during lone fatherhood than had reported experiencing stress.

The source of income, and whether or not the lone father was in paid full time employment, appears to have been related to the perceived adequacy or otherwise of income. The following table illustrates the general position:

156

Table 8.4
Relationship between full time employment
and self rating of adequacy
of financial position

	Full time Employment	
	Yes(18)	No(17)
Adequate (22)	13	9
Inadequate (13)	5	8

This data indicates, as would have been expected from previous research studies, that lone fathers who were in receipt of an income were more likely to feel that their economic position was generally adequate than lone fathers who were in receipt of benefits. The main reason for this, not surprisingly, appears to have been that generally wages yield higher, more adequate, incomes than benefits. All those who were employed and who rated their incomes as inadequate were in low paid jobs, with the exception of one case, Matthew HH, no. 34, who felt that his problem was his inability to budget and manage his income. The lie of the media image that scroungers are 'well off' is illustrated by these figures; the actual position was eloquently summed up by Al L, no.12, who said:

> You say you're better off (on benefit than working) but it's a load of crap; I've found myself saying it to people, but I'm not, you just say those things, you kid yourself really, because you're in a trap, I think everyone on benefits does it to survive, as a defensive thing, it's all kidology.

Those who were on benefits and felt that their income was adequate were not necessarily 'super budgeters'. Sometimes they were in receipt of assistance in kind from relatives, friends, or voluntary organisations; thus some spoke of small gifts of food, toys or children's clothing, for example:

> If my mother didn't help me with (the children's) clothes and shoes I don't think I could dress them and give them a good standard of food just with the money that I get, I'd have to sacrifice their appearance or their nutrition, it would be appearance, nutrition would come first. I'd probably get clothes from jumble sales, if it wasn't for the help that I get from my mother there wouldn't be enough. (Jeff S, no.19.)

Others (legally) supplemented their benefit entitlements from their savings, Ivan U, no. 21, quoted earlier, went on to add that:

> I'm £20 short every week, so I use my savings, when they run out I don't know how I'll manage.

George and Wilding noted that the impacts of 'motherlessness' on the financial affairs of the household are not necessarily immediate:

> In the period straight after the wife's death or departure the father somehow maintained his former job and his former hours. As the temporary situation assumed a greater air of permanency he has to adjust. The adjustment leads to the loss of earning power which is clearly evident in those motherless for one to six years. (p.109, George and Wilding, 1972.)

As everyone in this study had been in a 'motherless' state for at least one year, and in some cases longer than six years, in general the time for the transitions anticipated by George and Wilding had elapsed. The indications on the basis of this study are that, even in the case of a small sample, the economic positions of the families involved varied, in some cases lone fatherhood was being pursued in relative affluence, in other cases relative adequacy, and in a minority of cases in dire straits.

However, to understand the complexities of the different positions involved, it was not simply sufficient to know about the general perceived adequacy or otherwise of the sample's incomes. Consequently, evidence was obtained in respect of the sample's financial positions in three areas:

1   Day to day living expenses
2   Expenditure on larger items (here the examples given were cars, holidays, and maintaining the home.)
3   Savings.

The following table illustrates the lone fathers' perceptions of their financial situations in relation to these three areas.

Table 8.5
Detailed ratings of income adequacy

	All(35)	Divorcees(19)	Widowers(16)
Day to day living			
Very Adequate/Adequate	24	12	12
Barely Adequate/Inadequate	11	7	4
Larger items(e.g. equipment replacement,holidays.)			
Very Adequate/Adequate	16	6	10
Barely Adequate/Inadequate	19	13	6
Savings			
Very Adequate/Adequate	16	6	10
Barely Adequate/Inadequate	19	13	6

	All(35)	Patriarchs(25)	Pioneers(10)
Day to day living			
Very Adequate/Adequate	24	20	4
Barely Adequate/Inadequate	11	5	6
Larger items(e.g. equipment replacement,holidays.)			
Very Adequate/Adequate	16	14	2
Barely Adequate/Inadequate	19	11	8
Savings			
Very Adequate/Adequate	16	13	3
Barely Adequate/Inadequate	19	12	7

Table 8.5 indicates that more men in the sample rated their economic position as being very adequate or adequate in terms of day to day living than had given a similar rating in terms of the general adequacy of their income. This indicates that on the basis of self-ratings, on a day to day basis approximately two thirds of the households were in a financially adequate position, with one third being in a financially less than adequate position. Some men in the sample felt able to spend without budgeting, others remained solvent by budgeting carefully and/or cutting back their expenditure. Thus, typically the latter group spoke of:

Managing day to day by juggling money(Al L, no.12.)

159

Need(ing) to sit down and think what you can afford to spend, I didn't have to do that before, you need to make your ends meet otherwise you're bankrupt(Arthur T, no.20)

The precariousness of the financial positions of some of the families in the study was illustrated by the responses in relation to the costs of large items of expenditure. As well as expenditure such as paying for holidays - which in many cases could not be afforded - expenditure that was impossible or that caused economic hardships included such things as buying Christmas gifts and paying for or replacing more expensive consumer items such as washing machines or television sets. Here the economic position of more families in the study was less adequate, with a more than 50% increase in the number of ratings in the barely adequate/inadequate categories. Such larger expenditure was sometimes carefully considered and planned, typical of this was the case of Albert P, no. 16:

It can be a question of who you know, relying on favours and using informal contact for house repairs; for Christmas everything's planned out, I buy from catalogues, it can take 9 months to pay off £200.

Clearly, even relatively small amounts of additional expenditure demanded great foresight and months of repayment. This precariousness appeared to be more pronounced for families on benefits than families where the father was an earner, which accords with other research studies on the inadequacy of benefits. (Allcock, 1987,Bradshaw and Morgan,1987.) In some cases for larger household items or when moving house, those on benefits were assisted by the single payments scheme in operation at the time of the study under the Supplementary Benefits regulations. The Income Support scheme introduced since the time of this research does not enable such grants to be made, thus households in a similar position now would be relatively worse off financially as a result.

In relation to the sample's contacts with the DHSS, experiences of the 'social security' varied, however the majority who commented on this felt that they were helpful or at least not unhelpful:

When I got a council house and moved from my mother's with the children the DHSS were very helpful (Jeff S, no.19)

although others had the experience that when it came to welfare benefits

You canna get anything extra, I've tried everything, I can't get owt. (Arthur T, no.20).

However, the point made by those respondents on benefits who were managing was that they had to be both assertive and proactive to achieve an adequate standard of living; Jeff S, no. 19, summed this up when he spoke of his house furnishing:

Setting up this new home, the DHSS were very helpful, they paid for all the carpets and furniture - about £700-£800 - I got estimates and they paid them, for example, the settee was £25 from a second hand shop; I hunted all over the place for the bargains, but you need the energy and the capacity to use the system.

The above example is interesting in that there are resonances within Jeff S's approach to the 'problem' of equipping his new home, of his seeing the task almost as a job of work to be done, as a project to be systematically and methodically tackled and solved.

Economic positions pre -lone fatherhood and at the time of the study

Each lone father was asked to rate the financial position of the household at the time of interview compared with before they became lone fathers, on a five point scale 'much better off - much worse off.' The following table indicates their ratings.

Table 8.6
Financial position of households pre-lone
fatherhood and at time of study

	All sample(35)	Divorcees(19)	Widowers(16)
Much better/better off	14	9	5
About same	6	3	3
Worse/much worse off	15	7	8

	All sample(35)	Patriarchs(25)	Pioneers(10)
Much better/better off	14	11	3
About same	6	3	3
Worse/much worse off	15	11	4

The data indicates that almost as many lone father households were better off financially than were worse off in comparison to the pre lone fatherhood position. Those fathers who felt that they were better off, were so because either their financial resources had increased, or the demands on those resources had decreased, or they were managing better on more limited resources. Resources had increased for some widowers in that the death of the spouse had brought financial benefits in the form of insurance policies. Thus, an example of this was Andy R, no. 18, who reported that things were financially fine, and that he was better off because:

I've got a good job and my wife was well covered when she died.

Not everyone reported that they were better off because of specific items such as insurance policies, some lone father households had benefited from a general rise in living standards associated with pay rises (e.g., cases 17 and 29), and others reported being better off because they perceived that lone father households were financially less demanding. Thus, Tony V, no.22, despite experiencing feelings off grief and loss at the death of his wife, acknowledged that he was:

> Better off, I'm getting the same wage and (my wife) doesn't have to be fed. She'd pop out and buy a frock, things like that, that doesn't happen now.

Other lone fathers reported feeling better off because they perceived their previous partners had been poor at managing money or had spent money in ways they perceived as being unwise. Typical examples of this position are illustrated in the following quotes:

> (I'm) much better off now. My wife's drinking and the bills she ran up got us in a hell of a mess financially.(John Y, no 25)

> It's an amazing, ironic thing, that I'm financially better off on considerably less income. Before, I used to work overtime and everything, and she had a job in a pub as well, but those plastic cards...she went mad with them, and we never had anything left over; since I've been on my own I've been able to manage great. (Jeff S, no.19)

It is interesting that in both of the above cases the men concerned reported being better off even though in the process of the divorce as part of the negotiations they had agreed to pay off debts incurred by their wives, in the former case £1500, in the latter £2500.

However, for others the process of the divorce and financial arrangements and agreements directly or indirectly related to the divorce were reasons why they were worse off financially in the lone fatherhood state. 8 of the 19 divorcees in the sample reported some sort of financial arrangements related to the split. In half of these cases the lone fathers still felt better off financially, either because they were better managers of finances than their ex wives, as indicated above, or because of a general rise in their living standards during the lone fathering period. In the other four cases financial arrangements related to divorce had led to a worsening of the financial position, an example of which is illustrated by the experience of Jake BB, no. 28, who said that when they were married:

> Our dual income was much bigger, she spent a lot, but she earned a lot and there were some savings. We also had the country cottage (2nd home), which went to her in the divorce settlement. Even though she spent a hell of a lot there was still some left over at the end of the month, in that respect financially I'm worse off without her...sorting out the financial arrangements of the divorce was a major problem - including £15,000 legal fees - I didn't expect those to be so high.

Such financial concerns were in some cases related to housing, the above lone father was in the process of moving to cheaper housing as a way of improving his financial position, and three other lone fathers anticipated that, to 'buy out' their ex partner's property rights, they might have to sell the property involved.

How far were self assessments of changed financial positions related to whether or not the lone father was in paid employment? The general experience of the sample was to be in paid employment prior to becoming lone fathers, at the time of the study approximately half had become unwaged.

Table 8.7
Lone fathers rating of their financial positions
compared with pre-lone fatherhood,
and employment positions

	All sample (35)	F.T.emp.(18)	Unemp.(17)
Much better/better off	14	9	5
Same	6	1	5
Worse/much worse off	15	8	7

It can be seen that some lone fathers who continued in paid employment became better off, and a similar sized group reported that they had become worse off. For those lone fathers who had become unwaged by the time of the research, similar sized subgroups reported their positions as being better, about the same, and worse; with a slightly larger subgrouping in the latter position. In sum, there does not appear to be a simple relationship between financial position and working or not working. In terms of self-assessments, some lone father's economic situations improved despite them ceasing to pursue paid employment, whereas other lone father's economic situations deteriorated despite them continuing in paid employment.

It needs to be remembered that for some men in the sample their benefits were 'cushioned' by redundancy or other one-off payments, and for others who were in work they were in low paid jobs which at best afforded bare survival. It also needs to be remembered that some lone fathers were comparing their current situations with previous situations which they perceived their ex - partners as mismanaging, and thus subjectively they were better off because they appeared to feel more in control of their economic destiny.

Control was clearly a factor that influenced some lone fathers assessments and experiences of their financial situations - there were implications that as single fathers they had control over the household's financial resources which they had not had - or more correctly perhaps had not chosen to have - during their marriages. It seems that some men's memories were that, particularly during the later, often negative phases of

163

their marital relationships, their wives financial behaviours had been unpredictable. They recalled that, they had, for example, discovered credit card or hire purchase debts, and were thus, as lone fathers, subsequently more keen to be aware of the realities of their financial positions. The following quoted are typical illustrations of this:

> I'm better off now, because I know what money I have is mine, with (her) I never knew where I was, she would even forge the signatures sometimes to get money out of my bank account. (Dick X, no.24.)

> I was better off when I was working, I was quids in, compared with when my wife was budgeting. Now because I'm not working I'm worse off, but I'm better off than if I wasn't working and she was still with me, I find I can manage the money better than she could. (Cary M, no.13.)

It should not be thought however that lone fatherhood represented for all lone fathers an increase in control and financial satisfaction, the comments quoted earlier of Al L clearly showed it did not. There were others on benefits and in work who found financial matters a real struggle and felt that they were worse off than they had been pre lone fatherhood:

> It's difficult to make money stretch a week, we can't afford a colour t.v. or the licence for a colour t.v. (Jack H, no.8, on benefit.)

> It's a bit of a struggle, I had to give up the phone 2 months ago, prior to that I'd cut down and stopped going out for a drink. (Cliff J, no. 10, local authority labourer.)

> We used to manage Monday to Sunday and still sometimes have some left, but now I'm going out more for a drink the money runs out about Saturday lunchtime. (Keith G, no.7, on benefit.)

How then did the sample view their futures in relation to their financial positions? The following table illustrates their responses.

Table 8.8
Anticipated financial position one year
following interview

	Better	Same	Worse
Total sample(35)	8	22	5
Divorcees (19)	5	11	13
Widowers (16)	3	11	2
Patriarchs (25)	4	18	3
Pioneers (10)	4	4	2

164

The responses indicated that the majority of the sample expected their financial positions to be unchanged a year later, but nearly 1 in 4 felt that their financial position would be better, and 1 in 7 felt that their financial position would be worse. A larger proportion of pioneers(40%) felt their financial position would be better a year later than did patriarchs(16%).

Those who felt they would be better off, did so, it would appear, for one of two reasons. Firstly, they felt their responsibilities would remain the same but their assets would increase - either through wage rises, or through children leaving school and going out to work and bringing extra money into the house. Secondly, others felt that they were in the process of changes which would directly or indirectly put their financial affairs on a sounder footing. Thus, one father was in the process of moving to a cheaper house, another was envisaging debts incurred by him during the lengthy coal strike of the 1980s would be paid off, and at least two others anticipated that they would be married again, indirectly as result of which they would be better off.

A forthcoming marriage was one of the reasons why one man anticipated he would be worse off financially a year later - because of the costs of marriage, particularly the expenses of house purchase. The financial problems he was anticipating would be short term ones, the same cannot be said for the other 4 respondents who anticipated that the passage of 12 months would lead to them being worse off. In each of these four cases the men concerned were dependent on benefits, and in each case felt that they would 'struggle along' gradually accumulating debts which they foresaw no way of redeeming. None of them felt that their situation was critical, but, as one of them wryly commented:

> I don't think I'll be getting much pay rise from the social security (Rick O, no.15.)

Money, parenting, and masculinities

The above data and analysis has indicated that for lone fathers, money and financial matters were important influences on the quality of life potentially available. However, it is also clear that the relationship between money and quality of life was not a simple one, in that low income appears not to have guaranteed misery and high(er) income appears not to have guaranteed happiness. In what ways then is the area of money understandable in relation to issues of parenting and patriarchy, of men and masculinities?

The area is a gendered area, it is not simply the City in which men are dominant, men also tend to be dominant in relation to financial matters in two gender households. Thus, research by Brannen and Wilson (1987) shows the relative dominance of men, and the relative financial vulnerability of women, in such households.

165

What constituted a patriarchal orientation? Two elements appear to have been involved - how the money was obtained, and how the money was spent. Regarding the former, the patriarchal orientation was expressed by an expectation that the male would continue working to obtain money. In other words, the patriarchal orientation involves a primacy of the masculine role over the parenting role. It may well be that for many men who do not obtain or have care or custody of their children, such an orientation is a significant factor of influence. It appears that the popular assumptions that men should go out to work whilst women should stay at home are still not uninfluential in affecting the perspectives and perceptions of both men and women. Brittan has written:

> Most men have been brought up to see themselves as responsible for the bread and butter of daily existence, they find it almost impossible to accommodate themselves to the sight of their wives going out to work to put food on the table (p.189, Brittan, 1989.)

Lone fathers did not have to accommodate themselves to such sights, but if they were not working - were not responsible by their daily labours for the bread on the table - then they had to find ways of accommodating themselves to their changed roles as lone fathers and as men. Those who were able to continue in the traditional patriarchal role of paid employment were receiving 'pay-offs' in a variety of ways. They were continuing to do what men do, in relation to notions of hegemonic masculinity; they were earning the money; they were continuing to work and minimising changes in their lives; they were legitimating their absence from the home for at least part of some days, and were continuing to have paid employment as a potential source of meaning. However, whilst this analysis of the patriarchal orientation can be employed to the financial arrangements of those from middle classes and above, it is also possible to see how patriarchal orientations in relation to those from the working class, from lower paid jobs, can be seen by them to more readily accommodate a shift - albeit perhaps intended as a temporary one - to dependency on benefits. For such men, there may well be a previous history of some dependency on state benefits absent amongst their more middle class fellows. For them also, work has probably involved relatively small financial rewards, and dependency on benefits affords the possibility of a period of a different kind of activity for relatively similar financial rewards. As Keith G, no. 7 commented, whether he was in work - as he had been previously, or on benefits - as he had been since becoming a lone father:

> It's the same; money's always come and gone, I still can't seem to get too much.

Low levels of pay were also limiting in that they reduced the possibility of paying for child care out of income, thus reducing the availability of earned income as a way of supporting the family. It also needs to be noted that sometimes the only way that a living wage can be accrued is by overtime and shift working. For these reasons then the working class man might be have been less able to continue working, but felt potentially less diminished in his identity as a man by becoming 'dependent' on benefits - after all, low paid working class jobs are dependent on the fickle needs of the labour market and provide relatively sparse benefits in the form of mean wages and miserable working and service conditions.

The financial and economic arrangements of some of the sample supports the suggestion that some lone fathers in some aspects of their lives were imprisoned by the ways they defined and lived their gender roles. These were men who adopted a 'traditional' patriarchal orientation in relation to the area of finance but their parenting responsibilities led them to be unable to pursue paid employment - their parenting roles had primacy over their economic roles. However, this primacy was not, in many cases, a matter of choice; as lone fathers these men felt that their possibilities of choice, and domains of control, were limited and limiting in the areas of finance and economic matters. They would appear to have preferred to have continued in or returned to paid employment, leaving the bulk of parenting and child care responsibilities to a surrogate wife - but such arrangements were impossible for them to achieve. Thus, they were imprisoned on benefits, excluded from the world of paid work they desired. Eloquently expressing this perspective was Cary M, no.13, quoted earlier, when he commented somewhat bitterly about the mistake he felt he had made in giving up paid employment. It seems to be the case that such an orientation crossed class divisions, some middle class men were likely to exhibit this orientation. Thus, Aidan FF, no. 32, who had been in management recalled how becoming a lone father had meant he had:

> Had to leave work, to start off with my mother in law looked after the kids..it was clear after 3 months that it was too much for her, I had to give up work,

which financially had meant the family had become

gradually worse off, the level of benefit is too low.

In response to the financial difficulties being on benefit caused, Aidan FF had tried to return to work on a part time basis a year prior to the interview, but had found difficulties in relation to both child care arrangements and in performing the job satisfactorily - he felt that he had lost self confidence. Thus, he had not continued in paid employment, but consequently felt trapped on benefits, and worried about what would happen when major expenditure items arose - such as the necessity to replace an ailing washing machine or worn carpets. Therefore a middle class man, who had been in management, who lived in a house he owned, felt imprisoned at home.

167

Pioneering orientations

Pioneering orientations provided a means by which lone fathers asserted control over their life situations. In relation to financial matters the patriarchal orientation for those in employment afforded control by enabling the continued earning of an income; for those who were non - employed it led them to define their dependency on benefits as a state of powerlessness. In contrast, for those lone fathers who had come to act in ways which could be defined as adopting pioneering orientations to masculinities, they asserted a measure of control over their economic positions by the ways in which they were able to derive satisfactions and generate meaning in their lives.

These men gave a high priority to their parenting functions, implicitly perceiving that these roles were the ways in which they defined their identities and masculinity, and consequently financial matters became less of a test for them of their masculinity. Their priorities were different - they perceived themselves as being more the product of what they did with and for their children, than of the economic rewards they did - or did nor derive - from what they did in the domain of paid employment. Many men in the sample expressed attitudes which can be seen to show elements of a pioneering orientation in relation to financial matters; for many of them the transition to lone fatherhood had come to involve a change in their personal priorities. The views expressed by Fergus W, no. 23, (an example of a man with a patriarchal orientation to gender views who had developed more of a pioneering orientation in this structure of relations) typified this change in priorities:

> I realise now that people are more important than work, you can earn a lot of money but it's no good if it keeps you away from your family. I've had things put into perspective, if you miss your children's childhood you can never bring that back.

There were other examples of men whose priorities had changed. Indications of them were obtained in response to both direct questions about financial matters and the question which asked the sample if their personal circumstances had changed their thoughts about what was important in life. The following illustrative comments, from men who were in the category of pioneers in relation to masculinities and gender relations, were typical:

> I'm not materialistic like I used to be.(Chris Z, no. 26)

> When I was a teenager for me the most important thing in life was succeeding materially, mainly through jobs I suppose. Now, I don't see that as important, now, the important thing in life I see is relationships with people - with family in particular.(Jeff S, no.19)

Clearly, in relation to economic matters, a pioneering orientation did not go alongside feelings that the household was in dire straits financially -

the lone fathers needed to feel that the most basic needs of the household members were being met. Given that however, the evidence from this study appears to indicate that the processes and transitions involved in becoming and being lone fathers involved for some men a turning away from the pursuit of materialistic goals as the central raison d'etre of their lives. Thus, in these aspects of their lives there appears to be evidence that some men in the sample had been involved in changes in their orientations to masculinities. It is not being argued that the changes described necessarily flowed through to all aspects of their lives, the men involved could display a range of traditionally patriarchal orientations whilst in their workplaces, yet the meaning of their workplace to the 'pioneers' had changed, it had become less of a central mainspring of their masculinity and more of a means to an end. The pioneering orientation for those on benefits involved an appreciation that parenting was more successfully achieved for them by not engaging in paid employment, being on benefit was not a priori the second best solution to their situation. Connell has written:

> A hegemonic pattern of masculinity, in organizing the solidarity of men, becomes an economic as well as a cultural force (p.106, Connell,1987.)

In relation to economic and financial matters, some men in this sample were pursuing traditional patriarchal patterns of behaviour which were consistent with hegemonic masculinity. Other patriarchs, as a result of their structural circumstances and their subjective orientations to their lives felt that they were trapped; felt that they were not able to adopt patterns of behaviour consistent with hegemonic masculinity. Others, by the pioneering orientation they adopted, were living their lives in ways which challenged hegemonic masculinity in this area.

The question was asked earlier, how far were these orientations related to different economic positions; can men in similar economic positions develop, adopt or hold different orientations; or are these orientations largely economically determined? The evidence from this study appears to be that the economic circumstances created the broad boundaries within which these men lived their lives, but the economic circumstances did not dictate their orientations. In relation to the masculinities suggested, some men in similar economic circumstances had adopted and developed different masculinities, whilst others in different economic circumstances had developed similar masculinities.

Therefore, this chapter has involved a consideration of the economic positions of single parent households in general. Following this, the chapter has focused on the particular economic situations of the single fathers in this sample; and concluded with a discussion of the relationships between the areas of money, parenting, and masculinities. Such relationships do not occur solely within households, and the next chapter focuses on a consideration of single fathers, kinship and social networks, and the community.

169

9 Relationships of kinship, sex and sexuality

Lone fathers are not only members of households, they are also members of a range of social networks, and of communities, and it was anticipated that these social relationships would have impacts on their definitions and experiences of parenting and gender roles.

It is generally seen that gender is an influential variable in these areas, but the meaning of gender in such relationships is underresearched in relation to men. Women are generally recognised as being more involved in relationships outside the household that are family or community focused. Thus, Beresford and Croft, having surveyed the literature on the concept of 'community' argue that the term 'community' renders women, who they see as constituting the actual community, invisible. They note that:

> the home locality is very much the province of women. The 'community' is women's space, just as 'caring is women's work. Women are the 'community' patch social services' advocates are talking about when they speak of 'informal networks and care'. (p.80, Beresford and Croft, 1986.)

If women are seen to dominate the domain of the community and caring networks, then leisure and leisure relationships are seen to be the domain of men (Hargreaves,1989.) Lone fathers are potentially at odds with these perceived patterns: they are not living with female partners, and thus are perhaps more likely than other men to be involved in kinship, informal, and community networks and less likely to have time for and access to leisure activities because of this.

To establish if this was the case, and to explore the extent and meaning of such relationships for lone fathers, it is necessary to establish the nature and extent of the non-household relationships in which the members of the sample were involved. Six areas were examined:

170

1   Kinship relationships - in relation to close, and distant family members.
2   Ex partner relationships - in relation to the divorcees in the sample.
3   Sexual relationships.
4   Friendship, acquaintance and leisure relationships.
5   Community relationships.
6   Relationships with professionals and/or members of state agencies, in relation to lone fatherhood - to be discussed in a later chapter.

How then did the members of the sample describe their relationships in these areas? This chapter will focus on the more 'private' areas of kinship, ex-partner, and sexuality relationships, the next on the more 'public' areas of social networks and community relationships.

Kinship relationships

The experiences of the men in this study in respect of their involvement with family members other than their ex-partner and children varied considerably. Some men had little or no contact with any other members of their (or their ex-partners) families, others had a great deal of contact - in a minority of cases these family members were intermittently household members. There were also considerable variations in lone fathers' control of the contacts, some wanted more contact with family members but could not arrange it, others wanted less contact with family members but were unable, or felt unable, to arrange a reduction.

Morgan (1975) concludes that the main features of kinship in modern, urban settings are that:

    - Families are more properly described as 'modified extended families' than 'isolated nuclear families.
    - Such a family form is found amongst all classes, including the mobile middle classes, often perceived as the most isolated.
    - All kin relationships are not equal, some are 'selected' to be more intimate, on the basis of degree of relationship, geography, and personal choice.
    - Parents, then siblings, then others, is the preferential sequence in relation to degrees of intimacy; intimacy therefore is related to generational issues.
    - Women are most important in relation to the maintenance of kinship ties and the handling of flows of aid, information and resources. (p.66, Morgan, 1975)

Previous studies of lone fathers have either not focused to any large extent on issues related to kinship, or have looked only at contact with 'extended family' in terms of the help offered by such relatives to the lone fathers (the relationships, if examined, tend to be only seen as one-way.) Thus, George and Wilding (1972) refer to the fact that two-thirds of their sample received help from relatives at some point. They note that lone fathers were more likely to have contact with their own, rather than their ex partners, relatives, but have no data on the proximity, or frequency of contact with, relatives. Hipgrave (1982) refers to loneliness and social isolation as being potential problems for lone fathers, but does not indicate whether this was in any way related to an absence or presence of contact with relatives. O'Brien notes that the lone fathers in her sample had all:

> Moved into a world characterised by a close and continual connectedness to the home (p.227, O'Brien, 1982.)

but also presents no detailed data on this area. Greif, whilst stressing that his study was concerned to look at lone fathers from a 'systems framework', considering all the contextual influences on lone fathers, subsequently provides no data on this area and only mentions - in idealistic terms - the important of contacts with relatives:

> relatives supply continuity, love, and a feeling of belonging that the family may need more acutely after the break-up (p.89, Greif, 1985.)

As part of the interviews for this study, the respondents were asked about the geographical proximity and frequency of contact with family members outside the household. The following table illustrates how near the lone fathers lived to their nearest relative.

Table 9.1
Geographical proximity of nearest relative

Miles	All sample(n=35)	Widowers(n=16)	Divorcees(n=19)
0-1	21	10	11
2-4	8	4	4
5-10	2	1	1
11-99	0	0	0
100-199	2	0	2
200-999	1	0	1
999+	1	1	0

	All sample(35)	Patriarchs(25)	Pioneers(10)
0-1	21	16	5
2-4	8	5	3
5-10	2	1	1
11-99	0	0	0
100-199	2	2	0
200-999	1	0	1
999+	1	1	0

172

The data illustrates not necessarily the closest relative in terms of intimacy, but the closest relative geographically. Whilst some writers (Litwak, 1960; Harris, 1983) have argued that geographical separateness does not a priori reduce kin contact, nevertheless geographical proximity to kin makes face to face contacts by lone fathers with their relatives potentially easier.

Analysis indicates three main categories. 60% of the sample (21 lone fathers) had at least one relative living within a mile of their household, which is easy walking distance for an adult or child. 28.6% of the sample (10 lone fathers) had at least one relative living within 2-10 miles of the lone father household, not easy walking distance but not inaccessible by public transport or car. The remaining 11.6% of the sample (4 lone fathers) had no relatives nearer than 100 miles, thus physical contact by the lone fathers with these relatives would involve the expenditure of significant amounts of time, energy, and cash. Whilst membership of the first two categories was relatively equally comprised of widowers and divorcees, the latter produced 3 of the 4 cases in the third category. Social class membership does not indicate any particular differences between middle class and working class lone fathers in the first two categories; 3 of the 4 cases in the third category were middle class lone fathers.

With respect to patriarchal and pioneering orientations to masculinities, there were no clear differences between the two groups with regard to their geographical proximity to kinfolk - it might have been expected that kinfolk contacts could have been a traditionalising influence on lone fathers, making distance from kinfolk more likely to be associated with pioneering masculinity, but this hypothesis is not supported by the data.

Were there differences in the number of kin available for such face to face contact?

Table 9.2
Number of relatives with whom
lone fathers had regular contact

	Number				
	0	1-2	3	4-5	6-8
Total sample(35)	1	6	10	12	5
Widowers(16)	1	2	3	7	3
Divorcees(19)	0	4	7	5	3
Patriarchs(25)	1	3	8	8	3
Pioneers(10)	0	3	2	4	2

The majority of the sample had contact with between 2 and 5 relatives, with no clear differences emerging between the numbers of relatives mentioned by widowers or divorcees and patriarchs or pioneers.

173

Analysis by social class membership reveals some differences; working class fathers were more likely to mention a small number of kin, and middle class fathers a large number of kin.

As well as the geographical location and number of kin, estimates were sought on lone fathers' face to face contacts with any relations in a typical month.

Table 9.3
Numbers of face to face contacts
with relatives in an average month

No. of contacts	All sample(35)	Widowers(16)	Divorcees(19)
0	3	1	2
1-2	2	0	2
3-4	3	2	1
5-6	3	1	2
8-10	3	3	0
10-19	1	1	0
20-30	3	2	1
31-50	3	2	1
60	1	0	1
90	1	0	1
99+	12	4	8

	All sample(35)	Patriarchs(25)	Pioneers(10)
0	3	2	1
1-2	2	1	1
3-4	3	3	0
5-6	3	1	2
8-10	3	3	0
10-19	1	1	0
20-30	3	3	0
31-50	3	1	2
60	1	0	1
90	1	1	0
99+	12	9	3

Thus, there was wide variation in the amount of face to face contact lone fathers had with non-household relatives. In the average month a small minority of the sample had little or no contact with such kin (5 lone fathers in the 0-2 contacts range.) A larger minority had contact approaching at least once a week or more with such kin (9 lone fathers in the 3-10 contacts range.) A further small minority had frequent, albeit less than daily, contact with kin (4 lone fathers in the 10-30 contacts range.) Approximately half of the sample had the equivalent of daily contact with relatives (17) with more than a third (12) reporting an average in excess of three contacts per day.

174

Divorcees were relatively overrepresented at both ends of the contact continuum; widowers' contact patterns were fairly evenly spread across the continuum. Analysis by social class supports the conclusions of other studies regarding kinship network contacts in that no class differences emerged in relation to the amount of face to face contact.

How do these contacts compare with data on lone mothers contacts with kinfolk? Townsend (1979) records that 23% of his sample of lone mothers saw relatives most days, and another 44% saw relatives at least once a week. These figures show greater kin contact by lone fathers - approximately 50% saw relatives most days, and another 30% saw relatives at least once a week.

There were some differences between the kinship contact patterns of the two subgroupings of pioneers and patriarchs; pioneers tended to either have a low or a high level of contact with kinfolk, patriarchs were more evenly distributed across the range. Gender was related to contact in that the vast majority of contact was with female kinfolk, primarily mothers and sisters. O'Brien (1987) found that lone fathers contacts with female kinfolk were not gendered towards female kin, this study suggests the contrary. She also found a pattern of polarity regarding contacts with kin similar to the one found in respect of pioneers in this sample.

Statistical measures of kinship contacts give one kind of picture, but they do not illustrate the meaning of that contact for the participants. Just as a lack of such contact does not necessarily mean the existence of a feeling of isolation, so it is possible that a lone father could feel isolated despite frequent kinship contacts. Within the sample studied there were examples of each of four categories.

Firstly, there were some lone fathers who were isolated from kinfolk and who felt isolated, the former being directly or indirectly related to the latter. Perhaps the clearest example of this category was Ivan U, no. 21, whose nearest relative lived 1200 miles away, and who had no contact with any of his ex-partner's relatives. In reporting experiencing a great deal of stress, the main cause he saw was:

> The lack of contact with adults, not having someone you can really trust who (you) can sit down and have a good pow-wow with.

Such isolation was obviously not simply caused by the lack of kin contacts, but was related to the demands of caring for his young daughter, his recent split up from a girlfriend, and the fact that although he reported having 'hundreds' of acquaintances he did not feel that he had contact with anyone he could term a friend. For someone in Ivan U's position then, kinfolk contacts would have been potentially the basic safeguard against loneliness and lack of social contacts.

Secondly, there were some lone fathers who had very little face to face contact with kinfolk but did not feel isolated. An example of this category was James CC, no. 29, who estimated that he only saw relatives four times per year, yet did not feel lonely, partly because:

> In the early stages of the separation I wasn't lonely, I was too busy

and partly because he led an active social life, being a member of several different recreational clubs, and having a network of acquaintances and 6 people he termed 'real friends.'

Thirdly, there were numbers of lone fathers who had substantial regular face to face contacts with kinfolk and who did not feel socially isolated. A not untypical example of this category was Jeff S, case number 19, who saw his mother every day, and who, having had very close face to face contact with a female adult sibling prior to her moving away, had maintained that contact via frequent telephone calls. (In the high frequency of contact with kinfolk category, the order of frequency of contact tended to be the parent:sibling:other one referred to by Morgan , 1975.) Jeff S was typical of this category in that   analysis of his description of his situation indicates that his kinship contacts formed only part of the reason why he did not feel isolated, social contacts with friends forming the main remaining reason. Thus he said in relation to his kinship contacts:

> We go down to see my mother, who lives in the same street, every night (the children) enjoy seeing their grandmother, and apart from that, she buys them new clothes.... which is a considerable help financially; and with them being girls, especially the age they're getting to now, she's a great help.

In one sentence the social, financial and gender dimensions of kinship relations are illustrated. However, in response to questions about possible feelings of loneliness Jeff S did not see kinship relations alone being a guard against loneliness. When he was first separated and then divorced from his wife he and the children lived with his mother, yet he felt that had been the loneliest time, subsequently he had re-formed friendships with 'some of the lads' which he saw as being a bulwark against loneliness.

Finally, in the fourth category there were a number of lone fathers who had substantial regular face to face contacts with kinfolk and yet who did feel socially isolated. Typical of this category was Alan D, no. 4, who lived within two hundred yards of two brothers, with whom he was in daily face to face contact. Despite this frequent contact, he felt that:

> Every night when the kids are in bed and the telly finishes it's lonely - I've got my freedom but it's a lonely freedom

and he said he would

176

Like the family to be closer, like the...family nearby, where all the men go out for a drink every Saturday lunchtime, it must be great having the comfort and protection of a close - knit family.

What these comments indicate, and they were typical of the comments in this category, is that it was not the quantity but the quality of the contact with kinfolk that was perceived by these lone fathers to be important, regular contact did not banish loneliness. In fact, Alan D's contacts with his brothers could be termed instrumental - for them - in that he woke one for work every day, and cooked a daily meal for the other. It is possible, and the example he gave supports this, that less instrumental and more expressive contact with kinfolk would, for him, have reduced his loneliness.

In relation to kinship contacts, what were the connections with different forms of masculinities? Patriarchal orientations in this area were expressed by those men who had frequent contact with kinfolk, usually in relation to child care and their maintenance needs, who received a great deal of assistance from (usually women) kinfolk, and thus shared responsibility for, but retained control over, domestic matters. Thus, the men such as Jack H, no. 8, and Danny AA, no. 27, who were both in full time paid employment, and who both had daily assistance from their mothers in relation to child care, appeared to view such kinship contacts from the vantage point of a traditional patriarchal orientation. Others in the sample expressed a sense of their frustration in relation to kinship contacts, usually in one of two ways. Firstly, there were those who wished to receive more support from kinfolk and felt trapped into and by the performance of parenting duties because of the lack of such support (for example, Al L, no. 12.) Such an orientation represents an expression of a traditional form of patriarchal masculinity in relation to the domestic domain. Secondly, there were those who received support but felt that in so doing they had passed over an undue measure of control over their lives but were unwilling or unable to negotiate more appropriate arrangements for themselves (for example, Cliff J, no.10). Such an orientation represents in some ways a recognition of the losses potentially involved in pursuing traditional patriarchal masculinity.

What then constituted pioneering orientations in relation to contacts with kinfolk? It might be felt that such orientations would be likely to include less exploitative contacts with female kinfolk, related to an increased 'investment' on the part of the lone father in their parenting roles. However, the evidence is not strong for arguing that such orientations were widespread amongst the sample. Why might this be so? Perhaps, as pioneering orientations in relation to gender roles represent a break with tradition, it might be anticipated that more traditional orientations to gender and masculinities would be more prevalent in this area, as more personal historical socialisation precedents for behaviour exist in the area of kinship relations than in other areas. For patriarchs and pioneers, the overall impression of kinfolk relations gained from the data is of a generally high level of interaction with relatives who had traditional perspectives in relation to gender roles, and of lone fathers who felt they largely benefited from the support they were given from such relatives.

If contacts with relatives were marked by continuity rather than change, those men who were divorcees had experienced great changes in their relations with the women who had been their wives, and the area of contacts with ex-partners will now be considered.

Lone fathers contacts with their ex-partners

Nineteen lone fathers had ex-partners who were still alive and with whom they could thus potentially be in contact at the time they were interviewed. The contacts of the parent who has custody of the child(ren) of terminated marriages with the non-custodial partner are, it has been found, often difficult. Parkinson (1987), Smart and Sevenhuijsen, 1989, and Wallerstein and Kelly (1980, 1989) amongst others have outlined the difficulties separated or divorced partners can face in managing amicably their post break-up relationships. In most cases prior to the changes in child care legislation in 1991, custody of children was held by the mother on a sole custody basis. The 1988 Lord Chancellor's Report records that in 1987 only 8.3% of sole custody orders were granted to fathers, and the majority of the literature in this area is written about the statistically more frequent situations in which mothers have retained the care of the children and the fathers are the non-resident parents. Given that the divorced lone fathers in this sample all had the care of their children, what then were the number and nature of the contacts that lone fathers had with their ex-partners?

Table 9.4
Numbers of contacts lone fathers
estimated they had with ex-partner
in previous year

No. contacts	All(19)	Patriarchs(13)	Pioneers(6)
0	4	2	2
1-3	5	4	1
10-30	5	4	1
31-99	0	0	0
100	4	2	2
365	1	1	0

The figures indicate that there were some divorcees who had had no contact at all in the previous year with their ex partners. In two of these cases they had no idea of the whereabouts of the ex-partner. In the other two cases they knew where the ex-partner lived, and the adolescent children of the marriage had contact with their mothers that they arranged themselves without their fathers involvement. There was a slightly larger group of lone fathers who had only had between 1 and 3 contacts with their ex-partner in the previous twelve months. A similar sized group had contacts of between 10 and 30 times per year. The next group, in ascending order of frequency of contacts, was the 4 men who had approximately two contacts per week with their ex-partner; and there was a single lone father who had daily contacts with the ex-partner. The data does not indicate any substantial differences between the frequency of contacts of patriarchs and pioneers with their ex-partners.

Before the meaning of this range of contacts is discussed, it is important to consider other aspects of the contact. Not all of the contact was face to face, the following table indicates the type of contact.

Table 9.5
Type of contact with ex-partner

Type of contact	All(19)	Patriarchs(13)	Pioneers(6)
See and talk	8	6	2
See only	3	3	0
Phone contact only	3	1	2
Accidental contact	1	1	0
No contact	4	2	2

These figured indicate that less than half of the subsample of divorcees were in face to face contact with and talking to their ex-partners. The 3 cases where the lone fathers only saw their ex-partners were where children were being collected or delivered for access visits, ex-partners were seen only at the windows of houses or the steering wheels of cars. In three cases contact was by phone only, and in one case contact had occurred casually in the street.

What did lone fathers say were their primary reasons for their contacts with their ex-partners?

Table 9.6
Primary reason for contact with ex-partner

Reason	All(19)	Patriarchs(13)	Pioneers(6)
Access re. children	9	5	4
Financial matters	1	1	0
Casual contact	2	2	0
Mixture of above	3	3	0
No contact	4	2	2

It can be seen that the major primary reason stated for contacts was in relation to access matters, which to some extent possibly explains the distribution range in relation to the numbers of contacts lone fathers had with their ex-partners. Thus, if children were not old enough to make their own access arrangements, the negotiation and operationalising of

179

access meant that there were some lone fathers who of necessity had to have contact with their ex-partners. An interesting difference emerges in the above figures with respect to patriarchal and pioneering orientations, it seems that the pioneers involvements with their ex-partners were solely to do with access; perhaps this indicates the extent to which their lives were more likely to be focused on their children as a source of meaning than were the patriarchs.

The contact also varied in relation to the general 'tone' of the contact, and the following table indicates an analysis of the lone fathers responses in this area.

Table 9.7
Lone fathers assessment of tone of contact
with ex-partners

Tone of contact	All(19)	Patriarchs(13)	Pioneers(6)
Very friendly	2	2	0
Friendly	5	4	1
Neutral	3	2	1
Unfriendly	1	0	1
Very unfriendly	4	3	1
No contact	4	2	2

This table indicates that, on the basis of the lone fathers assessments, there was wide variation in the quality of the tone of the contact between ex-partners. Some lone fathers and their ex-partners had friendly or very friendly contact (36.8% of the subsample). In 5 cases out of the 6 cases where the contact was at least friendly the men involved were patriarchs. It might have been anticipated that pioneers would be more likely to have friendlier contacts with ex-partners than patriarchs, but this data indicates that this was not the case. If one assumes that in those cases where there was no contact the quality of the 'relationship' could be termed unfriendly, on this basis almost half the sample (47.5%) were in this category. The smallest group was those 3 lone fathers who described their relationship with their ex-partner as 'neutral.'

The geographical proximity of ex-partners in part determined the boundaries of the extent and the form of the contact that lone fathers had with them. Data has been given earlier in this chapter about the geographical location of relatives vis a vis lone fathers, the following table illustrates the location of lone father's ex-partners using the same physical intervals.

180

Table 9.8
Geographical proximity of ex-partner

Distance in miles	All(19)	Patriarchs(13)	Pioneers(6)
0-1	3	2	1
2-4	6	5	1
5-10	2	1	1
11-99	4	2	2
100-199	1	1	0
200-999	1	1	0
999+	1	1	0
Whereabouts unknown	2	1	1

Generally ex-partners were more geographically distant than kinfolk from lone fathers. These figures indicate that only a minority (15.8%) of the ex-partners were resident in easy walking distance, i.e. under a mile, at the time of the research, which compares with the position in relation to nearest (geographical) kin described earlier, where the figure was 60%. In total 58% of ex partners were resident within a ten mile distance. (corresponding total for kin was 88.6%), not easy walking distance but not inaccessible by public transport or car. The remaining ex-partners lived at distances of 30 miles (2), 50 miles, 120 miles, 300 miles, and 11,000 miles, (with the whereabouts of two ex-partners unknown). Face to face contact by the lone fathers with these ex-partners would involve the expenditure of significant amounts of time, energy, and cash.

The lone fathers who were in some form of contact with their ex-partners were asked if they would like to change the contact; 6 of the 14 said that they would - of these 3 wished that they could increase the level of contact and 3 wished that they could reduce the level of contact.

Overall, these figures indicate a complex picture in terms of lone fathers relations and relationships with their ex - partners. As indicated earlier, the perceived needs of their children was the major reason for many lone fathers still being in contact with ex - partners. However, there was a variety of ways in which relations between ex - partner and child were maintained. In some cases children were still able to have access to the absent mother even though there was hostility, or a total lack of contact, between the parents. In other cases there were frequent contacts between lone fathers and their ex - partners. The quality of these contacts ranged from friendly to unfriendly, and there were significant minorities wished to either increase or decrease the amount of contact.

How far were patriarchal and pioneering orientations to masculinities evident in the domain of contacts with ex-partners? It would appear that there was no simple relationship between the form of masculinity and the nature of the contact with the ex-partner. However, some suggestions can be made, although because of the small numbers involved in the different categories caution has to be exercised in the interpretations of the data.

Ex-partners, for lone fathers, constituted the women over whom they had formally and formerly had patriarchal power in the domestic setting. At the time of this research the primary focus for lone fathers' contact with their ex-partners was the children of the relationship. Some men did not want contact for themselves, but participated in ongoing contact for access reasons. Some men had little contact with their ex-partners, and chose to have little contact, often feeling angry towards them. A small minority of lone fathers appear to have wished for more contact with the ex-partner in the hope that such extra contact would open up the possibility of the relationship being re-established. A minority had been able to develop and maintain amicable relations with their ex-partners - in the main these were men who had, in relation to gender views, a patriarchal rather than a pioneering orientation. Why might this have been? Perhaps the answer is related to the interconnections between masculinities and parenting, and the extent to which contacts with the ex-partner represented a potential threat to a particular orientation to this area. Thus, integral to a patriarchal orientation to masculinity is the fact that a female 'other' is the main child carer. On this basis therefore, children's contacts with the ex-partner are congruent with this orientation, the ex-partner is another female 'other' whose contacts with the children do not a priori challenge patriarchal masculinity. A pioneering orientation however is related to greater involvement in parenting and child care, active parenting is a more substantial element of this form of masculinity. On this basis therefore, children's contacts with the ex-partner are less congruent with this orientation, the ex-partner's involvement represents more of a threat to the changed, more active, parenting role which is implicit in the pioneering orientation. It thus appears possible that for pioneering lone fathers, having a close relationship with the ex-partners, and having child care as a primary source of meaning, were in some ways mutually exclusive.

Lone fathers, sexual relationships, and sexuality

Being a lone father is a consequence of being in a prior heterosexual relationship. Following their becoming lone fathers some lone fathers had, or had had, further sexual relationships, others had not. Like the other forms of relationships, the non existence of sexual relations was for some as influential as the existence of sexual relations; and thus it is important to explore the issues of lone fathers, sexuality, and masculinities. Walby (1989) has argued that whilst sexuality and gender are interrelated, they are also separate concepts. Connell (1987) has argued for the link between heterosexuality and 'hegemonic masculinity', and other writers, such as Gross (1989), Lippert (1989), and Weeks (1989) have noted the relationship between male heterosexuality and masculinity. In reporting on their sexual lives these men were looking back over a substantial period of time when AIDS/HIV was not a concern, and did not act as an inhibitor on sexual activity.

In relation to this study, the single fathers were involved in a variety of patterns of relationships across gender boundaries, and were involved in a variety of different patterns of heterosexual relationships. Without exception, the members of this study described past and present sexual relationships as being heterosexual rather than homosexual. Thus, the inference drawn from this evidence was that all the members of the sample were heterosexual rather than homosexual. That is not to say that there are not single fathers who are homosexual, although research evidence about gay fathers is somewhat scarce. (Bozett, 1987.)

Whilst data about sexual relationships provides valuable information about lone fathers lives, to gain a fuller picture of gender and sexual relationships it was necessary to seek wider information. How far were lone fathers likely to have more contact with women than with men in relation to social networks? Did their changed roles as parents lead them to have contacts with more women than men? How far did they feel that they 'got on' better with men that with women? All these areas were considered in relation to gender and sexual relationships.

The following table illustrates the contacts the lone fathers had with other men and women.

Table 9.9
Relative amount of contact with other adults

	Total sample(35)	Divorcees(19)	Widowers(16)
More men	14	8	6
More women	4	2	2
Equal	17	9	8

	Total sample(35)	Patriarchs(25)	Pioneers(10)
More men	14	10	4
More women	4	2	2
Equal	17	13	4

The largest subgroup of lone fathers (17) had relatively equal amounts of contact with men and women. Another large subgroup of lone fathers (14) had more contact with other men rather than women, whilst the smallest subgroup of lone fathers (4) had more contact with other women than other men. Divorcees and widowers, and patriarchs and pioneers were relatively equally distributed throughout these different subgroupings. It might have been thought that the process of becoming a lone father, and the process of being a lone father, might have led the members of the sample to have more contacts with other women than with other men (O'Brien, 1987), on the basis of these figures this hypothesis appears to be not proven.

183

In terms of relating to the opposite gender, how did lone fathers rate themselves?

Table 9.10
Self assessment of gender relating

	Total sample(35)	Divorcees(19)	Widowers(16)
'Better with' men	10	5	5
'Better with' women	3	3	0
Same/no difference	22	11	11

	Total sample(35)	Patriarchs(25)	Pioneers(10)
'Better with' men	10	7	3
'Better with' women	3	2	1
Same/no difference	22	16	6

The largest subgroup of lone fathers (22) felt that they related equally well to other men and other women, commonly they spoke of it depending on the personality rather than the gender of the other person. The next largest subgroup (10) felt that they related better to other men, this appeared to have been sometimes related to some apprehension about women, as indicated for example by Roy F, no. 6:

I find it hard to speak to women

this, despite the fact that he had been married and was the father of four daughters, three grown up. Other men felt they related better to men for positive reasons, for example, talking about 'preferring men's company' (Keith E, no. 7.) A very small subgroup (3) felt that they related better to other women than to other men, one for stated positive reasons:

I love all women, I'd far rather chat with women than men(Alan D,no 4)

and the other two for stated negative reasons:

I prefer the company of women to the company of men, because politics, sex, and football get a bit monotonous (Len E, no. 5.)

I was never 'one of the lads', you couldn't have a decent conversation with them, they were all idiots (Albert P, no. 16).

All three men who felt they 'got on' better with women were divorcees rather than widowers, but, as can be seen, pioneers were not more likely than patriarchs to be in this small grouping. Their preferences were constructed as being to do with women being better company as conversationalists than men, rather than preferring women because, for example, of the possibility of sexual relationships and relations.

It is interesting to note that well over half the sample rated themselves as being able to get on equally well with both sexes. All the members of the sample felt that their membership of the above categories had not changed since they had become lone fathers - in other words, they felt, in response to specific questioning in this area, that their ability to relate to their own and the female gender had been unchanging despite any other changes that lone fatherhood might have wrought. The minority whose contacts with men and women had changed since becoming lone fathers had all experienced reduced contact with other men - as a result invariably of leaving paid employment.

What had been the experiences of the lone fathers in this sample with regard to close relationships with women since they had become lone fathers? The members of the sample were asked about this, 'close' was left to them to interpret rather than being defined in the question.

Table 9.11
Numbers of relationships with women
since becoming lone fathers

	Total sample(35)	Divorcees(19)	Widowers(16)
None	12	5	7
One	6	2	4
Two	5	4	1
Three	6	3	3
Four	3	2	1
Six	2	2	0
Twelve	1	1	0

	Total sample(35)	Patriarchs(25)	Pioneers(10)
None	12	9	3
One	6	5	1
Two	5	3	2
Three	6	4	2
Four	3	2	0
Six	2	1	1
Twelve	1	1	0

Thus 66% of the sample had had at least one relationship with a woman since they had been lone fathers. Widowers were more likely to have not had a relationship than divorcees - 44% (7) of widowers had not had a relationship, compared with 26% (5) of divorcees who were in the same category (and it has to be remembered that widowers on average had been lone fathers longer than divorcees, and had therefore had more time in which to develop such relationships.) Divorcees were more likely than widowers to have had three or more relationships, 42% (8) of divorcees were in this category compared with 25% (4) of widowers in the same category. No clear differences emerge from the data between the subgroups of patriarchs and pioneers. However, lone fathers who were engaged in manual labour were more likely not to have had any close relationships with women than middle class lone fathers; only 3 of the middle class fathers had had no relationships compared with 9 of the working class lone fathers. There is almost certainly no single reason for this latter difference, but possibly the likelihood that working class lone fathers would have fewer material resources at their disposal than middle class lone fathers may have been a factor in them feeling that they could not afford the cost of a heterosexual relationship.

Before considering further the meaning of these figures in more detail, it is important to note that all the above 'close' relationships had not, and were not, sexual relationships, as the following table indicates.

Table 9.12
Numbers of sexual relationships
with women since becoming lone fathers

	Total sample(35)	Divorcees(19)	Widowers(16)
None	15	7	8
One	5	2	3
Two	2	2	0
Three	5	2	3
Four	4	2	2
Six	2	2	0
Twelve	2	2	0

	Total sample(35)	Patriarchs(25)	Pioneers(10)
None	15	12	3
One	5	1	1
Two	2	0	2
Three	5	4	1
Four	4	4	0
Six	2	1	1
Twelve	2	1	1

The above figures show that not all close relationships were lone fathers had with women were sexual, and not all sexual relationships were seen as being close. They also indicate that pioneers were more likely to have had at least one sexual relationship than patriarchs. Some men spoke of companionship or friendship, or, in one case, of the fact that:

My fiancee's a lovely girl, we're waiting until we get married (to have a sexual relationship).(Len E, no. 5)

Such comments and attitudes indicate that models of masculinities that see men in relationships with women as only being interested in sex

186

oversimplifies and is misleading in relation to the complexities of some men's lives and relationships.

What of the men who had had a number of heterosexual encounters which had not been part of close relationships? In these cases the men felt, and it cannot be known what the women felt, not that they had exploited the women involved, but that the choice and benefits involved had been mutual- Cary M, no. 13, typified this perspective when he said:

> I wouldn't say that they'd been deep relationships (with women) but we've been friendly and I've slept with them - I think we've both got something out of it.

At the time of the study some men were involved in a relationship with a woman they rated 'close' and others were not.

Table 9.13
'Close' relationship with a woman
at the time of the study

	All sample(35)	Divorcees(19)	Widowers(16)
Yes	13	7	6
No	22	12	10

	All sample(35)	Patriarchs(25)	Pioneers(10)
Yes	13	10	3
No	22	15	7

Whilst there was relatively little difference between the experiences of widowers and divorcees, and patriarchs and pioneers, overall 37% (13) of the sample had a close relationship at the time of the study. It needs to be borne in mind that there is by definition likely to be a greater turnover of lone fathers who cease to be lone fathers in the former category than the latter, - several of the former category were actively planning marriage.

Finally in relation to this area lone fathers were asked what attitudes they had towards having a close relationship with a woman at the time of the study.

187

Table 9.14
Attitude to close relationship with a woman

	All sample(35)	Divorcees(19)	Widowers(16)
V.Important/ important	13	7	8
Interested if it happens	4	4	0
Neutral	1	1	0
Not bothered/ not interested	5	1	4
Mild avoidance/ avoidance	8	3	3

	All sample(35)	Patriarchs(25)	Pioneers(16)
Very Important/ important	13	9	4
Interested if it happens	4	3	1
Neutral	1	1	0
Not bothered/ not interested	5	3	2
Mild avoidance/ avoidance	8	5	3

This table indicates that there was a range of attitudes towards close relationships with women in the sample, with equal proportions of the sample feeling that such relationships were important, or to be avoided, or not interesting. There was a slight tendency for pioneers to be more resistant towards having a close relationship than patriarchs, which was perhaps related to the tension between orientations to masculinities and parenting discussed earlier.

All the men who were involved in a close relationship with women at the time of the research felt that the relationship was important to them. However, there were different perceptions of the meaning of the relationship. Thus, a few men saw the relationship as leading towards a future recreation of a more 'normal family life', typical of this group was Danny AA, no. 27:

> I used to say once bitten twice shy, but you change, you go crackers for a while with one night stands and then you settle down, I'm totally in love now, I wasn't with my first wife, we were too young and too daft. To me, the best thing in the world is to be settled and to lead a normal average life, that's all I want.

In similar vein, Len E, no. 5, said:

I've never gone out to find a wife, but I like being friendly with women and I've liked courting and the relationship that's grown with my fiancee, when (we are married) I hope it will be a nice family life again.

Some lone fathers then, all drawn from the patriarchs sub-group, saw intimate relationships with women as part of a process that was leading towards a new (renewed) family life. Others, including both patriarchs and pioneers, whilst valuing such relationships with women, appeared to see them more as an end in themselves. Typical of this group were the following:

I like having a close relationship but I wouldn't want to give up my independence, and she wouldn't want to give up hers; I take pleasure in entertaining a woman but I wouldn't want to get married - ever.(John Y, no. 25.)

I've a relationship at the moment, I wouldn't like to see it end, but whether there's a future in it is doubtful, I wouldn't want to make the mistake I made in my first marriage again, the idea of being happily married has its attractions, but it's not all that pressing, and I've seen a hell of a lot of second marriages that have come unstuck.(Jake BB, no. 28.)

The figures indicate that widowers and divorcees were equally represented in the group who had current intimate relationships with women. There were however two widowers, both patriarchs, who had had at least one intimate relationship with a woman, and were keen to have more, one for reasons to do with recreating 'the family', the other for the intrinsic satisfactions of a sexual relationship:

When I had a girlfriend we were a family again, we still talk about it even though it's over, I'd jump at the chance to get back tomorrow.(Ivan U, no. 21.)

I could leave it at one time, but now I'm woman mad at the moment, once you've got the taste again you can't leave it alone, I was quite happy being on my own, now I'm mad about women. (Dave C, no 3.)

The group who were interested in having a relationship 'if it happened', or felt neutral, were all divorcees. Typically, they described the non - existence of relationships with women because the opportunities had not arisen and they had not sought them:

I wouldn't knock back another relationship with another woman, but I'm not seeking one. (Matt K, no.11.)

I'd take it or leave it, I've nothing against marriage but with not working, I'm not secure in myself, as time goes on you get set and then it's going to be an upheaval, but if it happens it happens and I wouldn't run away from it. (Cary M, no. 13.)

Interestingly, this last comment links relationships with feelings of security with one's self, and it does appear that some men were seeking relationships partly as a way of making themselves feel more secure in themselves. Others were not actively seeking intimate relationships at least in part because they felt insecure within themselves, as indicated by Cary M above. This insecurity did not appear to be confined to members of the patriarchs or pioneers sub-groups. Some members of the sample who were not actively interested in having an intimate relationship, or who were avoiding such a relationship, saw such relationships as dangerous. Thus, divorcees such as Jack H, no.8, said:

I've not had any relationships with women, it's a case of once bitten, twice shy. I'm not bothered, if I'd wanted one I could have had one.

They're out of the question, I'm in enough trouble as it is, I've been bitten too many times by my ex-wife.(Arthur T, no. 20.)

Although I've not had any relationships I'm not totally averse to other women although the possibility of her walking out on me will always be at the back of my mind. I would be warier because of my ex-wife's deception, after 20 years of complete trust, to be deceived like that, that was the worst thing, and that obviously matters - you think, 'well, could I risk that happening again?' (James CC, no.29.)

Whilst some divorcees saw intimate relationships as dangerous, some widowers did not want another relationship partly because of fonder memories of their previous one. Typical comments they made included:

I've never wanted another relationship, people have encouraged me to, but I'd be looking for someone too much like (wife who had died.) (Cliff J, no. 10.)

It doesn't bother me, I've had one good relationship and I'm not really bothered about another.(Roy F, no.6.)

Other lone fathers were choosing not to have intimate relationships because of their perceptions of their children's needs. Thus, whilst it is perhaps popularly believed that lone fathers seek women partners at least partly for their children's needs, the evidence from this study is that at times the opposite is the case. Two comments that were typical of how lone fathers who described their positions thus follow. The first echoes symbolically how some lone fathers saw intimate heterosexual relationships as potentially dangerous, the second illustrates more the sense of denial felt by some lone fathers who were, at least in part, choosing not to have such relationships:

190

I've never really troubled, in fact, I've gone out of my way to avoid it, in fact, I know one who's trying to get her hooks into us - I think she's took the hint now; nice woman like but I don't think the kids would accept it, they've told me not to bring anyone in here.(Rick O, no.15.)

The reason why I haven't bothered with a relationship is that I don't want (my daughters) to see 'aunties' here - so I'm prepared to put up with not having a relationship; but it's something I look forward to in the future, but I'm prepared to wait until they're older, I've no intention of becoming a Trappist monk. (Jeff S, no. 19.)

In this latter case the perception of the lone father was children's needs leading to the need for deferred gratification in relation to intimate heterosexual relationships. However, it also appears from the evidence of this study that some men did not wish for intimate relationships with women because they had come to see more advantages without them than with them. It may be that men are conditioned to expect that every family needs a wife and a mother, the experiences of some lone fathers had led them to question whether reality needed to accord with such images, as typified by the comments of Al L, no. 12:

I've got my own ways now, I don't think I could live with another woman. I think there are a lot of women like that, who don't want to get involved again. When you've been single for a long time you get your own habits and your ways, when I was first single I thought about getting married again, but I had too much on with the kids... and now I wouldn't want to.

A picture has thus been drawn which illustrates that, whilst all the men in the sample were heterosexual, they were expressing a variety of forms of heterosexuality in their lives as lone fathers. Therefore, just as it has been argued that it is more appropriate to talk of masculinities rather than masculinity, so it appears to be more appropriate to talk about heterosexualities rather than heterosexuality. Whilst 'hegemonic heterosexuality' can be seen to exist in the same sense that hegemonic masculinity exists, the daily practices of the lone fathers in this sample - embracing and rejecting, desiring and fearing, searching for and avoiding intimate relationships with women - were not homogeneously uniform. Similarly, whilst it may be that in some ways heterosexuality is a form of patriarchal structure through which mens' dominance over women is asserted and maintained, the evidence of this analysis does not show that this is clearly the case in relation to the lives of all the men in this sample. Thus whilst some lone fathers were constructing and creating a patriarchal orientation in the realm of heterosexuality, at least some of this group were not seeking to recreate a traditional nuclear family household by this process, and gave the impression of being able to accept a heterosexual relationship without desiring patriarchal dominance within a single household. Others felt themselves to be in positions in which they were unable to attain the heterosexual relationships they desired, and to some extent perhaps the non existence of heterosexual relationships for this group represented to them some form of denial of patriarchal power. A third group were choosing not to enter into heterosexual relationships at all, either on a time limited or an indefinite basis. By not necessarily actively seeking to enter into heterosexual relationships these men were expressing a form of heterosexual masculinity which shows that 'ordinary men' - can quietly live their lives in ways which challenge the notion that:

> male sexuality (is) some kind of primordial force which sweeps everything before it. (p.46, Brittan, 1989.)

In this chapter then, the kinship, ex -partner, and sexual relationships of the men in the sample have been considered. As indicated at the start of this chapter, the lone fathers were also involved in a variety of other different kinds of relationships: with friends, acquaintances, and the community. The nature and form of these social networks will be considered next.

10 Lone fathers, social networks, and the community

Whilst relationships with relatives were, as illustrated, of great significance for some lone fathers, this study sought to examine the significance of the other social contacts of lone fathers. Apart from family networks, what were the other social relationships in which lone fathers were involved?

Friends, acquaintances, and lone fathers

Some men clearly distinguished between friends and acquaintances whilst others did not. Those who did differentiate tended to describe a situation in which they had contact with a relatively small number of people they would call friends, and a larger number of people they termed acquaintances. Those who did not distinguish between the two categories tended to describe a situation in which they had relatively few social contacts, thus, it was not that they described themselves as having hundreds of friends, rather they described a relatively limited pattern of friendship and acquaintanceship contacts.

What were seen to be the factors which separated out friends from other people? Knowledge and trust were two factors many lone fathers mentioned. Thus, typical comments in relation to friends were that:

> I know a lot about them, and they know a lot about me. (Cary M, no. 13.)

> A friend is someone you would discuss personal problems with, whereas an acquaintance is someone you might have a pint with and discuss general subjects.(Jake BB, no. 28.)

> A friend is someone you could tell things to, like personal domestic things you wouldn't tell anyone else. (Jeff S, no.19.)

The above quotes imply that friendship is related to trust and intimacy. They are also all quotes from lone fathers with pioneering gender orientations; did lone fathers with patriarchal orientations see friendship and acquaintanceship in different ways? The following are typical comments:

> There's lots of things I wouldn't tell an acquaintance, whereas a friend, I'd tell him owt and it wouldn't gan (go) any further.(Matt K, no.11.)

> A friend is someone you can really sit down and discuss things with.(Ivan U, no.21.)

It appears to be the case then that in terms of definitions of friendship there were no clear differences between patriarchs and pioneers. Friends were seen as people - invariably men - who could be trusted to receive and share personal information and confidences, acquaintances were people with whom one would, as one lone father said, 'pass the time of day.'

Lone fathers and friendship networks

Many writers, including Brown and Harris (1978) have argued that a lack of social contact with other adults is likely to be at least partially associated with feelings of loneliness or depression. George and Wilding (1972) found that a 'striking' number of their sample of lone fathers (66.5%) felt lonely or depressed at least occasionally, which they saw as being partly related to lone fathers isolation from other adults. Contact with other adults does not simply act as a defence against loneliness, it is one way in which social beings construct and affirm themselves as human. What patterns of contact with friends and acquaintances, in their lives as men and as lone fathers did the members of the sample report?

The members of the sample were asked about the similarities and differences in their friendship networks pre and post lone fatherhood.

Table 10.1
Friendship relationships pre and
post lone fatherhood

	More friends	No differences	Fewer friends
Total sample(35)	6	18	11
Widowers(16)	1	8	7
Divorcees(19)	5	10	4
Patriarchs(25)	3	13	9
Pioneers(10)	3	5	2

Whilst approximately half the sample had constant friendship relationships, a small minority had experienced an increase in the number of friends, and a larger minority a decrease. The figures also indicate that divorcees were the majority of the subgroup who had overall gained friends, and widowers the majority of the group who had overall lost friends. Patriarchs were more likely to have fewer friends than pioneers.

What explanations did the members of the sample give for these differences? For those men who reported no differences in their friendship networks the explanation appears to be that they had had, in Bott's (1957) terms, segregated conjugal roles, and had been less involved in joint friendship patterns with their partner prior to becoming lone fathers. Thus, they had been able to continue to pursue similar patterns of friendship relationships during lone fatherhood, often because a female relative was available to do evening childminding, or the children were old enough to be left by themselves. The following comments were typical:

> I've still got the same friends - drinking mates.(Keith G, no.7.)

> I've got lots of friends, I've had some for many years, some through the Lions Club, and some through the children. There's no difference between the friends I have now and when my wife was alive, some of the friends she had, who she saw, I don't see them. (Fergus W, no. 23.)

> I've got the same friends as I've always had, I see them more now with not working shifts.(Jack H, no.8.)

Clearly the above examples fit easily with the concept of a traditional patriarchal orientation in relation to the area of friendships, with the patriarch pursuing his friendships in male gender groups untroubled by the presence of female partners. What however of those who had pioneering orientations to gender roles and who had retained the same friendship networks? Analysis of their responses reveals no clearly different pattern emerging. Thus, they ranged from a lone father who had always been relatively isolated:

> I've always led an unsettled life, I've only ever made casual friends, with one constant real friend.(Albert P, no.16.)

through to others who had reported patterns similar to the 'patriarchs':

> There's no differences, I still go to the same club every week and I'm still friendly with the same people.(Roy F, no.6.)

> I've got the same friends, I see them fairly often at the bar.(Cliff J,no.10.)

and finally, one who reported a busy social life with both sexes:

I've got the same friends, I like to party, I like to dance, I like the local bar; the last few years of our marriage I used to go out by myself because most times she wouldn't come out.(Cary M, no.13.)

This last quote illustrates the common thread that ran through the descriptions of this subgroup. They, like the patriarchs who had retained the same friendship groups, had been involved in prior friendship relationships as individuals rather than as one half of a couple.

However, whilst equal proportions of patriarchs and pioneers had retained the same friendship networks, pioneers were over represented in the sub sample who reported an increase in the numbers of their friends, and under represented in the sub sample who reported a decrease.

In the former case, 30% (3) of the pioneers had developed more friends, as opposed to 12% (3) of the patriarchs. Whilst these numbers are small, they do warrant further consideration. Without exception, the pioneers in this subsample were all divorcees, had all been in unhappy marriages, and had all not been involved in a busy social life as part of a partnership with their spouses. Thus, Jake BB, no.28, said:

We didn't have many friends before my wife left because her behaviour was so odd at times we didn't dare make friends; now, I've got 2 very close friends.

and another member of this subgroup described at length the processes he had experienced:

When I was married I didn't really go out at all, the people I'd known before had got married, and I sort of drifted away from them, so I found that, when we first split up, all of a sudden I didn't know anybody. I found myself wandering around old haunts, expecting old faces to be there, and of course they weren't, so I suppose loneliness at first was one of the main problems. During the last few years, several of my friends have become divorced as well, so I've come back into contact with them - there was 5 of us who used to knock about together, and now 3 of us are divorced, so I see them most weekends, when the kiddies are away at their mothers.(Jeff S, no. 19.)

These last comments show how marriage can be limiting in relation to the continuance of friendships. Illustrated clearly is how the establishment of an intimate cross gender partnership can lead to a reduction in same gender relationships, and how the deterioration and collapse of the cross gender partnership can then provide the opportunity, for a reestablishing of same gender relationships (sometimes, as indicated, facilitated by custody arrangements.)

196

What of the patriarchs who reported increased friendship patterns? 2 of the 3 were widowers, in both cases they had spent long periods 'working away', thus, from this group Dave C, no.3 said:

> I've many more friends now locally than I used to have, before, I was busy working away and never used to bother with anybody.

The other member of this subgroup, Dennis Q, no. 17 recalled a set of experiences that were not dissimilar to those of Jeff S, no. 19, above:

> We used to knock around a bit with other couples before, I rarely see them now, they were more her friends than mine. I've got lots more friends now, I knock around with people from work, they're mostly single guys.

Finally, what conclusions can be drawn about the lone fathers who reported a decrease in the numbers of friends they had? The majority of this group came from the category defined as patriarchs rather than pioneers (9 out of the 11.) One theme which emerged in some of their comments was that friendships had previously been pursued as part of a couple, and these friendships had then diminished partly or wholly after the men in the sample had become lone fathers. Typical of this group was James CC, no. 29, who spoke at length:

> My friendships have changed, I miss out on a lot of social activities, particularly social functions that we used to go to as a couple. When there's been dinner-dances and that sort of thing I've tended to give them a miss, being on my own, but I still maintain contact with lots of the same people, but perhaps I don't go out as often as I used to. All my friends rallied round initially (after wife left) but they gradually drifted away.

Others, also spoke of the difficulties they experienced being no longer part of a couple, as the following two quotes typify:

> We had an active social life, but all the people who were friends with us were couples, it seems like they don't want to know when you're on your own, perhaps they're frightened you'll run off with their wife, you don't see them.(Ivan U, no.21.)

> I never see them now (ex-friends) mebbe they think they would be interfering, or opening up old wounds, but I never see the couples we used to know.(Tony V,no.22.

Other traditional patriarchs who appeared to have had, prior to becoming lone fathers, segregated conjugal roles, had subsequently been unable to continue to pursue similar patterns of friendship relationships as lone fathers, because of the unavailability of evening childminding, or a lack of financial resources. Typical of this latter position was Kevin GG, no.33, who said:

197

I haven't got as many friends as I used to have, I can only go out for a drink once a week now, before, when I was married, I used to go out at least three times a week.

Another representative of this category was Dick X, no.24, who, in reporting a reduction in his friendship network, also reported the only example of a lone father whose friendships had changed substantially in relation to moving from contacts with men to contacts with women:

It's changed a lot, it used to be Friday night with the lads, and then going out a lot as a couple, now, I feel that I have more contact with the women round here, going round to coffee during the day.

Whilst it is not appropriate to generalise from this single case example, it can be noted that it seems clear that Dick X was only able to adopt this changed friendship pattern because he was not in paid employment, thus, such social activity in the community appears to be possibly related to non full time employment. It is also interesting to note that the focal activity described was a low cost one, other lone fathers had the time available for more friendship contacts but felt they did not have the income to sustain them. Thus the two pioneers who reported a reduction in their friendships post lone fatherhood in both cases were not engaged in paid employment but reported financial difficulties in coping on benefit. Whilst money shortage appears to have been influential, they also both reported feeling that others attitudes had changed towards them as a result of their becoming and being lone fathers. Alan D, no. 4, commented that in relation to friendships he had experienced:

Vast differences, before I was working, had lots of friends, and ran a football team, now I'm just a single guy, I'm a guy with the plague, people all socialise as couples, as a single guy I'm an oddity

and Aidan FF, no.32, remembered that:

For the first six months to a year our old friends used to come round, then they dropped off, because I was single they didn't seem to treat me as normal, which irritated me, perhaps they picked that up.

How far were differences of social class apparent in relation to lone fathers friendships? Analysis indicates that the main difference was that working class lone fathers were more likely than middle class fathers to report an increase in the numbers of friends they had. The explanation for this appears to be related to availability for friendship contacts. Prior to becoming lone fathers the working class men in the sample had included men who worked long hours, and/or shiftwork, and/or worked away. Lone fatherhood had meant for many in this group either ceasing paid employment or ceasing to work away from home or reducing shift work or overtime work. Whilst it is true that for some men work is a place in which friendships are formed and sustained, perhaps the extent to which workplace contacts can be seen to constitute friendships can be

198

overestimated, certainly those who had left their jobs reported that they had not retained contacts with ex-workmates.

In respect of friendships, for different individuals and groups of lone fathers a number of themes were apparent. Some men had continued to have the same friends, who tended to have been the man's friends rather than the couple's friends. Other men had created new friendship networks, or recreated old friendship networks, in both cases primarily with other men rather than with both genders. Other men had lost friends, and not created new friends, and in many cases this position also was, for them, related to perceptions that as individuals they did not readily fit into 'couple' friendship networks. Divorcees were more likely to have retained or made friends, widowers more likely to have not retained friends,and it might be that issues to do with bereavement, both the feelings of the bereaved, and the difficulties others have in relating to the bereaved, were a factor in this. In relation to forms of masculinities, lone fathers with pioneering orientations were more likely to have increased the size of their friendship networks than were lone fathers with patriarchal orientations.

However, perhaps the clearest finding that emerges from the analysis of this data is that lone fathers, be they patriarchs or pioneers, widowers or divorcees, working class or middle class, overwhelmingly tended to have friendships within, rather than across, gender boundaries. This is not to say that some lone fathers did not have friendships - of a non-sexual nature - with women, clearly in some cases they did, either with individual women or with couples which included women. However, at least one other study reports that lone fatherhood involves a 'shift' from male friendship networks to female friendship networks (O'Brien, 1987). The evidence from this data does not support such a finding. It may be that the way O'Brien's sample was constructed, involving as it did the use of lone parent organisations membership lists, therefore led to a sampling bias towards lone fathers who were involved in largely female friendship networks. What does not appear to be common on the evidence of this study is a process by which lone fathers move into female friendship networks as a result of the changes associated with their becoming lone fathers. It thus appears that different orientations to masculinities are not consequential on, or causal of, different patterns of gender friendship - it was not the case that patriarchs had more men friends, and pioneers more women friends.

Lone fathers contacts with other lone parents

How much contact did lone fathers have with other lone parents? During one period, membership of formal single parent organisations was not possible for lone fathers, Jackson has written that:

> in the early stages of organisations representing single parent families men were actually denied admission. (p.167, Jackson, 1982)

Whilst men are not denied admission to such organisations any longer, did the lone fathers negotiate admission to the informal organisation of the female friendship networks which it has been argued constitute a large part of the 'community'? There are some indications that women who are lone parents often become members of extensive lone parent friendship and informal support networks (Cashmore, 1985, Marsden, 1969, Townsend, 1979.) In relation to lone fathers contacts with other single parents, the data obtained indicates that, having left the social world of two parents households, in the main they do not enter the social world of single parent households.

Table 10.2
Amount of contact with other single parents

	A lot	A few contacts	None
Total sample(35)	8	6	21
Widowers(16)	3	5	8
Divorcees(19)	5	1	13
Patriarchs(25)	6	4	15
Pioneers(10)	2	2	6

It can be seen that the majority of the sample had relatively little or no contact with other single parents, and there is no evidence that pioneering orientations were associated with the amount of contact with other single parents. In fact, the data is somewhat misleading in relation to the information that 8 of the sample had a lot of contact with other single parents, because in the majority of these cases the contact referred to was the result of a heterosexual sexual relationship with another single parent, rather than more general non sexual contacts. Why then were lone fathers not active in single parent organisations such as Gingerbread? Out of the sample of 35 lone fathers, 1 man attended Gingerbread meetings regularly, 2 men had been attenders at Gingerbread meetings, and 2 men had been involved in a Cruse bereavement group which had largely consisted of bereaved single parents.

In respect of Gingerbread attendance, in all three cases, the men involved had not been part of extensive friendship networks at the time. Albert P, no 16, Ivan U, no 21, and Danny AA, no 27 all appear to have been motivated by feelings of loneliness and a desire for company to join Gingerbread. Ivan U was still a regular attender at their functions, as the lone father of a pre school child he found that:

It's good for the little girl we go on daytrips.

Albert P had attended regularly for a brief period but recalled that:

I was put off by the internal politics, there was a clash of personalities between the chair of the local group and the treasurer,

200

and I got fed up of the arguments, and by then I'd started going out with (a woman he met at Gingerbread) so I stopped going.

Similarly, Danny AA, no. 27 recalled how:

I went to Gingerbread, I was desperate and on the dole, I went for a few weeks but people there were a bit erratic and scatter brained, they were going through their divorces and I thought 'Oh dear, I can't handle this' so I stopped going .... I was the only man there.

Therefore one lone father appears to have found Gingerbread to be a source of ongoing support whereas the other two who tried it did not. The other lone fathers in this study had either not thought about becoming involved in the organisation, had felt it was not relevant to their needs, or had not felt able to join. Thus, many men said that they had not considered it, others said such things as:

I didn't fancy it.(Dave C, no.3.)

I sometimes wish I had joined Gingerbread, but I wouldn't have wanted to be the only man in the group.(Alan D, no.3.)

I nearly joined Gingerbread, when I was down, but I started pulling round, I thought it might be a bore.(Cary M, no.13.)

The majority of men in this study either did not know much about single parent organisations such as Gingerbread, or what they did know about them did not attract them sufficiently to motivate them to join. By their comments the men indicated that they felt Gingerbread was a women's organisation, clearly, whilst the majority of single parents are women, a minority are not, and it does appear on the basis of this evidence that they did not feel that any existing single parent organisations represented an attractive proposition for them. The second point is related also to gender and gender images. It might, as suggested, have been felt that one of the influences in moving men to pioneering orientations would have been membership of social groups in which they would be open to new influences on their perceptions of mens' and womens' roles, and it might have been thought that single parent organisations such as Gingerbread could have been the location for such informal gender renegotiation and reconstruction. Clearly, this did not apply in the case of the men in the sample, as instanced by the fact that only Albert P, quoted above, of the 10 lone fathers with a pioneering orientation had been involved at all in the organisation.

Lone fathers and leisure activities

Leisure is both an existential and a social reality; existential in that it is related to the freedom to choose, social in that it occurs in the social world (Kelly, 1983). Burns (1967), quoted earlier, has stressed the wider meaning of leisure for men, and Tolson (1977) has noted how leisure is seen to be **men's** reward for (proper) 'work'. His argument that leisure time is when men are able to 'be themselves' is reflected in Williamson's perception that his collier grandfather's 'time off':

> expressed his basic sense of himself and reflected his priorities, interests and values. (p.103, Williamson, 1982.)

This gendered quality of leisure activities is acknowledged in the literature on the sociology of leisure. Parker writes that:

> there are pronounced differences in the leisure patterns of males and females (p.86, Parker,1976.)

and relates the lower involvement of women in leisure to a mixture of ascribed role expectations, and less availability of free time. However, he argues that if the definition of leisure is widened to include such activities as church going and cooking, the differences between the sexes in relation to leisure activity time is less. He concludes, contentiously, that caution should be exercised in assuming that family responsibilities stop women getting their 'fair share of leisure,' and Kelly (1983) has also argued for the proposition that men and women are approximately equally involved in (different) leisure activities. Hargreaves has expressed what would perhaps be more generally be agreed to be the case:

> without doubt, men possess greater cultural power than women. In leisure activities in general, and in sport in particular, men spend more time and have access to a wider range of activities than women. (p.130, Hargreaves, 1989.)

The implication of this position is that part of the leisure advantages that men have are at the expense of women; whilst men are at the pub or playing football women are at home engaged in child care and domestic activities. However, as has been seen, the members of this study were generally more involved in child care and domestic management activities than they had been prior to lone fatherhood. How far had this involved changes in leisure activities, how far was leisure a way in which the men in the sample developed and retained a sense of self? The following table illustrates the lone fathers' responses in relation to changes in leisure patterns pre and post lone fatherhood.

202

Table 10.3
Changes in leisure activities compared with pre-lone fatherhood

	More	Same	Fewer
Total sample(35)	10	12	13
Widowers(16)	2	8	6
Divorcees(19)	13	6	7
Patriarchs(25)	7	9	10
Pioneers(10)	3	4	3

Whilst relatively equal proportions of the sample were involved in more, less, or the same leisure activities, the changes appear to have been slightly greater for divorcees than for widowers, in that they were less likely to have continued in the same leisure patterns. It appears that patriarchal or pioneering orientations to gender roles were not directly related to leisure activities. Combining the reason for lone fatherhood with orientation does suggest the possibility of a relationship in that all three of the pioneers who reported increased leisure activities were also divorcees.

How did the lone fathers describe their leisure activities? Those who were engaged in more leisure activities than they previously had been involved in appear to have experienced leisure as a source of enjoyment and fulfilment. The following comments are typical:

> Snooker, theatre, the local history society...I've got more time now for leisure activities than I ever had before, I reckon I've got an easy life now, there was a time when I never had a moments free time, but that's not the case now.(Jake BB, no.28.)

> I watch tv and play sport more than I did before, I also collect old records, I couldn't do that before, my wife didn't like records.(Chris Z, no. 26.)

> I didn't have any time for leisure when I was married, now, I go out for a drink on Friday nights and go to the match on Saturdays.(Jeff S, no.19.)

Whilst 9 lone fathers were categorised as being involved in the same leisure activities, they can be divided into two groups, those who had continued in the same activities at the same level, and those who had developed some new activities but overall were involved in what they perceived as being the same level of leisure activities. How did the former group describe their leisure?

> It's the same as before, I go out for a drink regularly. (Rick O, no.15.)

203

Drinking, the allotment, messing about with motors - the same as before.(Keith G, no.7.)

I go to the club at 9.30 every night for a pint, I always have done.(Matt K, no.11.)

The latter group's experiences were typified by such comments as:

I play the odd game of snooker and go for a drink 4 or 5 nights a week, that's similar to before, then I would have gone out 2 nights by myself and 2 nights with the wife.(Kev N, no.14.)

and the comments of Jack H, no.8, whose house contained numerous darts trophies indicated the impact becoming a lone father - with for him the consequent dependence on benefits - had brought:

I do more or less the same as I've always done, football, playing darts - but I used to play in a bigger darts league and I've had to move down to the local league because I can't afford the cost of travelling and so on.

The third group of lone fathers were those who reported a decline in their level of activity in comparison with pre lone fatherhood, more than a third of the sample. There were examples of men whose leisure activities had been interconnected with those of their ex-wives, and for whom becoming single had meant the loss of these couple activities, as instanced by the comments of James CC, no.29, earlier. There were other lone fathers who had been involved in leisure activities whilst married that had not involved their wives, but who found that as single fathers they did not have the resources of time or money or both to pursue them as they had done previously. Comments from lone fathers in this category included the following:

I used to go sea fishing every Sunday, I've only been able to go once in the past year because of my family commitments.(Len E, no.5.)

I still keep my racing pigeons, but I can't do the gardening I used to do now, and I've had to cut down on the amount of time I spend with my pigeons.(Joe II, no.35.)

What conclusions can be drawn about leisure activities and lone fathers? How far was leisure for these men as Kelly (1983) has argued, an existential and a social reality? It has been suggested that for some it was existential in that it was related to the freedom to choose, as a result of being lone fathers they were more able to 'choose leisure' because the change in their domestic responsibilities created a space for leisure. Jeff S, no.19 described his increased leisure occurring at weekends, when his ex-wife had their daughters on access visits, showing how the change in the form of parenting had created the possibility for changing masculinity outside the domestic setting. Other men had more time for leisure because

204

becoming lone fathers was for them partly related to/or coincided with, more availability of 'free time'. Such factors as a reduction in working hours or the increasing maturity of growing children meant that for some waged and unwaged lone fathers lone fatherhood did not mean all work and no play. Other lone fathers experienced a reduction in their choice regarding leisure, sometimes because of domestic commitments that previously had been fulfilled by their partners, sometimes because of cost, showing how the change in the form of parenting had reduced the possibilities for changing masculinity outside the domestic setting.

The questions asked of men in relation to leisure were open ended in terms of definitions of leisure, and the overwhelming majority of the activities described were 'masculine' rather than 'feminine' - snooker, football, pigeon racing, sea fishing, messing with motors, going to the club for a pint - are traditional masculine activities. They are also social activities which to some extent are expressions of male bonding, activities which take place in masculine rather than feminine arenas. Tolson (1977) has argued that leisure time is when men are seen to 'be themselves', the selves that the sample were being in their leisure, or wishing to be if they had the resources, were gendered selves, and relatively traditional gendered selves. What then were the reported experiences of the lone fathers in relation to the communities in which they were resident?

Lone fathers and their communities

The term 'community', not unlike the term 'family' is open to a multitude of interpretations (Hillery, 1955, Stacey, 1969, Williamson, 1982.) Two aspects of the social relationships which can be seen to constitute 'community' have already been considered - 'community' in relation to kinship contacts and networks, which showed a variety of experiences for the lone fathers in this study, and 'community' in terms of a 'community of interest' (Barclay, 1982). Lone fathers, it has been shown, did not in the main have any substantial contact with, or experience themselves as members of, the community of lone parents in general or lone fathers in particular.

The focus in this section will be on community as geographical, community as locality, as the spatial and local social entity in which much of the daily lives of the lone fathers and their children occurred. How long lone fathers had been resident in their localities, what they thought of their locality, and what they thought members of their local community thought about them, are amongst the questions that will be explored.

There have been those who have written somewhat romantically about the community, particularly the working class Bethnal Green/Hunslet type stereotypical 'organic' communities (Young and Willmot, 1957, Hoggart, 1957). Other writing has noted how the community can constrain those defined as deviant. (Thompson, 1968.) Thus, the 18th and 19th century practice of 'rough music' was a way in which the community expressed

205

its displeasure against those whose lifestyles were deemed unacceptable to the wider community, be they cuckolds or wife beaters, adulterers or petty criminals. More recently, feminist writing has noted the power the community attempts to assert on those women who are behaving in ways which challenge traditional notions of femininity.

Community membership and community pressure then can be a central part of peoples' lives. It has been indicated by other writers that lone fathers may be in somewhat isolated and marginal positions in their communities, Jackson in his review of the literature on single parent families notes that being and becoming a lone father:

> Is a counter swirl in the patterns of society and an utterly different experience...the man may have to cope with an atmosphere in which his decision and his lifestyle are sensed as odd and peculiar. (p.167, Jackson, 1982.)

In relation to community relationships what then were the experiences of the lone fathers in this sample, were their experiences that the community perceived them as 'odd and peculiar', did they meet resistances, or did they experience their community relationships in other, perhaps more supportive, ways? Firstly, how far were lone fathers long term residents of the geographical areas in which they were living at the time of the study.

Table 10.4
Number of years resident in area

	All sample(35)	Patriarchs(25)	Pioneers(10)
0 - 5 years	3	2	1
6-10 years	1	1	0
11-20 years	2	1	1
21-30 years	3	1	2
30 plus years	26	20	6

	All sample(35)	Divorcees(19)	Widowers(16)
0 - 5 years	3	2	1
6-10 years	1	0	1
11-20 years	2	1	1
21-30 years	3	1	2
30 plus years	26	14	12

The above table indicates clearly that the vast majority of this sample were living in areas in which they had been resident for some considerable time, in the majority of cases all their lives. As can be seen, there were no clear differences between the subgroupings of widowers and divorcees and patriarchs and pioneers. If then the majority of the sample had lived within the same area for some considerable time, how far had geographical mobility taken place within these areas?

Table 10.5
Distance in miles lone fathers were
living from birthplaces

	All sample(35)	Patriarchs(25)	Pioneers(10)
0-4	26	20	6
5-10	2	1	1
11-99	3	1	2
100-199	3	2	1
200-999	0	0	0
999 plus	1	1	0

	All sample(35)	Divorcees(19)	Widowers(16)
0-4	26	16	12
5-10	2	0	2
11-99	3	3	0
100-199	3	2	1
200-999	0	0	0
999 plus	1	0	1

It can be seen from these two tables that the cumulative evidence is that the lone fathers in this study were in the main living near their birthplaces, their communities of origin, and had been so resident for considerable time periods - the mean length of time for residence in the area was 34.6 years. Pioneers were marginally more inclined to have been born more than 4 miles away from their place of residence at the time of the study than patriarchs.

The major conclusion to be drawn from this data is that in the majority of cases the men were living in areas with which they were familiar. They may have been, as lone parents, living a 'totally different experience', but the experience was rooted, in the overwhelming majority of cases, in localities which they knew well. However, a slight difference emerges between the categories of patriarchs and pioneers if the data relating to the moves of household since the birth of the first child is examined.

207

Table 10.6
Moves of household since birth of 1st child

	All sample(35)	Patriarchs(25)	Pioneers(10)
0	8	8	0
1	15	9	6
2	7	5	2
3 or more	5	3	2

	All sample(35)	Divorcees(19)	Widowers(16)
0	8	2	6
1	15	8	7
2	7	2	3
3 or more	5	5	0

It can be seen that there was a sizable sub group of patriarchs who had not moved house at all following the birth of the 1st child of their previous partnership, but all the pioneers had moved at least once since then. Might this mean that pioneers were more open to change in areas such as gender and parenting, having adapted to more moves of housing than some patriarchs? On the basis of such relatively small numbers such a conclusion is at best tentative, but it does point towards the possibility of pioneers having been more likely to experience, and adapt to, change than patriarchs. The data also shows that widowers were more geographically settled, and divorcees more geographically mobile.

What of subjective experiences, did the men in this sample like the areas in which they were resident, or did they dislike them?

Table 10.7
Feelings about living in the area
in which resident

	All sample(35)	Patriarchs(25)	Pioneers(10)
Like	24	19	5
Neutral	8	5	3
Dislike	3	1	2

	All sample(35)	Divorcees(19)	Widowers(16)
Like	24	12	12
Neutral	8	4	4
Dislike	3	3	0

It can be seen that the majority of the sample liked the area in which they were living, with a minority feeling neutral about it, and only a small number actually disliking it. Patriarchs more frequently expressed a liking for the area of residence than did pioneers; with regard to cause of lone fatherhood only divorcees expressed a dislike of the area in which they were resident.

Of those who liked the area, convenience and security appear to have been major factors that of importance. Thus, typical comments included:

I like it around here, I feel settled.(Len E, no.5.)

I like it round here, it's quiet and it's pretty central, you can walk down town, and if you miss the last bus ever you can walk home.(Dick X, no.24.)

I like the area, it's central, you can get the bus to anywhere.(Tony V, no.22.)

The above comments also indicate that in terms of the concept of area, the men questioned defined the concept fairly narrowly when perceiving why they liked an area - they did not for example generally say that they liked the area because it was in the north of England, their judgements were much more related to micro issues particularly transport and convenience. Perhaps this latter was partly related to the stresses of being a lone father; if being a lone father involves for many juggling potentially conflicting responsibilities, access to transport, convenience for shops, and convenience for schools etc. are all important issues in the fight for daily survival. However, underpinning these daily issues perhaps were for some more basic issues, in living in areas for a long time they had in some cases developed security via a sense of place, of being and belonging to the areas in which they were resident.

Other lone fathers either felt neutral towards the areas in which they were living or disliked them. Their stated reasons are illustrated in the following typical quotes:

I'm just used and accustomed to it.(Jack H, no.8.)

It's alright I suppose, it's not a fantastic place to live, but the kids enjoy it and all their friends are here.(Dennis Q, no.17.)

I don't particularly like it, I find it depressing, but all my family and friends live here.(Danny AA, no.27.)

To be quite honest I think it's a dump, I don't like it - I would like nothing better than to just up and move down south, but I don't want to go away from me mother, and I don't want (my daughters) to lose contact with their mother or Grandma, and that's the only thing that's keeping me here.(Jeff S, no.19.)

The members of the study were living in a variety of kinds of accommodation - 12 in council housing, 19 in property which they were purchasing (in 3 cases ex - council property) and 4 in privately rented property. High levels of satisfaction with their accommodation were recorded, only 2 members of the sample said that they disliked their accommodation, and only 3 members of the sample could think of any particular changes that they could wish to be made to the property they were resident in to improve it.

Thus, a picture emerges in which the overwhelming majority of the sample were satisfied with their accommodation and had been resident for some time in the area in which they lived. Homelessness had not been a major feature of the mens' lives, only 2 of the sample had ever been homeless, and in neither case had they been homeless since assuming the care of their children. However, in several cases they had gone to live with relatives at the time of the break-up of the marriage. Those who had subsequently been involved in negotiations with local authority housing departments to obtain accommodation had in general found the housing departments to be sympathetic and helpful. Did lone fathers feel settled in their accommodation, and by implication in their communities? The evidence is that they did, only 4 men in the sample thought it was possible they might move in the two years following the time of the study. Patriarchs appeared to be more settled, or to wish to be more settled, than pioneers - 12 patriarchs (48%) envisaged staying in the same accommodation 'forever', compared with only 1 pioneer (10%) who rated himself in this category. This seems to indicate a wish to avoid the idea of change on the part of a substantial subgroup of patriarchs, and a corresponding ability to be more able to accept the idea of change on the part of the majority of pioneers. It was earlier suggested that lone fatherhood was sometimes seen in 'crisis' terms, with this perspective in some ways a patriarchal orientation could be said to be an attempt to impose a 'steady state' on the crisis, in part by seeking to stay in the same housing forever. A pioneering orientation, marking as it does a break with traditional hegemonic masculinity, could be seen to be more of an approach which sought to maximise the opportunities in the crisis, as indicated in part by a readiness to see that the future does not lie in the same place forever.

What attitudes did the lone fathers perceive had been displayed by neighbours?

Table 10.8
Neighbours feedback of them as lone fathers

	All sample(35)	Patriarchs(25)	Pioneers(10)
Very good/good	10	5	5
Neutral	8	8	0
Poor	1	1	0
No specific feedback	16	11	5

	All sample(35)	Divorcees(19)	Widowers(16)
Very good/good	10	3	7
Neutral	8	5	3
Poor	1	1	0
No specific feedback	16	10	6

Widowers were more likely to receive positive feedback on their parenting than divorcees, perhaps in part this was an indication of sympathy to the bereaved. An interesting aspect of the above figures is the lack of negative feedback the lone fathers received - in the one case where the feedback was negative, Keith G, no.7, described a feud between one of his children and a neighbour's son. It may be that this presented the neighbour with the opportunity to criticise Keith G, and it may also have been that there were instances in which neutral feedback or a lack of feedback masked negative criticisms of the lone fathers which were not voiced. What were voiced, and were recalled by some lone fathers, were positive comments on them, and the following are a typical selection:

> (They) tell me that I'm doing well, they say 'I couldn't do what you're doing' to which I reply if they were in my position they would do the same - I think I'm doing reasonably well, I've never had a sleepless night and I've never had a wet bed (with the children) so something's going alright.(Fergus W, no.23.)

> They say 'I don't know how you manage' and 'You're coping very well.'(Tony V, no.22.)

> They often say they wonder how I've managed so well. (Frank B, no.2.)

> They seem to think I'm doing a good job, they always praise me for what I'm doing.(Dave C, no.3.)

The above are all quotes from lone fathers with patriarchal orientations, and it is interesting to note that there was an element of surprise expressed in the comments from neighbours, perhaps that men placed in the position of lone parents were able to cope at all. An element of encouragement was also present in the comments, and it is perhaps hard to imagine that single mothers are likely to receive the same kinds of comments.

The following represent examples of neighbours comments in relation to lone fathers who had pioneering orientations:

> They admire us in every way, saying you've brought them lads up great, you've nothing to be ashamed of, it makes me feel great and that all the struggle's been worth it. (Cliff J, no.10.)

> I think they tended to think that you couldn't cope, but once things were organised it was alright: one bloke said he couldn't believe you could cook and wash and iron, with me being a bloke.(Cary M, no.13.)

> They view me with respect for what I'm doing, but also with suspicion because I keep myself to myself and don't often mix.(Albert P, no.16.)

An element of being on trial as competent parents is implicit in the above statements in a way which it is not present in the comments made by the patriarchs quoted above. Perhaps this implies that pioneering lone fathers were more conscious of their parenting positions, and the vulnerability of their positions to judgements by others, than were the patriarchs. This dimension of judgement by neighbours was present in the comments of another of the pioneers - Burgoyne (1987) has commented about men's visibility when 'pegging out washing' - which relates to the experience of Jeff S, no.19, who said of his being a lone father:

> Nobody mentions it at all, I got some funny looks when I first moved in here, they couldn't believe it I think, they were looking thinking 'where's the woman' - and when I was hanging washing out, they were looking, they were obviously very puzzled and couldn't work it out at all.

As a group pioneering lone fathers were clearer about and more aware of their local community's perceptions of them than were those with more traditional patriarchal orientations. Thus, pioneers either knew that there was positive feedback from neighbours or that there was no feedback; in contrast a significant subgroup of patriarchs felt that feedback about them was neutral.

A number of fathers did not receive comments from their neighbours about their situations, commonly they said that neighbours 'never say anything' (Rick O, no.15) or that 'Nobody's ever said anything, they've just been quite normal.' (Jack H, no.8.) Where neighbours said nothing, lone fathers felt that it was perhaps sometimes because the neighbours did not know of the changes, and this applied even in cases where lone fathers were resident with their children in the ex-matrimonial home (e.g., John Y, no.25, Jake BB, no.28,). Others felt that norms of privacy appropriately constrained neighbours or other community members from commenting.

How far were neighbour's attitudes different in relation to the men in this sample between the period prior to their becoming lone fathers and at the point of the study?

Table 10.9
Differences in attitudes to lone fathers
on part of neighbours from attitudes to them
prior to their becoming lone fathers

	All sample(35)	Patriarchs(25)	Pioneers(10)
More positive	3	2	1
No difference	7	7	0
Worse	1	1	0
Don't know	24	15	9

	All sample(35)	Divorcees(19)	Widowers(16)
More positive	3	2	1
No difference	7	3	4
Worse	1	0	1
Don't know	24	14	10

Whilst there was a slight tendency for neighbours to have more positive attitudes, in the majority of cases lone fathers could not make an assessment. This was for one of four reasons; in some cases the man concerned had only been peripherally involved in the community prior to becoming a lone father, often because he worked away (e.g., Dave C, no.3,) thus the neighbours had little idea of the before to contrast with the after. The gendered dimension of parenting in two parent families led some other fathers to believe that before, as instanced by the words of Al L, no.12, the neighbours:

Didn't really know me, I was just an ordinary family man.

Other lone fathers felt that because neighbours and other members of the local community had known them all their lives, their assessments and opinions of them had been formed over years, the most important influence in their assessment of the lone fathers concerned would be this long held knowledge. By contrast, in the fourth category were those lone fathers who had moved since becoming lone fathers to a situation in which they weren't really known, so pre and post assessments could not be made by neighbours because they did not have knowledge about the earlier phase.

What is the significance of this information about the local communities attitudes towards lone fathers? Perhaps the main impression that emerges from the data is that the common experience of the lone fathers was that they did not experience their local community as hostile towards them - sometimes encouraging, sometimes indifferent, sometimes inquisitive, but rarely hostile or negatively judgemental (at least overtly). Whilst it does not appear that in general lone fathers had become more extensively involved in their communities as a result of becoming lone fathers, in some cases they felt that they were more known to their neighbours, partly because of their being lone fathers (and therefore different), and partly as a result of some of the changes in their child care arrangements occasioned by their becoming lone fathers. Whilst it might have been the case that if more of the members of this sample had been parents of pre-5 children they might have become more heavily involved in community networks via the networks that develop in taking a pre-school child to clinics etc., the minority of men in this sample who were lone fathers of pre school children did not appear to be experiencing such changes.

Whilst the relationship between being a member of a community and being a lone father might not appear to have been a particularly significant one for the men in this study, that in itself is significant. The evidence is that they did not experience particular resistance as lone fathers from their local communities, they did not to any great degree as individual lone fathers have to do what Jackson predicted they might have to do, and:

cope with an atmosphere in which his decision and his lifestyle are sensed as odd and peculiar. (p.167, Jackson, 1982.)

Earlier it was argued that the experiences of the lone fathers who made up this sample should be seen within the particular economic and social regional context of the North of England in the 1980s. Byrne has written that:

If the debate about locality has any value, it is in that it identifies some sort of spatial locality for the working out of history in the way that base and social being add up to produce the potential for action. (p.138, Byrne, 1989.)

Within the spatial locality in which lone fathers were living, what were the conditions of the base during this period? With regard to economic and gender factors, despite the dramatic decline in full time male employment during the 1970s and 1980s, studies have indicate that there was a widespread perception that men in two parent families should properly be 'at work.' (Morris, 1987, 1990, Wheelock, 1986, 1990.) How does this accord with the perceived tolerance by localities to lone father households? It would seem that lone fathers in relation to community attitudes are likely to be in privileged positions and may be seen as a 'special case.' There would appear to be likely to be tolerance towards them because of the nature of their household; rather than being 'odd and peculiar' they are more likely to be seen to be 'doing well' in doing what is taken for granted if done by a single parent mother. If they are in employment they are doing well to combine paid worker and parental roles, if they are not in employment then they are not perceived as a counter swirl in what is happening in the region anyway (i.e. men not 'working.') Consideration of lone fathers in the locality, in their kinship, friendship, leisure and community context suggests that their positions can therefore be best understood by employing a perspective which has regard to both interactionist and structural issues.

At the start of this chapter it was noted that women are seen to dominate the domain of the community and caring networks and leisure and leisure relationships are seen to be the domain of men. It appears from the evidence of this study that in relation to these areas there was a range of different patterns of social relationships experienced by lone fathers. Whilst there was a general tendency for men to be more involved in non-work social relationships than they had been prior to becoming lone fathers, this involvement was clearly a gendered experience - the men, as a result of becoming lone fathers, did not move into the worlds of womens' relationships. Whilst for some their contacts with women kinfolk for example increased, these contacts were clearly on the basis of them being lone fathers, and not of them being surrogate mothers. Thus, patriarchal or pioneering orientations to lone fatherhood were expressed through the domain of these social networks, but do not appear to have their origins in the lone fathers' activities in these domains. Whilst some fathers had experienced major changes in their lives in these areas of activity, others had not. In general there had been more continuity in relation to kinfolk contacts and geographical locality than there had been in relation to sexual relationships and friendships. There was some evidence that pioneering orientations were associated with change in place of residence and increased level of friendship activity, and pioneers appeared to be more aware of their neighbours perceptions of them than were patriarchs.

A key area of lone fathers lives that remains to be explored is their relationships with professionals employed on their or others behalf - including the State - and this will be considered in the next chapter.

215

11 Lone fathers, the state, and professionals

This chapter explores 'public' involvement into the privacy of households by examining lone fathers' relationships with social workers and other professionals, particularly representatives of the law, health, and voluntary sector welfare agencies. It includes a consideration of the nature and meanings of these contacts for the lone father households, looking at similarities and differences between the experiences of widowers and divorcees, and patriarchs and pioneers. It concludes with a brief discussion of the implications of these findings for the services and professionals considered with regard to parenting and masculinities.

Men and social work

It can be argued that social work is a service primarily provided by women for women and children, with the involvement of men being largely, but not insignificantly, confined to the management of the services. (Brook & Davis, 1985; Burden & Gottlieb, 1987; Dale & Foster, 1986; Davis, 1985; Hale, 1983; Hanmer & Statham, 1988; Hudson, 1985; McLeod & Dominelli, 1982; Marchant & Wearing, 1986; Walton, 1975.) If social work services are largely delivered by and for women, it appears to be possible that lone fathers potentially are in marginal positions in relation to these services, being male carers.

However, as the heads of lone parent households, they are more likely to be the focus of intervention by social welfare agencies than are adults in two parent households (Ferri, 1976, Jordan, 1984.) Whilst there is a common perception that lone fathers will 'do better' in obtaining the services of social welfare agencies because of their gender than will lone mothers, Hicks has argued that:

> most men carers are no more effective in their dealings with the welfare bureaucracy than are women. (p.162, Hicks, 1988.)

Ambiguity arises because there is evidence that welfare agencies, possibly because they are more usually involved with carers who are

216

female, tend to be much less likely to understand the particular needs of male carers. Thus McConchie, writing about fathers of mentally handicapped children has written of:

fathers' relative invisibility in policies of care and education(p.162, McConchie, 1982.)

and Parton, 1990, and Hearn, 1990, have noted how responses to child abuse have tended to be framed in a context that assumes that women have responsibility for childcare and child protection with men's roles and responsibilities being somewhat overlooked.

There is one area however in which men are increasingly seen to have a central role that relates to social work involvement, and that is the area of physical, and particularly sexual, abuse of children. The mass of the available research evidence is that sexual abuse within families tends to be predominantly the abuse of children, particularly girls, by fathers or stepfathers. The fieldwork for this study took place immediately prior to the publicity surrounding responses to child sexual abuse in Cleveland, and thus these results were not influenced by those events.

Whilst child sexual abuse within families has been a recent focus for state intervention, intervention into families for other reasons has been a long-standing central feature of social work agencies activities. Statutory social work services in England and Wales in the last quarter of the 20th century have been centrally concerned with the support and surveillance of families. The 1968 Report of the Committee on Local Authority and Allied Personal Social Services (the 'Seebohm Report') argued for the creation of:

a new local authority department, providing a community based and family oriented service (p.11, HMSO, 1968)

and local authority Social Services Departments were established in England and Wales in 1971. Subsequently, work with families by these social welfare agencies has increased, particularly in relation to child protection work. However Jordan (1982) has argued that agencies' lack of resources, and enforced emphasis on 'policing' rather than 'prevention' has resulted in an inability to respond appropriately to the increasing diversity of family types.

In relation to lone father families therefore, two strands within recent social work policies interact. The first is that whilst men are seen to have ultimate authority in relation to their families, the day to day responsibilities, including the involvement with social work and social welfare agencies, tend to be seen to fall within the province of the female adult. Marsh, in a pioneering review of the area of fathers and social work, has written:

217

Social work practice has not been in the forefront of developing a father aware practice....our body of knowledge is..growing but there is a very long way to go. (p.194 - 195, Marsh, 1987.)

Most of the literature in relation to social work - and most of the legislation - is not simply father blind but gender blind, it is based on the implicit assumption that women will act as carers. One notable exception is found in the work of Hanmer and Statham (1988). Writing from a feminist perspective, they, having criticised the concept of the 'fit mother', go on to note that in relation to men:

there is no corresponding 'fit father' role for social workers to use in their assessment and planning...unlike motherhood, social workers are not expected, and do not expect, to monitor or improve expressions of fatherhood in the families they visit. (p.56, Hanmer and Statham,1988.)

In the case of lone father households, the absence of a female adult/ mother figure means that the families do not accord with social work's stereotype of families, which assumes women have a central, indispensable role with regard to child care. The consequence of this might be that social work activities would seek to negotiate either the return of the children to the mother, or a suitable mother figure, or the admission of children to care. Whilst comprehensive statistics are not available, it is clear that some children from lone father families do enter care, and some children do enter care rather than becoming part of lone father families. However, in this study, at the time of the research all the men studied were caring for children as lone fathers. Thus, one area this chapter will explore is to consider how, from the viewpoint of the consumer, social work agencies and social workers interact with the 'unusual' family type that lone father households represent?

The second issue in relation to recent social work policies is that, rather than having preventative or 'social care planning' (Barclay Report, 1982) strategies, local authority social services departments have increasingly been driven, by a combination of political and economic pressures, to reactive crisis intervention in families, particularly focusing on 'dangerous families' (Dale et al, 1986) It has been argued that lone parent families are more likely to be seen to be 'at risk', Parton has noted that whilst in the last decade 'families' were seen by the dominant politicians and policy makers to be a 'good thing', and the source of 'health' in society:

Not all families are to be so praised and seen as the main source of good in our society. Single parent families are seen as a cause of poor results in school, vandalism, football hooliganism, to name just a few social problems, and pose a threat to the 'health of society.' (p.34, Parton, N., 1990)

This scapegoating of lone parent families has continued throughout the 1990s and has been a major theme of the 1993 Conservative party conference and subsequent speeches by members of the government. Whilst the target has been primarily lone mother families, the rhetoric has sought to create a climate in which all 'different' forms of households are to be feared and condemned.

Lone fathers and social work

How far then were the lone fathers and their households the focus of intervention by social work agencies; how far did it appear that they were being perceived as being a threat to the 'health of society' and dangerous? One previous study suggested that:

> the personal social services are at best peripheral to the problems of most motherless families. That fathers managed to look after their children owed little to the personal social services. (p. 149, George and Wilding, 1972.)

Ferri found that one parent families had had a range of contacts with the pre-Seebohm social work agencies:

> Altogether about one in three of both the fatherless (35%) and the motherless (31%) families had been involved with at least one service compared with only 8% of families in which both parents were present...the official social services appear ill-equipped to assist in many of the problems facing the family which loses a parent. (pp.87 & 92, Ferri, 1976.)

Murch, in writing about the reasons for the development of a Motherless Families Project to offer assistance to lone father families, noted that:

> investigations showed that there was not very much that the statutory agencies had been able to do to help them, apart from the drastic offer of receiving the children into care. (p.365, Murch, 1973)

It is perhaps therefore not surprising that the Finer Report (1974) argued that personal social services could play a more positive and supportive role in relation to single parent families than they appeared to have been doing.

Whilst some work has begun to take place on the ways in which social work might begin to consider and respond to the links between social problems and masculinities.(e.g. Hearn, 1987, 1990, Metcalf and Humphries (eds) 1985, Parton, 1990), there appears to have been little recent social work intervention focused specifically on lone fathers.

219

What then were the experiences of this sample of lone fathers of social work agencies? Such involvement with lone father households might be expected to have occurred prior to them becoming lone father households; prior to and subsequent to them becoming lone father households; or subsequent to them becoming lone father households. It was anticipated that involvement by social work agencies would also have been likely to have been for a reason other than simply the fact that the household was a single parent household.

Table 11.1
Households' contact with social workers
prior to becoming lone father households

	Contact	No contact
Total sample(35)	10	25
Widowers(16)	5	11
Divorcees(19)	5	14
Patriarchs(25)	5	20
Pioneers(10)	5	5

It can be seen that a substantial minority of families had had some contact with social work agencies pre lone fatherhood. In the majority of cases - 8 out of 10 - this had been contact with local authority social services departments, and as the table indicates, equal numbers of the households of future widowers and divorcees had social work involvement (given the smaller number of the former in the total sample proportionally therefore there had been more involvement with them.) Analysis of the data in relation to patriarchs and pioneers shows a similar division, 5 patriarchs' and 5 pioneers' families having involvement with social workers prior to lone fatherhood. Proportionally this represents a much higher involvement in families where subsequently the lone father adopted a pioneering orientation.

The men were asked to assess what they felt had been achieved by the social work contact. Responses were relatively evenly divided into those who felt social work had achieved what the family wanted (2), what the social worker wanted (1), what both family and social worker wanted (2), what neither wanted (2), and those who could not be really sure and were unable to assess the outcomes (3). Men who were subsequently to become widowers had a greater sense that something positive had been achieved than men who were to become divorcees, 4 of the 5 men who felt the contact had achieved what the family, social worker, or both wanted being in this group. In contrast, 4 of the 5 men who were subsequently to become divorcees felt the involvement had led to what neither wanted, or were unable to assess it. Perhaps this indicates a difficulty on the part of social workers in making it clear to those with whom they become professionally involved of their perceptions of the possible outcomes of the interactions - certainly in responding to these questions even the lone fathers who were able to rate the outcomes of the interventions did so with some difficulty.

The focus of the involvement by social workers varied. In several cases they had been involved in short term service delivery arrangements connected with the illness of the dying partner - for example arranging a home help or giving advice regarding practical issues. In the case of Desmond EE, no. 31, social workers arranged a home help and nursery place for a child because of his wife's illness, he subsequently felt in relation to social workers that:

> They're always there if anything does come up.

Other lone fathers had short term help but then chose to manage by themselves:

> A social worker came to arrange a home help when my wife was dying, after she died I didn't keep her on, I thought about it, but decided not to, I'm too independent.(Frank B, no.2.)

In other situations, usually where the marriage ended in divorce, social work intervention had taken place focusing on marital relationship or child care difficulties. Thus, when Jeff S, no. 19's, children were unilaterally placed in care by their mother before she disappeared for several days, this proved to be the event that marked the end of the marriage - he took them out of care and went to live with them at his mother's. In another case, John Y, no. 25, recalled how a child guidance social worker had been briefly involved with his eldest daughter when she was 7 or 8 because of behavioural difficulties she was having, which with hindsight he felt had been related to the poor marital relationship in the home at that time.

With regard to the provision and delivery of more practical services, in many cases where this happened there appeared to have been general satisfaction from the recipients. There does not however appear to have been any significant amount of more 'therapeutic' input by social welfare agencies prior to lone fatherhood, it does not appear to have been sought or offered either by those in relationships which were in difficulty, or by those in relationships where one partner was dying.

If this was the position in relation to social work contact prior to the households becoming lone father households, what was the position in relation to contacts during the period of lone fatherhood?

Table 11.2
Households' contact with social workers
subsequent to becoming lone father households

	Contact	No contact
Total sample(35)	16	19
Widowers(16)	5	11
Divorcees(19)	11	8
Patriarchs(25)	11	14
Pioneers(10)	5	5

It can be seen whilst the overall numbers of families with whom social workers were in contact increased compared with the pre lone fatherhood period, the involvement was much higher for lone father divorcees than lone father widowers. In relation to patriarchs and pioneers, proportionally similar numbers had contact with social workers, which marked an increase in social work involvement with patriarchs compared with the situation prior to lonefatherhood.

Overall nearly half the sample had some form of contact with social workers during the period of lone fatherhood; the type of social worker with whom the lone fathers had contact was somewhat different from the earlier phase. Prior to lone fatherhood, 8 families had had contact with local authority social workers and 2 with voluntary agency social workers. After becoming lone fathers, 8 of the families had contact with local authority social workers, 2 with voluntary agency social workers, and 9 with probation officers (usually in the role of court welfare officer.) There was also a cross gender component to much of this contact; in 75% of cases the contact was with female, rather than male, workers.

Experiences of those who had no contact with social workers

Before looking in more detail about the nature of the contact with social workers, it is important to consider briefly why some families did not have such contact.

Table 11.3 Reasons for nil contact
with social workers (n=19)

Reason perceived by lone father	Number
Didn't consider it	3
Didn't know how to make contact	8
Problems not serious enough	1
Expected social workers to make contact	4
Don't know	3

The data indicates that for social work intervention to have taken place in some of the lone father families the agencies involved would have had to have been more proactive in terms of initiating contact or advertising their services. A majority of the lone fathers did not know how to make contact; or expected the approach to come from the social work services; or the image of social work services was such that the lone fathers did not consider that social work services could offer them anything. This tends to support a number of previous findings into social services departments images that there is a lack of clarity amongst citizens about the nature and purpose of social services departments. (e.g. Rees, 1978) Whilst a number of statutory agencies have recently sought to provide more information about the services they are offering, clearly many in the past have not got their message across. This point also relates to the wider debate about the proper position of social work services in late 20th century Britain - to be slimline, reactive, and statutory work focused, or more proactive, expansive, and preventative. (Barclay, 1982.)

Some comments from members of this study reflected this uncertainty about the functions and roles of social services and social welfare agencies; thus when asked whether they had considered contacting them they said such things as:

It never passed through my mind, I never bothered anybody, I don't know what social workers do.(Trevor A, no.1.)

I just never thought about it, I don't think there's anything they could do for me, as far as I know they help old people with meals and that, general help and visiting and God knows what.(Rick O, no.15.)

Those lone fathers who had not had contact with social workers were asked about their perceptions of social workers and social services roles and services.

Table 11.4 Perceptions of nature of social work
services by those who had not been in
contact with social workers

	Total(19)	Pioneers(5)	Patriarchs(14)
Child care/abuse work	10	3	7
Mixture of client groups	5	1	4
Don't know	4	1	3

	Total(19)	Widowers(11)	Divorcees(8)
Child care/abuse work	10	5	5
Mixture of client groups	5	3	2
Don't know	4	3	1

Thus, the majority of lone fathers who had not been in contact with social workers had at least a partially correct perception of the nature of social work services, and an awareness that the service was potentially related to their own situation - i.e. children and families.

It is sometimes perceived that social work intervention is a potential intrusion, and that people have a right to be left to their privacy unless they request otherwise. The following typical comments from representatives of this sample indicate that some felt that they would have welcomed at least an initial contact from social services:

> I would have liked them to visit when my wife died, but they don't bother with you. I think it's wrong that nobody came. You're on about social workers, they never came. You don't know that they're there, they never bothered with me, they should have known that I was a single parent.(Andy R, no.18.)

> I was surprised really that (a social worker) hadn't visited after the wife had died.(Tony V, no. 22.)

Other lone fathers felt that social welfare agencies were failing in their duties by not ensuring that everything was satisfactory in new lone father households. As such, they appear to have been partly seeking external validation of their 'fit fatherliness':

> I just thought that in the light of all the unfavourable publicity within the last three years about children being abused and in care etc. that all social services would investigate new single parents to see if the circumstances were alright and to see the children to find out what their feelings were. Even though I think I'm doing a good job now, I think someone should be periodically asking the children 'Is there anything you think your father should be doing that he's not doing?' (Fergus W, no.23.)

> If my children were behaving in a manner to create the attention of social services then I'd accept it, I'd accept that there was something wrong.(Albert P, no.16.)

Such interventions would have significant resource implications for social welfare agencies, and, during a period when resources have been squeezed in the public sector, many agencies have had to target statutory work. The consequence of this can be that those who seek assistance may find that they are not perceived to be sufficiently in need, as was the experience of Danny AA, no.27:

> I did try to contact them, but they said they couldn't help, they never even visited, they said if the kids weren't being looked after they could help.

Some situations fall into a high priority category for intervention by social work agencies. In the last twenty years, partly as a result of a series of inquiries into child abuse deaths (e.g. DHSS/HMSO, 1982, London Borough of Brent, 1985, London Borough of Lambeth, 1987, London Borough of Greenwich, 1987,) agencies have developed procedural guidelines for intervention that specify the involvement that must take place in suspected cases of abuse.

In this sample, in four cases social work intervention had taken place following suspicions that children were being not cared for adequately or were being ill-treated. Where the allegations had been felt to be unfounded, the lone fathers concerned subsequently reported no animosity towards social services:

> I did have a visit from a social worker one Friday night, following an anonymous letter to them; I thought that in a way the letter was good because it could have been genuine and I could have been doing something to the kids for two years.(Tony V, no.22.)

> Three months after I'd had the kids I think I was reported because someone saw a bruise on one of them, a social worker visited and things were OK.(Aidan FF, no.32.)

In the two other cases the social work involvement had continued after the initial intervention and the lone fathers concerned had more ambivalent feelings about social work. In both cases prior to the involvement about child abuse children from the family had had periods of residential care as a result of them being 'beyond the control' of their parents. In one case, Keith G, no.7, the care episodes were in relation to 2 stepchildren. In the other case, Arthur T, no.20, the 11 year old son of the lone father concerned had been admitted to a social services observation and assessment centre, at his fathers request, for 3 days.

At the time of the research both these lone fathers were experiencing being monitored by social services in relation to their parenting. In the case of Keith G, his 7 year old son he found more difficult to control than his 8 year old daughter, and he perceived that social services were considering court action to remove the children from his care: supervision orders having been made some months previously as a result of him beating his son as a form of discipline. Keith G considered the social worker involved had been very unhelpful throughout this period.

In the other case Arthur T had also physically disciplined his son who had told his mother about this and social services were assessing the case and considering whether or not to remove the child. Both lone fathers felt that their legitimate rights as parents were being diminished by social work involvement:

If I can't chastise my own kids there's something wrong - (social services) want to know why he's running away, it's because he knows if he comes in he's going to get wrong, so he goes to his Ma's, he knows he can play one off against the other.(Arthur T, no.20.)

I marked him one day with a slipper, I made him black and blue, and social services got to know, and I was in front of them. They say there's other ways of dealing with (his behaviour) but they don't say what they are, so I've got to judge what way I can check him without them finding out. I'd like to tell them 'look, I want you away from my house' but I cannot because of the supervision orders. (Keith G, no.7.)

Whilst openness and honesty between workers and clients can be achieved in child protection work, they appear to have been not achieved in these cases. It has been argued that:

Members of the helping professions remain uneasy about imposing themselves and their authority on what are usually involuntary clients, although parents, sometimes after initial anger and hostility, generally prefer an honest and straightforward approach. Often a parent's abusive behaviour has resulted from loss of control, and external controls are not only necessary for child protection work but can also be reassuring for the parent. (p.11, DOH, 1988)

Whilst the above is undoubtedly true in many cases, in respect of those cited here, although the period of initial anger and hostility had had time to pass it was still present in the two men concerned. Perhaps this was a reflection on the quality of social work input, perhaps this was a reflection of the men's anxiety that their children would be removed, or perhaps the threats to the men's parenting and autonomy were such that honesty and openness were unlikely to ever exist. Clearly, it was at least possible that the children in the families involved were better cared for, and safer, as a result of social work intervention. From the lone fathers perspectives however, the results were that social workers interventions were perceived to be:

A waste of time, I wouldn't entertain them.(Arthur T, no.20.)

Very unhelpful; if you tell her the truth she gans and reports it, but now I'm not saying owt to her, if she comes and asks how he's been I say he's alright, I'm not going to let them know nowt now.(Keith G, no.8.)

Both these men were in the group of lone fathers who had traditional patriarchal orientations to gender roles. It can be seen how in some ways the social work interventions - in both cases by female social workers - were framed and experienced by them as a challenge to their legitimate patriarchal rights. Thus, their experiences at the micro level at a structural

226

level can be seen as a form of state challenge to the excesses of hegemonic masculinity. Patriarchal power in domestic relationships is enshrined in the law and in cultural practices. However, to legitimate the particular form of society it is necessary to have checks on the worst excesses of any (overt) abuses of power, hence social work involvement in the kinds of situations described. It may be argued however that whilst this involvement is legitimate and vital to protect children, it frames child abuse and child protection as an individual, familial process, and overlooks and ignores institutional and structural abuse. (Barker & Moran, 1990.)

Lone fathers and court welfare officers

What of the other lone father households in which social work involvement had occurred? As indicated, probation officers had been involved in 9 of the households. In all cases this involvement had been related to decision making regarding the custody of the child/ren (additionally a probation officer had been involved subsequently in relation to motoring offences committed by a child in one family.) Under English law, at the time of this research, the courts had a duty to to ensure that when a divorce is taking place and custody is being decided:

> the arrangements proposed for the children are satisfactory, or the best that can be devised in the circumstances. (Section 41, Matrimonial Causes Act 1973.)

In 1985 over 100,000 custody orders were made in England and Wales, and probation officers were involved in approximately 25,000 inquiries, having responsibility to act as court welfare officers to investigate the circumstances of each case, and, if appropriate, make a recommendation to the court regarding the future care and custody of the child/ren. It has been noted (Parkinson, 1987.) that there is some tension in the role of the court welfare officer. On the one hand, they may be seen to be acting as a facilitator and possibly mediator between family members, thus the intervention is seen to be largely therapeutic, and may involve counselling and family therapy sessions. On the other hand, they may be seen to be acting as advisors in respect of an adversarial contest, advising the court of the best and least damaging (for the children) ways of resolving custody disputes. What is not in dispute is that the court welfare officer is in a powerful position in relation to care and custody decisions, and the lone fathers who were assessed by such social workers were clear about the powers these professionals had in the legal decision making processes.

The evidence of consumers views was that it does not appear from this study that the court welfare officers were framing their roles primarily as mediators, the perceptions of the lone fathers were that they were there to recommend to the court custody arrangements. (At the time of this study there was no formal conciliation service in the geographical area in which the men lived, subsequently such a service has been established.) In all but one of the cases it appears that custody was recommended to go to the father. Some lone fathers saw the process of engagement with the court welfare officer as a necessary evil, the following quote illustrates and is typical of this position:

> I could have done without them, I realised that they were there to do a job, and I'd got to cooperate or else I'd lose the children, so I treated them with respect. To be honest I didn't feel I needed them to do anything for me..(but) you've got no option, he was vital to my case, you've got to cooperate and persuade him because as a man you're always faced with the bias of the court, 90% of cases end up with women having the custody so you need the probation officers. To be fair, they were doing a good job, the first one in particular was a bit non-committal, I couldn't get which way his mind was working, it preoccupied me for 6 to 8 months, but I couldn't get any indication from him whether he favoured me having custody or not, even up to the day of the court hearing I didn't know which way his report would go.(James CC, no.29.)

In many lone fathers cases there was respect and appreciation of the court officers role:

> I wanted to have the kids, he would never tell you what his report was going to be, but he sort of intimated without saying so...they were very helpful to me.(Jeff S, no. 19.)

> I can't complain because I got the children, everything she said made me look as though I'd already got my halo, she said that there was nothing to support any of the allegations my ex-wife made, I was very happy with the report and the children liked her, she was a real pro - she interviewed every relevant person.(Jake BB, no. 28.)

Other lone fathers, whilst indicating some resentment at the surveillance element of the role of court officer, also spoke of the process as a form of validation of the legitimacy of their having care and custody of their children:

> The welfare officer visited from court 4 or 5 times and inspected the home, it made me angry, she even looked under the beds, but I knew that everything was OK and I'd nothing to be afraid of..it gave me self confidence, it was like sitting an exam and passing it - if they said I was good enough then I must have been good enough; it helped me with my self doubts at a time when I was having self doubts.(Alan D, no.4.)

In all but one case the court welfare officer's eventual recommendation in relation to custody appears to have been in favour of the lone father. In the case which had not, Kevin GG, no 33, the reasons for the recommendation of the court officer that custody should go to the mother were unclear to him. Kevin GG felt that possibly the court welfare officer had recommended it because it was 'the usual thing to happen', he was

228

not sure why the court had accepted his arguments rather than the court officer's recommendation, but was clear that when he did get custody awarded it was 'the best day of my life.'

Apart from surveillance and court welfare interventions, the only other case in which there had been extensive statutory social work involvement during the period of lone fatherhood was that of Dave C, no 3. During this period, as a result of a medical condition and the consequent treatment, his son had developed a very substantial physical disability. A combination of fieldwork and medical social work involvement had taken place, all were rated by Dave C as 'very helpful', as he said:

> There's nothing else I'd like to get them to do that they haven't done.

Lone fathers contacts with voluntary social work agencies

Social welfare services are not solely delivered via the statutory sector, there is a range of informal and formal voluntary organisations providing social work and social welfare services. (Wolfenden, 1977). It can be argued that in some cases advice or assistance offered by a voluntary sector agency can be more easily targeted and shaped for particular individuals and groups that fall into particular (problem) categories. Hadley and Hatch have suggested that:

> Altogether this array of voluntary organisations constitutes a substantial and indispensable element in the overall pattern of community care. In addition it is significant that in the one field where there is a fast-rising demand - that of advice and counselling - the voluntary sector is the main provider of services. (p.95, Hadley and Hatch, 1981.)

It might be hypothesised then that lone fathers would be likely to be significantly involved as consumers of voluntary sector services. They are, as Hadley and Hatch would define them:

> single parents...people with a problem that sets them apart from everybody else (p.95, Hadley and Hatch, 1981.)

and they are potentially in a situation of greater comparative need in relation to advice and counselling. Was this hypothesis about involvement with voluntary sector services proven on the basis of this study? The short answer is that it was not, for the periods either prior to lone fatherhood or during lone fatherhood.

During the former period there was little if any evidence of the members of this sample seeking or receiving assistance from voluntary sector agencies. It might have been felt that Relate would have been involved with some of the couples in relation to the collapsing marital relationships, in fact they were not used by any members of the sample.

Subsequent to them becoming lone fathers, a minority of the men in this sample used the services of voluntary agencies, but only a minority. The majority of lone fathers were not seeking, or availing themselves of, counselling services from the voluntary sector after they become lone fathers. Two of the 16 widowers in the sample had attended group counselling sessions for the bereaved. In both cases they had seen newspaper articles about Cruse, had made contact, and had been going to regular meetings for 9 and 12 months respectively. Both found the meetings to be helpful:

> I've found that it's helped me to talk about things generally, the more I've been able to talk the less painful it has become.(Aidan FF, no.32.)

> It's been helpful, the contact with people, and talking about my own feelings and hearing what other people are feeling, you get feedback both ways.(Desmond EE, no.31.)

In both cases then the men involved had taken initiatives to get help with their life situations, they had felt they wanted to talk about their positions to other than family and friends, and had found the results of their initiatives to be positive. Both men were in the pioneering category, whilst it would be wrong to generalise from such tiny numbers, it may be that they were more able to consider talking about their feelings than others in the sample who had more traditional patriarchal orientations. It does seem that they would not have made contact with the service involved had they not seen the written account of the services, which possibly has implications for social welfare organisations publicising their services.

No other voluntary social work agencies appear to have been used to any extent by the lone fathers in this study. A number of men however had been in contact - during the process of their becoming, or after they had become, lone fathers, with organisations or professional groupings that had helped or hindered them.

Contacts with other organisations and professionals

The professional groupings or areas of service that will be considered under this heading are the legal profession; the medical and health services; and other services.

The lone fathers in the sample were asked who - apart from relatives, friends, social workers and probation officers - had been particularly helpful or unhelpful, and were shown a checklist as an aide memoire. The results of the responses are shown in table 11.5.

Table 11.5 Professionals or services that were helpful or unhelpful

Total Sample

	Helpful(18)	Unhelpful(8)
Solicitor	3	3
General Practitioner	3	1
Health Visitor	2	3
Vicar, priest	4	1
Personnel officer	3	
CAB	1	
Samaritans	1	
Student counsellor	1	

As can be seen, solicitors were the most mentioned grouping. In fact, given that solicitors had not been included in the aide memoire shown to lone fathers, the fact that they were the most mentioned grouping indicates the influence or impact they had had on the lone fathers lives.

Those lone fathers who had been involved in divorces had had contact with the civil legal system and members of the legal profession. It might have been assumed that all the men in the sample would be happy with the legal services and professionals, having had their right to the custody of their children given or approved by the law. In some cases they felt the contact had been helpful, in others the involvement within the legal domain appears to have been peripheral, and in others the involvement was perceived by the lone fathers as unhelpful.

Some lone fathers talked about solicitors being 'very helpful.' Amongst those in this category was Jeff S, no.19, who said:

> The solicitor was very helpful, he advised me about an affiliation order..when we first split up he advised me that we needed a woman in the background, and all I wanted was to get the kids, so that's why we lived at my mothers.

The theme of winning or losing the case in relation to custody emerged in other responses. The role of possible women supporters/mother substitutes also loomed large in other lone fathers legal experiences - thus one father's mother was quoted as a good mother substitute for his ex-wife by the solicitor in court.

Other lone fathers were critical of solicitors, they seemed to feel that the solicitors were doing what they decided was best rather than ascertaining and trying to achieve the wishes of their clients. John Y, no.25's, solicitors appeared to him to have decided that they didn't approve of lone fathers:

The solicitors weren't supportive at all, they seemed to be frightened of a father looking after his kids, they put so many obstacles in the way - the girl's puberty, me working - they tried to get me to give up my job. They interviewed my girlfriend to check that she was a good mother substitute. They're no good at all, and you have to be forever visiting their offices.

Whilst not apparently exhibiting such moral judgements, James CC, no 29's solicitors annoyed him because they took control of events:

I felt that they misled me - for instance the two solicitors, hers and mine, signed an agreement about the access arrangement that I'd never even seen, which caused problems the first weekend there was access. When my wife complained it was the first time I knew that the agreement had been signed, which actually made arrangements contrary to what I'd discussed with my solicitor..the fact that they'd done it without coming back to me caused a problem with access right from the start.

The adversarial nature of divorce proceedings was a source of some regret and concern for some lone fathers. The one who felt most abused by the system was Jake BB, no.28, as indicated earlier. He felt that his wife had used the legal system to pursue a vendetta, changing solicitors several times when the ones she was using were nearing reaching a legal outcome, with an enormous bill for legal services being the consequence for him. However, not all lone fathers were heavily involved in adversarial legal disputes, there were some who had little if any contact with solicitors, they and their ex-partners having come to agreements about the nature of custody and any division of property.

Overall, those lone fathers who had been involved in the legal system where agreements had not been reached by them with their ex-partners did not appear to have experienced the process as helpful - at best they had 'won' their cases, sometimes at the expense of considerable time and money. If the experience of some members of the sample was typical, being involved in legal processes appears to be adversarial - adversarial in relation to the ex-partner and her solicitors, and, in a minority of cases, adversarial in relation to the lone father and his own solicitors. There are also indications that in the latter relationship some solicitors had difficulties with the concept of a 'lone father', and sought to show the courts not so much that the men were 'fit fathers', but that there were mother substitutes in the situation who could be deemed 'fit (substitute) mothers', which is probably a reflection of how gender roles and responsibilities are perceived in the legal domain. Smart (1989) has argued that in custody issues, partly as a result of pressure group interests (e.g. 'Families need Fathers.'), a de-gendering process has taken place, which has been part of a process of patriarchal reconstruction. She argues that men's rights in custody decisions have come more to the fore, at the expense of maternal rights. It can be seen that one analysis is that the granting of custody to lone fathers is a process by which the legal framework of the state asserts patriarchal authority in the domestic domain. In the case of this sample custody decisions did not appear to be being made as a form of assertion of patriarchal power, they were experienced by the men in this sample as being made on the basis of the needs of the children involved. Their experience of the legal domain was not that the processes in which they were involved had been degendered, they felt that the fact that they were patriarchs was a disadvantage rather than an advantage.

If the lone fathers experiences of solicitors and legal services were variable, did the same apply to their experiences of health services? It is perhaps surprising that relationships with health professionals appear to have not loomed very large in most lone fathers lives. Two categories of health professionals were mentioned - general practitioners and health visitors. The former were rated positively by 3 lone fathers and negatively by 1; the latter positively by 2 lone fathers and negatively by 3. GPs were praised for their availability and interest, and were criticised for a lack of interest. It might have been expected that health visitors could have occupied a key role in the lives of a number of lone fathers, given their central concerns with child care and parenting. It is thus interesting that the common experience of lone fathers, even those who had been caring for pre school age children during their lone fatherhood, was to have had no contact with health visitors. Only two lone fathers had had helpful contacts with health visitors, three had had unhelpful contacts:

She was no help at all, I asked her for help, she was no good at all.(John Y, no. 25.)

The health visitor called once to give (my son) an injection, apart from that she didn't call, nobody was bothered.(Dick X, no.24.)

It was, in fact, a source of surprise to some lone fathers that they had not had more - or in most cases any - contact with health visitors. Even though many of the children cared for during the period of lone fatherhood were of school attendance age, it might have been felt that health visitors would have been a source of practical advice and emotional support for lone fathers, some of whom were struggling to develop parenting skills. On the basis of this study it appears that such opportunities for health visitors to intervene positively and proactively were not taken up by them, for reasons which are unclear.

As the data indicates, a number of other professionals or organisations were reported as having been helpful. 4 lone fathers had had pastoral assistance from vicars or priests that they had found helpful, 1 had had interventions that had been unhelpful. Clearly, even in what is perhaps wrongly seen to be an increasingly secular society, representatives of organised religion are perceived as offering a valued service to some at a time when they are in need or in crisis. Personnel officers at the place of lone fathers employment had been helpful in 3 cases, in assisting lone fathers to continue in paid employment. The CAB had been particularly helpful to 1 lone father (in relation to legal advice, he felt they had been far more helpful than his solicitor), and 1 lone father at a time of stress had contacted the Samaritans and had found the experience to be a helpful one. It can thus be seen that lone fathers were involved in a variety of different ways with a variety of different professionals and organisations, both statutory and voluntary.

Lone father households and agency and professionals' involvements

It can be argued that social work, health and related agencies on one level represent helping activities, and on another level represent a form of 'policing of families' (Donzelot, 1980.) Usually, this helping and policing, this supporting and surveillance, are channelled through the adult female members of families, hence the emphasis on 'fit mothers', whilst the male adult - the patriarch, is engaged in the world of paid employment. Even where the male adult is not engaged in paid employment, the activities of social work, social welfare, and health agencies still tend to be based on the assumptions that women are responsible for 'family matters.' In the case of lone father households there is however a dilemma for agencies, given that they are often households without adult women. Thus, agencies that interacted with the adults in the households in this sample were relating to adult males not adult females.

In fact, in the majority of cases the agencies and professional groupings considered in this chapter did not intervene significantly in the lives of the lone fathers. If lone fatherhood is a state of crisis, the evidence largely is that social work and other agencies were not involved in crisis intervention. Where interventions did take place, there were some indications that traditional patriarchal orientations, carried to excess, could lead to problems - for example, the men who felt that their rights to discipline their children physically were being challenged and undermined by social services involvement. In relation to those who might be perceived to have adopted more pioneering orientations, there was little evidence that they were encouraged or enabled to reflect on their gender or parenting roles with regard to domestic work and child care with the assistance of state or voluntary organisations.

In relation to the professionals and organisations themselves, the picture is somewhat mixed. There is evidence to show that some of those who had had contact with social services departments felt positively. Perhaps however the clearest message was that there was not a clear message to the lone fathers in relation to the aims and objectives of the social work involvement. Thus, those who had had contact with social workers in the main found it hard to be clear about the nature of the contacts in other than fairly general terms - the aims and objectives of lone fathers and social workers appear to have been implicit and possibly therefore different, rather than explicit and agreed. There was also a lack of clarity for many lone fathers about the network of services potentially available, many lone fathers were not clear about the detail of what social services departments actually did. This seems to indicate that there is a need for social services departments in particular to publicise their services more widely. Some authorities have begun to do this, the more services are publicised however (as required now by the 1989 Children Act) the more the underfunding of such services will be exposed.

One group of social workers whose role was clear to the lone fathers who had involvement with them was the court welfare officers. Their role, in relation to custody decisions, was clearly understood by the lone fathers as advisers to the court, not as possible arbitrators between or counsellors of separating and divorcing couples. In general, they were seen to act professionally and appropriately in preparing their reports for the courts. The other professionals working in the legal domain with whom many lone fathers had had contact were solicitors, and given that these lone fathers had been successful in obtaining custody it might have been expected that they would have been been more content with the services they received than many of them were. Clearly, the legal system was seen as adversarial, and solicitors in some cases were seen to be making moral judgements about or marginalising their clients. Solicitors also at times appear to have - perhaps unwittingly, perhaps pragmatically - been keen to show that lone fathers would only be able to cope with custody because mother substitutes were available, which seems to imply a presence within legal circles of images of masculinity which do not allow for competence in child care.

With regard to other state services, a small number of lone fathers felt their general practitioners had been helpful, and there was a surprising lack of involvement by health visitors in the lives of the lone fathers and their children. Whether this was the result of mismanagement, a respect for patriarchal rights to authority and privacy, difficulties in (female) health visitors relating to (male) parents, or some other cause, is unclear. It does appear however that at least a sizeable minority of lone fathers felt they would have benefited from some professional being available to give them advice and validation in their parenting roles, health visitors would have been ideally placed to have adopted such roles, and some lone fathers were surprised that they had not.

In relation to contact with voluntary organisations, the indication is that the minority of lone fathers who had had contacts with services for the bereaved felt positively about them, clearly there is potential for such services to be offered more widely. Contacts with one parent family organisations, with one or two exceptions, had been either non existent or unsatisfactory. It may be that such organisations do not offer services that are perceived by lone fathers as 'lone father friendly'; there is a difficulty in running organisations that cater for the needs of the majority of (female) lone parents, estimated at 90.1% at the time of this study, and the minority of (male) lone parents, estimated at 9.9% at the time of this study (National Council for One Parent Families Annual Report, 1989.) It may be however that such organisations could consider whether they wish

235

to attract more lone fathers to membership, and if so, what the implications are for their practices and policies.

This chapter has considered the involvement in lone father households of agencies of the state, and of voluntary organisations. The impression is that such individuals and institutions were slow to invade the privacy of lone father households, in fact, at times, slower than many lone fathers felt was legitimate. It was not the case that 'fit fatherhood' was being nurtured or monitored, except in a small minority of households where patriarchal force appears to have been exercised too physically. There is little evidence that the men in this sample were encouraged or enabled to reflect on their gender or parenting roles with the assistance of state or voluntary organisations. Attention has and is being focused on creating a form of social work which is experienced as 'a genuinely woman centred practice' (Hanmer and Statham, 1988). It appears however that the process of giving consideration to the issues involved in creating, in appropriate circumstances, 'male centred practice' which takes gender and masculinity seriously, has only just begun. Hudson (1989) has written of the need for social worker to consider how to engage with families where:

> the 'problem' is often that men are positioned, or place themselves at the periphery. (p.85, Hudson, 1989.)

In lone father families as has been indicated men are invariably not at the periphery, yet the impression from this data is that social welfare, health, and legal agencies were not engaging with lone father households in ways which were grappling with the complexities of gender issues.

Overall, many lone fathers would have liked to have had more involvement and support, or the offer of more involvement and support, than they had experienced. This could have been in a number of forms, to do with practical issues such as advice about legal matters and benefits; to do with personal issues such as loss and bereavement; or to do with parenting issues such as advising and validating lone fathers performances. The personal social services, health services, and voluntary organisations were 'at best peripheral' to the problems of many lone fathers, and further implications of this will be discussed in the concluding chapter.

12 Conclusion

In this concluding chapter the main themes of this research study are summarised and discussed. The study has looked at the situations and experiences of a small sample of lone fathers and considered their positions in relation to issues of parenting and masculinities.

This study has sought to develop the research process with regard to the area of the family and the household in a form which is congruent with the guidelines for such studies suggested by Harris:

> What is required if the place of the family in industrial societies is to be better understood is that a new generation of studies comes to exist which examine the patterns of relations between the private and public domains and regards the household as the site of their articulation. (p.247, Harris, 1983.)

The study has indicated that there was no single, universal pattern of lone fatherhood. It has been suggested that the differences between lone fathers can be best understood as the expressions of different forms of masculinities operating within the different patriarchal structures of society. The study theorises a six fold division of patriarchy into the patriarchal relations of the domestic setting, the economic setting, community and neighbourhood, sexuality, the state, and culture. With regard to parenthood, patriarchy and masculinities, it has been suggested that, whilst all men are the beneficiaries of patriarchal power, on the basis of orientations to gender roles two forms of patriarchal masculinities were being practised within the different settings. Traditional patriarchs tended to adopt an orientation to masculinities and parenting that saw child care as more properly women's work than men's work. As such, they tended to meet their child care and parenting responsibilities with the assistance of (female) others, or, where such assistance was lacking, regretted that they were having to manage as fathers without mothers. They were more likely to report difficulties with child care, particularly in relation to issues regarding the disciplining of children, and gender issues related to rearing girls. In contrast, gender pioneers had orientations to masculinities which prioritised child care and parenting as being important for men as

237

well as for women, and they tended be generally more child centred in the ways in which they generated a sense of meaning and purpose in their lives. As parents, they were generally inclined not to regret the additional responsibilities of lone fatherhood, and tended to perceive that they had become 'softer' in their relations with their children as a result of being lone fathers.

An important finding of this research has been that both traditional patriarchs and gender pioneers were more involved with their children and the day to day management of their households than they had been prior to lone fatherhood, and virtually all the men in the sample were more 'active' as fathers and as workers in the domestic setting than men have generally been found to be in studies of two parent families. Thus, this research illustrates that in certain circumstances 'men can mother', that fathers can take primary responsibility for tasks and activities that are traditionally seen to lie within the feminine domain. In taking on such responsibilities lone fathers did not feel either particularly diminished in their sense of masculinity or assert that they were behaving in 'ideologically sound anti-sexist practices' - they did not appear to see themselves as 'Old Women' or 'New Men'.

Overall, the degree of difficulty experienced by lone fathers in relation to child care was less than might have been expected. In general, as indicated earlier, the demands and rewards of child care do appear to have been more central to the lives of pioneers than of patriarchs. The former orientation was associated with according children and their needs a central position, with taking responsibility for child care and child tending, and with developing a role in relation to parenting and fathering that marked a form of discontinuity from past parenting influences. The traditional patriarchal orientation to masculinities was associated, not with a neglect of child care and children's needs, but with perspectives that were at times less child centred, which gave equal or greater primacy to social interactions and obligations in the other structures of patriarchal social relations. This orientation to masculinities was more associated with sharing child care responsibilities with others, and was more likely to involve the pursuance of a fathering role that was influenced by the lone father's own parents' examples.

With regard to the management of the domestic setting and housework, whilst having noted the increased involvement of virtually all the sample members in this area, it has been suggested that patriarchs tended to have had a relatively lower level of involvement in housework, and were satisfied that others were taking some responsibilities for this area. Pioneers tended to have a higher level of involvement in housework, to have been more likely to have developed routines for doing housework, and to experience some aspects of the activity as satisfying. For them, the meaning of housework appears to have been part of a process of being 'good fathers', of a process of self validation and a concrete means by which they were able to assert some control over their life situations.

238

All the sample members were in full time employment or its equivalent at the start of lone fatherhood, at the point of the research nearly half were unwaged. The impression from the data is that pioneers were more likely to have experienced such a process as not negative, and to have invested more in the domestic setting as a means of generating and having a 'sense of self.' Lone fathers with traditional patriarchal orientations to masculinities appear to have experienced their unwaged states more negatively, either because they felt in some ways diminished by being unemployed, or because they experienced being on benefit more negatively than pioneers.

Thus, some lone fathers appear to have been relatively content with a situation in which they were unemployed and doing domestic work, whilst others appear to have felt more stressed and diminished in experiencing what were objectively very similar situations. For some their perceptions of the importance of paid employment had diminished, whereas for others the experience or the idea of paid employment still had a central significance in their lives. Clearly on the evidence of this data it is a mistake to assume that there were no orientations to employment other than the dominant model of the traditional patriarchal form of masculinity, and clearly some lone fathers had developed an orientation to employment which, implicitly rather than explicitly, in its daily practice challenged the dominant, yet narrow, concepts of masculinity. Paradoxically to be a 'good man' in terms of paid employment is not in many ways congruent with being, or being available to be, a father. For some men the regional economic situation had, during their time as lone fathers, played an important part in enabling or leading them to exploit the wave of redundancies during this period to allow them to adopt more active day to day parenting roles.

The evidence indicates that the processes and transitions of becoming and being lone fathers involved for some men a turning away from the pursuit of materialistic goals as a raison d' etre of their lives. It has not been argued that the changes necessarily flowed through to all aspects of their lives, yet the meaning of their workplace to the pioneers had changed, it had become less of a central mainspring of their sense of masculinity and more of a means to an end. The pioneering orientation to those who were on benefit involved an appreciation that parenting was more successful for them by their not engaging in paid employment, being on benefit was not a priori the second best solution to their situation Thus, some men were pursuing traditional patriarchal patterns of behaviour which were consistent with hegemonic masculinity. Others, as a result of their circumstances and their orientations to them felt that they were trapped, felt that they were not able to adopt patterns of behaviour consistent with hegemonic masculinity. Others, by their adoption of pioneering orientations, were living their lives in ways which implicitly or explicitly challenged hegemonic masculinity. Whilst the individual economic circumstances created the broad boundaries within which the men lived their lives, the economic circumstances were not directly causal of, and did not dictate, orientations to masculinities. Thus, some men in similar economic circumstances had adopted and developed different masculinities, whilst others in differing economic circumstances had developed similar masculinities.

With regard to sexuality, it has been shown that, whilst all the men in the sample were heterosexual, they were expressing a variety of forms of heterosexuality in their lives as lone fathers. Therefore, just as it has been argued that it is more appropriate to talk of masculinities rather than masculinity, so it appears to be more appropriate to talk about heterosexualities rather than heterosexuality. Whilst 'hegemonic heterosexuality' can be seen to exist in the same sense that hegemonic masculinity exists, the daily practices of the lone fathers in this sample - embracing and rejecting, desiring and fearing, searching for and avoiding, intimate relationships with women - were not uniform. Similarly, whilst it may be that in some ways heterosexuality is a form of patriarchal practice through which mens' dominance over women is asserted and maintained, the evidence of this analysis does not show that this was clearly the case in relation to the lives of all the men in this sample. Thus whilst some lone fathers were constructing and creating a patriarchal orientation in the realm of heterosexuality, at least some of this group were not seeking to recreate a traditional nuclear family household by such a process, and gave the impression of being able to accept a heterosexual relationship without desiring patriarchal dominance within a household. Others felt themselves to be in positions in which they were unable to attain the heterosexual relationships they desired, and to some extent perhaps the non existence of heterosexual relationships for this group represented to them some form of denial of patriarchal power. A third group were choosing not to enter into heterosexual relationships at all, either on a time limited or an indefinite basis. By not necessarily actively seeking to enter into heterosexual relationships these men were expressing a form of heterosexual masculinity which shows that 'ordinary men' - can quietly live their lives in ways which challenge the notion that:

> male sexuality (is) some kind of primordial force which sweeps everything before it.(p.46, Brittan, 1989.)

With regard to kinship contacts, patriarchal orientations in this area were expressed by those men who had frequent contact with kinfolk, usually in relation to child care and their maintenance needs, who received a great deal of assistance from (usually women) kinfolk, and thus shared responsibility for, but retained control over, domestic matters. Others expressed a sense of their frustration in relation to kinship contacts, in one of two ways. Firstly, there were those who wished to receive more support from kinfolk and felt trapped into and by the performance of parenting duties because of the lack of such support. Such an orientation represents an expression of a traditional form of patriarchal masculinity in relation to the domestic domain. Secondly, there were those who received support but felt that they had thus passed over an undue measure of control over their lives in the process, but were unwilling or unable to negotiate more appropriate arrangements for themselves.

240

What then constituted pioneering orientations in relation to contacts with kinfolk? It might be felt that perhaps such orientations would be likely to have included less exploitative contacts with female kinfolk, related to an increased 'investment' on the part of the lone father in their parenting roles. However, the evidence is not strong for arguing that such orientations were widespread amongst the sample. Why might this be so? Perhaps, as pioneering orientations in relation to gender roles represent a break with tradition, it might be anticipated that more traditional orientations to gender and masculinities would be more prevalent in this area, as more personal historical socialisation precedents for behaviour exist in the area of kinship relations than in other areas. For patriarchs and pioneers, the overall impression of kinfolk relationships gained from the data was of a generally high level of interaction with relatives who had traditional perspectives in relation to gender roles, and of lone fathers who felt they largely benefited from the support they were given from such relatives.

The major primary reason stated for contacts with ex-partners was in relation to access matters and children, yet less than half of the subsample of 19 divorcees were in face to face contact and talking to their ex-partners. There was wide variation in the quality of the tone of the contact between ex-partners, some, generally patriarchs, had friendly or very friendly contact. It might have been anticipated that pioneers would be more likely to have friendlier contacts with ex-partners than patriarchs, but this data indicates that this was not the case. It would appear that there was no simple relationship between the form of masculinity and the nature of the contact with the ex-partner. Ex-partners, for lone fathers, constituted the women over whom they had formally had patriarchal power in the previous relations in the domestic setting. As such, their contacts with these ex-partners at the time of this research were on a different basis, and the primary focus for their contact with their ex-partners was the children of the relationship. On this basis therefore, children's contacts with the ex-partner were less congruent with the pioneering orientation, it was suggested that the ex-partner's involvement possibly represented more of a threat to the changed, more active, parenting role which was part of the pioneering orientation. It thus appeared possible that for pioneering lone fathers, having a close relationship with the ex-partners, and having child care as a primary source of meaning, were in some ways mutually exclusive.

In relation to social networks, it was found that whilst approximately half the sample had constant friendship relationships, a small minority had experienced an increase in the number of friends, and a larger minority a decrease. The figures also indicated that divorcees were the majority of the subgroup who had overall gained friends, and widowers the majority of the group who had overall lost friends. However, whilst equal proportions of patriarchs and pioneers had retained the same friendship networks, pioneers were over represented in the sub sample who reported an increase in the numbers of their friends, and under represented in the sub sample who reported a decrease. Working class lone fathers were

241

more likely than middle class fathers to have reported an increase in the numbers of friends they had, and it was suggested that the explanation for this appears to have been at least partly related to availability for friendship contacts. In relation to forms of masculinities, lone fathers with pioneering orientations were more likely to have increased the size of their friendship networks than were lone fathers with patriarchal orientations. It was clear that lone fathers, be they patriarchs or pioneers, widowers or divorcees, working class or middle class, overwhelmingly tended to have friendships within, rather than across, gender boundaries. What does not appear to be common on the evidence of this study is a process by which lone fathers move into female friendship networks as a result of the changes associated with their becoming lone fathers. It thus appears that different orientations to masculinities were not consequential on, or causal of, different gender patterns of friendship - it was not the case that patriarchs had more men friends, and pioneers more women friends. Similarly, the majority of the sample had relatively little or no contact with other single parents, and there is no evidence that pioneering orientations were associated with the amount of contact with other single parents.

Whilst there was a general tendency for men to be more involved in non-work social relationships than they had been prior to becoming lone fathers, this involvement was clearly a gendered experience - the men, as a result of becoming lone fathers, did not move into the worlds of womens' relationships. Whilst for some their contacts with women kinfolk increased, these contacts were clearly on the basis of them being lone fathers, and not of them being quasi mothers. Thus, patriarchal or pioneering orientations to lone fatherhood were expressed through the domain of these social networks, but do not appear to have their origins in the lone fathers' activities in these domains. In general there had been more continuity in relation to kinfolk contacts and geographical locality than there had been in relation to sexual relationships and friendships. There was some evidence that pioneering orientations were associated with change in place of residence and increased level of friendship activity, and pioneers appeared to be more aware of their neighbours perceptions of them than were patriarchs.

It has been suggested that many lone fathers would have liked to have had more involvement with and support from welfare services, than they actually experienced. What might this involvement have constituted? It would seem that it could have been in one of a number of forms. Some lone fathers suggested that they would have welcomed involvement related to practical issues such as advice about entitlement to benefits or legal matters. For some, the start of lone fatherhood was particularly a time of personal crisis when they would have welcomed practical advice, and when they did not feel able or motivated to seek out the relevant professionals or agencies concerned. With regard to state financial support, the DHSS supplementary benefit system in operation at the time of the fieldwork for this study has been subsequently replaced by the DSS social funds system. This latter appears to be less generous than the former system, and the discretionary grants and single payments which had been so vital for the quality of life and economic survival of some lone father families would not be payable under the new system. It also appears that the current benefit system disadvantages widowers in comparison with widows, special payments to which the latter are entitled are not payable to the former, and this gender differential appears to have no logical justification.

Some lone fathers indicated that they would have found it appropriate had there been intervention with regard to parenting issues such as advising on and validating their fathering. Such attitudes might indicate a lack of experience and or a lack of confidence in parenting and fathering. It also needs to be remembered that this sample represents successful lone fathers, in that the men were all looking after their children, in the vast majority of cases very competently.

There was little evidence that the men in this sample were encouraged or enabled to reflect on their gender or parenting roles with the assistance of state or voluntary sector welfare or health agencies. In some ways this was not perhaps surprising, given that since the 1970s there has been a squeeze on resources available to public sector welfare and health agencies, with the consequence that agencies have been only able to deliver those services seen to be the most needed - and required - by statute. It can be argued however that services that begin to engage with issues concerning masculinities and fathering should be a high priority, given the damage that unchallenged hegemonic masculinity can be seen to create for women and children. Connell has written that:

> We live in a world shaped by the collective failure of our forbears to abolish gender inequalities.(p.279, Connell, 1987.)

The fact that the personal social services, health services, and voluntary organisations, were generally peripheral to the experiences and problems of the majority of lone father households indicates that such agencies were not grasping the opportunities that involvement would have afforded to begin to enable the processes of challenging gender inequalities.

This is not to suggest that patriarchal and parent child relationships are not continually in the process of being reshaped and restructured. One means by which such restructurings occur is the legislation that relates to, and regulates, family life. The 1989 Children Act, which came into force in October 1991, replaced the concept of parental rights with the concept of parental responsibilities, and sees mothers and fathers as having equal responsibilities towards their children throughout their children's lives. If these legislative aims are to come closer towards realisation, the suggestion from this and other studies is that welfare and other services will have to consider more carefully the meaning and impact of gender processes and gender differences on their work than currently appears to be the norm. The 1989 Children Act also requires local authority social services departments to seek out and meet the needs of children in their areas and to publicise the services that they are offering to such children more widely. If these intentions are realised it may be that welfare services will become more available and more accessible to all, including lone fathers and their households. However, for the Children Act changes to be fully realised it will be necessary for there to be both a change in attitude on the part of welfare service deliverers, and the availability of additional resources to implement the changes. It is not clear at the time of writing if either or both of these are likely to happen. The evidence of the 1980s is that the changes in attitudes towards how services should be offered to the public may be easier to attain than increased resources to deliver services. Shortly after this research took place, in the area from which this sample was drawn, one local authority SSD faced losing one out of eight of its employees, and another a £4 million cut in its annual budget, because of central government penalties on their perceived overspending. These are merely two of countless examples of the attacks on public spending which threaten the development of adequate and appropriate services.

Parenting, patriarchy, and masculinities

Morris, having reviewed the UK and US literature on domestic life and gender roles concludes that:

> The evidence from both Britain and America indicates an absence of any significant change in established gender roles.(p.189, Morris, 1990.)

The data presented in this study suggests that the lone fathers in this sample had experienced changes and were engaged in the processes of reshaping gender roles. However, it is oversimplistic and wrong to see lone fathers as self made New Men, the position was both more complicated and more interesting than that. In relation to their daily practices, it can be seen that in general lone fathers were highly involved in the care of their children and the management of their domestic settings, much more than they had been prior to becoming lone fathers, and much more than would have been expected from the evidence of the studies cited by Morris (1990.)

With regard to orientations to gender roles, this study has argued that, on the basis of attitudes to gender relations, lone fathers could be categorised as traditional patriarchs or gender pioneers. Examination and consideration of their practices in the different patriarchal structures however indicates that individual men were not homogeneously traditionally patriarchal or gender pioneering. In comparison with their expressed orientations towards gender relations, at times traditionally patriarchal lone fathers appeared to be acting in ways which were somewhat progressive, and gender pioneering lone fathers in ways which were traditionally patriarchal. Substitution of masculinities for masculinity affords a means of understanding such contradictions, indicating as it does

244

that different behaviours can occur in different contexts. However, it should not be thought that such an approach leads to a view of men as no more than a series of fragmented, post modern multiple personalities. The contradictions of different masculinities are present at a structural level, and at the level of the individual the men in this sample were struggling to resolve the contradictions of masculinities and parenting, of being lone fathers, within a patriarchal society, influenced by the cultural theme of hegemonic masculinity.

It has been suggested in this research that a full understanding of the positions and processes experienced by lone fathers can only be reached by including a consideration of patriarchy in the analysis. As a number of writers have noted, patriarchy is generally considered to be such an all pervasive factor in social relationships as to lack sophistication as a descriptive or analytical tool at other than a macro level. In arguing a six fold division of patriarchy into the patriarchal relations of the domestic setting, the economic setting, community and neighbourhood, sexuality, the state, and culture it has been suggested that different forms of masculinities can be practised by men in these different patriarchal settings. Thus, for example, a man might be employed in manufacturing industry in which setting he adopted a traditional patriarchal orientation, and engaged in the domestic setting where he adopted a gender pioneering orientation. Exactly why and how such differences become manifest is more difficult to explain; on the basis of this study it is possible to begin to suggest that such processes do however occur, and this study has begun to describe and unpack these processes.

Was the fact that in some of the patriarchal structures some men adopted pioneering orientations to masculinities whilst others were traditionally patriarchal in their orientations connected in any ways with the concept of crisis discussed earlier? The evidence suggests that the pioneers were more able to cope with change, and were more able to respond proactively to changed circumstances, than were the patriarchs. Pioneers tended to have been more likely to have experienced change in relation to place of residence and friendship patterns than patriarchs, and patriarchs tended to feel more settled in relation to physical location - 50% felt that they would be likely to remain in the same house forever, compared with 10% of pioneers.

Another factor related to orientations to masculinities appears to have been the increased child focussedness of the pioneers. This did not take place within the personally experienced boundaries of traditional fathering, the pioneers did not use their parents' behaviour towards them as role models for their own parenting in the way that many of the patriarchs did. The patriarchs also experienced greater problems with child care than did the pioneers, indicating that a traditional patriarchal orientation to masculinities is not a priori a recipe for success when a matriarch is not also present. A pioneering orientation to gender roles therefore appears to have been related to lone fathers being more able to have interactions with their social situations which led to outcomes which

245

they could experience as positive. For example, whilst structural factors, such as the declining economic and industrial situation in the region impacted on many men in the sample, the concept of different orientations to masculinities was crucial to understanding how members of this sample experienced these impacts. It is not too simplistic to suggest that lone fathers who were patriarchs who became unemployed or redundant experienced such processes as negative, and as a loss, whereas lone fathers who were pioneers experienced such a process as positive and an opportunity. In Viney and Beattie's 1980 study, they suggested that positive adaptations to the crisis of lone parenthood were associated with the satisfactions of getting more involved with children:

> they cope by accepting the limits of their new situation and working within them. (p.349, Beattie and Viney, 1980.)

Negative adaptations were associated with a withdrawal into 'anxious self pre - occupation', and an increased focus on the problems and pressures of lone parenthood. They suggest that such differences are related to the psychological meaning of the crisis of lone parenthood for the subjects. However, this study suggests that structural issues may also be involved. The positive orientation they describe is similar to the gender pioneering form of masculinity, whilst the negative orientation they describe can be best understood not as individual deviance or failure to cope, but as a consequence of the contradictions inherent in traditional patriarchal masculinity, particularly that of wishing to exercise power but being dependent on female others to take responsibility. Lone fatherhood represented a crisis of masculinities for lone fathers who adopted a traditional patriarchal orientation to the domestic setting and who were unable to call on female labour to provide for the household's needs. For those men, and for those lone fathers who adopted such orientations and who were able to use female labour, lone fatherhood can also be seen to be part of the wider crisis of masculinities in that such orientations are supportive of the continuance of gender inequalities which are ultimately damaging for men as well as for women.

This latter illustrates how the experience of lone fatherhood can be best understood as an interplay of the symbolic interactionist and structural elements of their social realities. Clearly gender was a major factor in the experiences of the members of the lone father households, but the impacts of gender within and without the households were both subtle and complex, the monolithic gender differences suggested by functionalism, marxism, and early feminism were not evident in this study. The only way that the gender processes could begin to be understood was by seeking to understand gender as both an individual and a structural factor.

This research has provided some answers in relation to lone fathers, parenting, and masculinities, but, equally importantly, has also provided some questions which would provide opportunities for further research in these areas. As one famous fictional creation commented in respect of his scientific methods and their results:

One forms provisional theories and waits for time or fuller knowledge to explode them. (Sherlock Holmes, on p.1039, 'The Penguin Complete Sherlock Holmes', Sir Arthur Conan Doyle, 1981.)

In seeking to describe and understand more about lone father households this study has intentionally focused on the experiences and perceptions of the lone fathers themselves. Further research into the experiences of different samples would be of value. Research which explored the experiences and perceptions of the children of such households, and the ex-partners of lone fathers, would be invaluable. Such research would be interesting both to let them 'tell their own stories', and to see the ways in which the similarities and differences of their accounts from those of lone fathers' accounts illuminated the data in this study. It would also be interesting to obtain more information about men who had been lone fathers who subsequently formed households with women partners, to see how far any changes in orientations to gender, and patterns of behaviour arising from the experiences of lone fatherhood were sustained or modified as a result of the recreation of a two parent household. It would also be interesting for studies to be done which focused on adults who had been raised for some parts of their childhood in lone father households to see if there appeared to be any relationships between such experiences and adult gender roles.

This research has focused on a sample of lone fathers that was an all white, relatively able bodied, group of men. It might be anticipated that lone fathers who were also black, or lone fathers who also had some form of physical handicap, would experience lone fatherhood differently because of such factors, and research which considered the experiences and situations of such men would be interesting.

In looking to highlight some of the possible relationships between patriarchy and masculinities this research has looked at the private and public experiences of lone fathers in a way which has focused more on the private, and its implications for the public, than vice versa - not least because the site of the research interviews was the household setting of lone fathers. In furthering understanding of the links between forms of masculinities and patriarchal relations, research which sought to observe and understand the ways in which masculinities were expressed in the more public structures of patriarchal relations would be valuable. It would also be interesting if there was more research into the ways in which children experience and are influenced by the implicit and explicit messages regarding masculinities and parenthood which are expressed through such structures as the patriarchal relations of the state and of culture.

Currently approximately one marriage in three ends in divorce. It is clear that often divorced parents have difficulties in post divorce relationships with each other and with their children. The 1989 Children Act seeks to create by legislation post divorce relationships where the

247

divorced parents retain ongoing parental responsibilities towards their children. Whether such desired arrangements are sustainable in the majority of cases, and what combinations of factors work towards supporting or undermining such arrangements, will need to be monitored and evaluated and legislative policies and practices reviewed in the light of the findings. It should not be assumed that changes in gender and parenting patterns will inevitably facilitate more cooperative post divorce parenthood relationships. The tentative evidence from this study is that men who became more 'involved' as lone fathers and who had pioneering orientations to gender also had less positive feelings towards their ex-partners and their involvement with the children than did men who remained less involved and more traditionally patriarchal. Whether this is a general pattern, and the implications for post divorce arrangements if it is, needs to be established by further research.

In relation to the 'involvement' of fathers, it has been argued that:

> Popular belief in the more 'involved' father must therefore be seen as something of an illusion. (p.88, Backett, 1987.)

There seems little doubt that the men in this sample were more 'involved', in absolute terms, and in relative terms compared with when they had been fathers in two parent households. Some were so whilst holding traditional patriarchal orientations to masculinities, whilst others appeared to have developed gender pioneering orientations. There were contradictions experienced and expressed by the sample members however, sometimes with pioneers at times acting in traditionally patriarchal ways, and sometimes with patriarchs at times acting in gender pioneering ways. Connell (1987) has criticised many discussions of gender and sex roles for having been based on hypothetical normative standard cases rather than primary data. The results of this study are based on primary data, and as such are not tidy nor neat nor easily packaged. Perhaps if the results were presented in the form of a neat model they would less accurately reflect the diversity of the lives of the respondents. It is sometimes popularly felt that if the social sciences became more like the physical sciences and concentrated on developing neater, tidier models of human activity there would be an increase in their utility and respectability. Such views misinterpret the creative enterprise that is natural science, as the Nobel Prize winning joint discoverer of DNA has written:

> No good model ever accounted for all the facts, since some of the data was bound to be misleading if not plain wrong. A theory that did fit all the data would have been 'carpentered' to do this, and would thus be open to suspicion. (Francis Crick, 'The Guardian', 9.4.1990)

This study, in seeking to understand the interconnections between lone fathering, parenting, and masculinities, has indicated that there was a variety of ways in which the members of the sample were struggling to negotiate and make sense of their social realities. In so doing, at times their practices were at odds with their stated ideological orientations to gender, and in experiencing these gaps between beliefs and actions they were expressing some of the contradictions inherent within and between being a lone father, being a parent, and experiences and images of masculinities. Being an adult responsible for the care of children is not an easy process in industrial capitalist society, and there are increased difficulties for lone parents. The lone fathers in this sample did not experience the gender disadvantages and sexism that lone mothers experience, but they struggled at times to cope with lone parenthood, and in so doing nevertheless suggested that men can successfully parent and can perform functions which traditionally are seen to lie in the domain of mothering. In the course of their careers as lone fathers, some had become more aware of gender inequalities in society, and appeared to be more content, particularly within the patriarchal relations of the domestic setting. Other lone fathers, with traditional patriarchal perspectives, appeared to experience more difficulties particularly with regard to the patriarchal relations of the domestic setting.

Increasingly, as post industrial Britain enters the 21st century, households types appear to be becoming more diverse. The evidence indicates that this is not necessarily such a new development; if there ever was a golden age of stable, nuclear families then it was probably a relatively short one, and probably it contained many households touched more by misery than was apparent to the casual observer. Lone father households are one example of this diversity - and as such in many cases appeared to be confronting the challenges of meeting the needs of the household's members successfully. Therefore, there appears to be no logical reason why, purely on the basis of household composition, they, like any other form of single parent household, should be attacked.

Thus, whilst this study has suggested that lone fatherhood is not the last - or the first - haunt of the New Man, it has also suggested that lone fatherhood is one of the sites within the patriarchal relations of society of interesting developments in parenting and masculinities.

Appendix

The following descriptions of the lone fathers in the sample have been disguised to ensure confidentiality. The numbers and names are those used in the main body of the text, the descriptions relate to the time of interview.

No.1. Trevor A

A 59 year old father of a girl aged 15 and a son aged 28 (who live at home) and a daughter aged 30 and a son aged 23 (who live nearby.) Mr A's wife had died 5 years previously after 26 years of marriage. She had collapsed suddenly and was admitted to hospital where she died six weeks later. He was told her condition, cancer, was terminal 2 weeks before her death. Subsequently Mr A worked for 2 years as a faceworker in the local colliery, his daughter living during the week with relatives nearby and with him at weekends. He had taken voluntary early retirement 3 years previously to enable his daughter to return to live with him. Mr A lives in a modern private semi-detached house on the outskirts of a small fishing and mining town, he has lived in the house for 12 years, and the town all his life. He has had no relationships with women since his wife's death, and has wished for none. Although he did not feel life was stressful, particularly compared with the first 2 years following his wife's death, he quickly broke down and started crying as soon as he started talking about her. He felt that the future would be neither better nor worse the present 'unless my health starts to change - but I think it will be the same.'

No.2. Frank B

A 57 year old father of a girl aged 15 and sons aged 23 (living at home), 20 (away at University in term times) and 31 (living away from home.) Mr B's wife died of cancer 10 years previously, following a mastectomy 18 months prior to that. They had been married for 23 years; he knew his wife was terminally ill 6 months prior to her death. Mr B had worked at the local pit for 35 years. Previous to his wife's death, he had done rotating shift work, after her death he worked permanent nights as that

250

fitted in better with his child care responsibilities, but eventually the strain of regular night work made him ill and he readily took early retirement when the chance arose 18 months previously. He lives in a semi-detached private house in a coastal village 3 miles away from the nearest small town. He has lived in the same house for 25 years, and in the region for all his life apart from the ages of 12 to 21 when he lived in Canada, having been evacuated there in wartime, and having returned home to be nearer his ageing parents. Mr B has a large circle of male friends, and has not sought a relationship with a woman since he became a widower. He did not feel life was stressful, the most stressful time for him had been when his wife was dying, after that things 'just slipped into place.' He expected the future to continue to be the same, although he was keen to see all his children secure and established.

No.3. Dave C

A 35 year old father of a girl aged 13 and boys aged 10 and 8. After 11½ years of marriage, his wife died 2½ years ago of cancer. She had had bowel troubles for 9 years, but it was believed that a colostomy operation had solved this. However after a further 2 years she was admitted to hospital for an exploratory operation and died 5 days later. A year later the eldest boy was admitted to hospital for an operation on a brain tumour, which has left him permanently blind. Mr C works part time as a mini-bus driver. Prior to his wife's death he had worked as a long-distance lorry driver and coach driver. He lives in a terraced council house on a busy main road in a suburb of a large conurbation. He has lived in the region all his life, and in the immediate locality for 5 years. He has had one relationship with a woman since his wife's death, and was saddened by its' recent breakup. His inability to have the satisfactions he had derived from a long distance driving job was his major reported source of stress, he was hopeful that the future would be better and was determined that, having just had one relationship with a woman terminated 'I'm going to make sure I find somebody and settle down.'

No. 4. Alan D

A 43 year old father of a boy of 15 and a daughter aged 19, both of whom live at home. His wife had left him 6 years previously, 2 days after he had discovered she was having an affair with one of his friends. Apart from a 4 day reconciliation some weeks after that, they have not lived together since, and neither he nor the children have seen her for 5 years. He won the court case to get the custody of the children, having previously successfully applied for them to become wards of court. He and his wife were officially divorced less than a year ago, she has written five times in the last five years asking for contact with the children, but they and he have refused to let her. He believes she is now living 350 miles away. His son has had behavioural and emotional difficulties in the past few years, and has received some child guidance services. After a career in catering and pub management jobs, Mr D has been unemployed, partly through choice, since he was made redundant from a supervisory

251

job in catering 2 years previously. He lives in a terraced council house on the edge of the inner city, he has lived in the same area all his life, and the same house for the past 15 years. Although he has had 5 or 6 relationships with women since his wife left, he has not had one since he stopped paid employment. He currently finds life 'very, very stressful', citing the lack of a close relationship with a woman as the main cause of the stress. He expected the future to be 'better - we're climbing up now and in years to come we'll all be working - even if we're all on a low wage we'll share everything and we'll be a lot better off.'

No.5 Len E

A 34 year old father of girls aged 9 and 7. Mr E's wife had died 18 months previously of cancer, which had been diagnosed 6 months before her death, she having had two hospital admissions in the year previous to that for tests. Mr E knew she was terminally ill for the last six months, his wife wasn't told. His mother-in-law, who he described as 'a lonely widow looking for a role' lived with the family for the last few months, to help care for her daughter and grandchildren and enable Len E to continue working. However, after increasing arguments between them - 'she wanted everything her way' - Len E told her to leave 3 months after his wife's death. Since then he has continued to work and care for the children with the assistance of neighbours, a childminder, and his parents. Mr E has worked for the large organisation for which he is currently a service engineer for the last 18 years. He has lived in the region all his life, currently in the private semi-detached house in a small coastal town he and his wife moved to a year before her death. (They had previously lived 5 miles away.) He has had three relationships with women since his wife's death, the first two being women who were going through divorces at the time, the third (which he stressed is non-sexual) is with a younger woman who he plans to marry within the next year. He finds being a single father a lot harder than he had imagined it would be 'having to come in and start working at home after working all day, with no other adult to talk to or unwind with' but 'since I've got engaged I feel a lot better now' and hopes that the future will be 'a nice family life again.'

No.6. Roy F

A 51 year old father of a girl of 9 who lives with him, and nearby married daughters aged 24, 22, and 20, the last one of which left home 2 years previously. After 21 years of marriage Mr F's wife died suddenly 4 years previously. She had had had bronchial trouble for years, but when she had an attack of breathing difficulty and died in the ambulance on the way to hospital it was completely unexpected. For 2 years Mr F continued with his job as a craftsman in heavy engineering, with help with child care from his extended family. However he increasingly found this a strain, and readily took the chance of redundancy when it arose then as a result of recession in the industry. Apart from his 10 years in engineering he had spent the rest of his working life as a miner, with three years in the army as a young man. He lives in a modern small council maisonette in a working class community which forms part of a larger industrial conurbation. He has lived in the same maisonette for 13 years, and in the same community all his life apart from his time in the army and a 2 year spell 15 years previously when he moved to work at a pit in the Midlands. He has neither had nor sought a relationship with a woman since his wife's death, at times he still felt 'a longing' for his wife but 'I've had one good relationship and I'm not really bothered about another'. He expressed reasonable content with his life, feeling that the future might get better when his daughter became old enough to enable him to look for a job - 'when you've worked since you're 15 it's a funny thing not to work.'

No.7. Keith G

A 45 year old father of a girl of 8 and a boy of 7., and a stepdaughter of 18 who lives with the family with her baby. Another stepchild, a boy of 11, lives with foster parents. Mr G and his wife had parted 5 years previously, she had been having an affair for some time of which he had known, He said when her boyfriend had hit their children he had fought him, and then told his wife to choose between her boyfriend and her children. She left, and they were divorced the following year. His wife did not seek custody, the children were made the subject of matrimonial supervision orders, with his wife being given weekly access. She and her boyfriend now have a child and live 2 miles away, Mr G and his wife are not on speaking terms with each other. Both stepchildren went into care 2 years previously, the girl because she was beyond his control, the boy because of non-attendance at school. Mr G and his family live in a council house in an inner city area which is generally agreed to be disadvantaged. He has lived in the same house for 8 years, and in the neighbourhood all his life. For the 5 years prior to his marriage breakup he had worked in a semi-skilled labouring job, when his wife left he had to give up work to look after the children. He had in the previous few weeks established his first intimate relationship with a woman since then, but was unsure about its future. He was ambivalent about whether life was more or less stressful as a single father; whilst it was less stressful 'because I don't have to put up with her any more' he found it difficult to manage on state benefit and was worried about child care. He found it difficult to look after the children but was at the same time worried that they might be taken into care because he wasn't caring for them adequately. Nevertheless he said he didn't think about the future and didn't worry about what would happen so long as he could continue to 'get out for a few pints.'

No.8. Jack H

A 42 year old father of a girl of 16 and a boy of 14. His wife had left him 9 years previously after 7 years of marriage. She had been spending nights away from home prior to her leaving; one evening he returned home from work to discover her taking her things out of the house. He has not seen her since, and says he has no idea where she lives. He was granted custody of the children in the divorce proceedings the following year, his wife did not come to court and has not used the 'reasonable access' facility the court awarded her. Mr.H had been a miner for 5 years prior to his marriage ending, since then he has not worked because of his child care responsibilities - having been sacked when he stayed off work to care for his children. He lives in an old and draughty terraced council house, in which he has lived for the past 10 years, and has lived all his life in the same isolated pit village (the pit closed a few years previously.) He has 'not bothered' to have any relationships with women since his marriage breakup, and currently finds life less stressful than it was when the children were younger. He did not expect to be ever able to get a paid job again, and expected that in the future 'I'll be a shade worse off - I don't know how much benefit I'll get - unless a miracle happens and I get a job - which I won't.'

No.9. Wally I

A 54 year old father of a girl aged 12 and a son aged 20, both of whom live at home - both children were adopted when they were 6 weeks old. His wife had died 1½ years previously, having been ill for 9 months prior to her death from cancer - he was told that she was terminally ill 6 months prior to her death, she was never told. Mr I works as a foreman in the construction industry locally, a job he has taken since the death of his wife. He had worked in a variety of similar jobs in different parts of this country and of the world, and he prefers to 'work away.' He lives in a small semi-detached private house in a town which forms a distinct part of a larger conurbation; he has lived in the same house for 17 years, and the immediate area all his life. Mr H has not had and does not wish for a relationship with a woman, and has a pessimistic attitude about the present and the future. He fears his children will grow up and move away; 'my health will deteriorate and I'll eventually have to give up work, my standard of living will fall. I'll never get over missing the wife, I'll never get over losing her, I can live with it but I can't accept it.'

No.10 Cliff J

A 47 year old father of a boy aged 15, with sons aged 27 and 24 who lived elsewhere. His wife had unexpectedly died 3 years previously 8 days after a sudden admission to hospital with back pains. Mr. J works in an unskilled job for the local authority, as he has done for the previous 18 years. He lives in a council house in a 'respectable' suburb of a large city, he has lived in the area all his life, and the immediate area for the past 28 years. 2 years previously he moved 100 yards from another council house to his present home as he felt it would be an easier house to manage. He has not got, nor has he had, a relationship with a woman since the death of his wife. Whilst he felt trapped in his current situation, not least because his parents spent a great deal of time at his house 'helping him', he hoped that in the future life would get better and he would 'find a good partner, but it would have to be the right one.'

254

No.11 Matt K

A 39 year old father of a boy of 14, and girls aged 16 and 17. Mr and Mrs. K's 16 year long marriage ended 4 years previously - he said she had a drink problem and was a spendthrift. For 2 years after he moved out the children lived with their mother in the matrimonial home, but as she increasingly neglected them they asked to come and live with him. By that time he had moved from his original bedsitter to a flat and was thus able to have them. He successfully applied to have custody of the children transferred to him. He says that she has not really accepted the fact that they are divorced, she is now an inpatient in a psychiatric hospital where he visits her. Mr K lives in one of a pair of flats he is buying in a working class area of an industrial town. He has lived in the area all his life, and in the immediate locality for the past 20 years. After a career in factory work, he has worked as a driver for a large public company for the past 4 years. His mother who lives nearby gives the 2 younger children their midday meal, all the children their evening meals, and looks after them in school holidays. Mr F, who described himself as 'not a good mixer', has had no relationships with women since he became a lone father. He experienced life as a lone father as being much better than when he was married - fewer arguments, more money, less stress, and expected that life would get better, particularly as he was moving to a better paid job in the same organisation.

No.12 Al L

A 41 year old father of girls aged 16 and 12 (living at home) and 20 (living away from home.) Mr and Mrs L's 16 year old marriage had ended 4½ year previously. She was a barmaid at a local club when she 'fell in love with another bloke', after amicable discussion they were divorced 4 months later. The children wished to stay with him, it was agreed that he should have custody, with Mrs L having reasonable access. He and the children are on friendly terms with the ex - Mrs L, seeing her at least once or twice a week. For 6 months following the split up Mr L continued working in the clerical job he had held for 21 years for a state enterprise, due to child care difficulties he decided to give up the job. This was the 'biggest mistake I ever made' as within the space of a year or so he felt he could have combined child care and paid work; by then he was unable to get his job back, and has been unemployed since. Mr L's main sources of stress are his financial position. He has lived in the region all his life, 8 months prior to the interview he had moved to his present suburban council house - which he is delighted with - from the 'sink' council housing estate in which he had been living. He has had several short term casual relationships with women since his divorce, but felt that these had not been serious and had mainly been for both party's sexual needs. He now feels that he has 'got my own ways, I don't think that I could live with another woman.' Whilst he was careful not to think about the future, he was relatively pessimistic but 'you keep hoping it gets better that's all, that's what keeps you going, thinking things might get better next year.'

No.13. Cary M

A 41 year old father of a son aged 16 (living with him) and daughters aged 14 (living with his ex wife) and 19 (living away) and a son of 18 (living away). After a marriage of 18 years Mr M and his wife had parted 3 years previously - she left him to live with another man, 2 weeks after he discovered she was having an affair. Mr and Mrs M were awarded joint custody and the children chose who they would live with, the eldest 3 chose their father, the youngest girl her mother. Mr M has lived all his life in the region, and for the last 20 years on a small council estate in a rural setting some 3 miles from a small coastal town. Mr M describes his current relationship with his ex wife as non existent, he has not seen her for a year but 'if she gets on the phone it's always bother.' He has frequent contacts with the children not living with him. He has worked intermittently as a semi-skilled factory worker for the past decade, being made redundant a year after his marriage broke up. Since then he has worked briefly on a fishing boat, but had to give this up as it involved his youngest son being relatively unsupervised. This son was involved in a motoring offence recently and was nearing completion of a short youth custody order. Despite having had a heart attack a year previously, Mr M described his health as being better and his life as being less stressful than when he was married. He described himself as a sociable man, he had had a series of short term relationships with women since his wife left, but felt that he was 'shying away from' more long term relationships. Whilst he was worried that he could not guarantee financial security for the future, he was nevertheless optimistic about the future.

No.14. Kev N

A 34 year old father of twins (a boy and a girl) aged 4½, Mr N's wife had died 12 days after giving birth 3 months prematurely. The pregnancy had been a difficult one but the death unexpected. Mr N's brother and sister in law moved in to help him with child care. Some 6 months prior to the interview they had bought a house a few doors away and the twins divide their time between living there and living with Mr N. Due to the twins' initial health problems, when they were born Mr N had to give up work to care for them - he had been working as a supervisor in the building trade all around the country for the previous 5 years. In the past 6 months he has started working again as a self-employed craftsman. Born some 100 miles away, he has lived in the present area for the past 28 years, and in the same private terraced house in a small coastal town for the past 10 years. He has had one serious relationship with a woman since he became a widower, and was planning to get married and move to a larger house in the same town in the immediate future. Immediately after he was widowed he found that the physical demands of caring were particularly stressful. Whilst he expected that the future would be a lot better, he was not completely certain that he would be able to have the twins back to live with him permanently full-time 'it's got to happen in the next 6 to 9 months, it's certainly practical, but I'm not sure that it's possible.'

No.15. Rick O

A 53 year old father of a boy aged 13, with 18 year old sons living at home, and daughters aged 28 and 21 living away from home. Mr O.'s wife had died of cancer 6 years prior to the interview. 7 months prior to her death an investigation of chest pains had revealed that she had cancer, Mr O remembered that 'they didn't tell her that, they told me it and told me to tell her that she'd got a collapsed lung.' She gradually deteriorated and had several short spells in hospital before she died, Mr.O was told 2 months before her death that she was terminally ill. Mr. O. had taken voluntary redundancy from the shipyards (where he had worked for 33 years) a year before 'so that left me able to look after the kids, it's a full time job.' The family live in the coastal industrial city Mr.O has lived in all his life, in a council house of which he has been the tenant for the past 28 years. Mr. O has had no relationships with women since his wife's death- 'I've never really troubled, in fact, I've gone out of my way to avoid it, I know one whose trying to get her hooks into us..I don't think the kids would accept it, they've told me not to bring anyone in here.' Mr.O missed his wife, particularly when he was not busy with child care or household tasks; paradoxically his biggest source of reported stress was having to do everything by himself without the support of a wife. He didn't expect the future to get any better, feeling that it would be 'about the same, but I'm not getting any younger.'

No.16. Albert P

A 35 year old father of boys aged 15 and 13. Mr and Mrs P's marriage had 'broken down' over a long process. He and his wife were legally separated for 2 years following 7 years of marriage. They then were reconciled and lived together again for 2 years, following which he worked for a year in Europe which he described as being a solution to financial difficulties and also a 'test of the marriage.' On his return he and his wife decided that the marriage was over, and she stayed in the matrimonial home with the boys whilst he moved 60 miles further north to his present house. After a year, 3 years ago, relationship difficulties between the boys and their new stepfather led to the boys asking to go move to live with him and custody was subsequently transferred. Mr P says he had always felt this would be the likely, and his preferred, outcome. Mr P has worked as a craftsman in the building trade, he has not been able to work since he assumed custody of his sons. He has had a steady girlfriend for the past year, and feels it may lead to marriage when his sons become independent. He is very keen to give his boys a better start in adult life than he had. He had a troubled childhood, with his mother committing suicide when he was 2 and his father when he was 12. After that he lived with relatives and a series of short term foster homes; then married young to get 'a family atmosphere.' Apart from the difficulties of providing for his sons in the way he would wish to within the limitations of state benefits, Albert P felt that he had few stresses in his current life, feeling that the future is 'going to gradually get better.'

No 17 Dennis Q

A 35 year old father of boys aged 13 and 12. His wife had left him 2¼ years previously, having had an affair 2 years prior to that. Although the marriage had been deteriorating, her departure was sudden and unexpected, the first he knew of it was a note from her when he returned home from work one evening. She is now living 120 miles away, they having been divorced 18 months ago. He has continuously looked after the children since his wife's departure, she did not apply for their custody but sees them every 6 - 8 weeks for the day at her mother's house nearby. His relationship with her was 'strained' after she left, then friendlier, is currently 'quite strained and very tense' related to a dispute over her being paid money for her share of the matrimonial house. Mr Q, a manager, has been employed for 18 years by the same company. He lives in a modern semi-detached private house in a suburb of a new town some 10 miles from a large conurbation. He has lived in the locality for four years, and the region all his life. He has had a stable relationship for the past 8 months with a woman, and sees life getting better, particularly if this relationship continues 'I hope the relationship I'm in now leads to marriage - mainly for myself now because the kids are growing up.'

No.18. Andy R

A 42 year old father of a girl aged 13, and boys aged 17 and 15. His wife had died unexpectedly 3 years previously after 20 years of marriage. At the time he had been working on the North Sea oil rigs, he had returned home from a tour of duty to find she had died a few hours previously of a smoking related thrombosis. He had continued in his engineering job in the N.Sea oilfield, on a 2 weeks on, 2 weeks off basis - with his wife's parents moving in and caring for the children when he was away. However, they stopped doing this after 18 months when he started going out with the woman who is now his fiancee, and his parents then took over the same function; which will be taken over by his soon to be wife. Mr. R has always worked away in the engineering industry, he has recently left the N.Sea for an engineering job which involves him being away from home from Monday to Friday lunchtimes. He has lived in the same small industrial community which is part of a larger riverside conurbation all his life, moving into his present very large expensive old house some 5 years previously. (He also owns a country cottage.) He reported being particularly lonely for the year following his wife's death, and had then found the rift between himself and his wife's parents when he started going out with his now fiancee particularly stressful. He also felt it was particularly hard that there was no one from outside the family to offer help or advice when he was first widowed 'I was lucky, I had money to start with. I found it very, very, hard; I would have found it unbearable if I didn't have money.' Having had a happy 1st marriage, Mr R expected that his new marriage would be successful and that the future would be better 'I'll be more relaxed and more settled down'.

No.19. Jeff S

A 36 year old father of girls aged 11 and 10, Mr.S and his wife had split up slightly over 5 years previously and had been divorced four months later. He described how their marriage had deteriorated following the birth of the children, and how his wife - who he described as a compulsive spender - had started going out at nights while he stayed at home to look after the children ' at one time she disappeared for a couple of weeks.' When she 'did another of her disappearing acts, and left the kids with my mother, when she came back I'd moved in with my mother and the kids' and started to sue for divorce. Custody, which was contested, was granted to him, his wife has the children to stay every weekend. For 3½ years following the divorce Mr S and his children continued living with his mother, largely on the solicitors advice so that there would be a mother substitute and therefore lessen the chances of him losing custody if the case went back to court. 18 months previously he had moved with the children into his present council house, which is ¼ mile away from his mothers, and in the same working class part of the large industrial conurbation that he has lived in all his life - apart from the 9 years of the marriage when they lived 5 miles away in a similar area where his wife originates from and still lives in. Relationships with his ex he described as 'amicable, polite, and very formal'; his daughters like going to see their mother because she lets them stay up late and gives them treats. Mr.S had been in clerical employment for a large state controlled industry for most of the marriage, at the time that the marriage broke up he was at a local college full time doing a social science degree, and has been unemployed for the last 3 years since he successfully finished that. 'When I first finished college I applied for over 80 jobs because I think I thought it was expected, but I knew I couldn't take one up if I got one; so I just gave up because I became convinced that because of the children I couldn't take a job anyway.' Financial problems he reported as being the cause of minor stress, but life was 1000% better than when he was married, and he had managed to clear £1000 of the £2500 debts his wife had incurred in his name during their marriage.Because of the children he had not sought any relationships with women since his divorce 'It's something I look forward to, but I'm prepared to wait until they're (the children) older.' When the children got older he also expected he would return to paid employment, and therefore the future he thought would be 'materially better, I think for myself personally it will be a little sad that this part of my life will be over..even though I haven't got a job or my own house, I'm quite happy.I don't think I'll ever be this happy again.'

No.20. Arthur T

A 36 year old father of a boy aged 12 and a girl aged 11, Mr.T had been separated from his wife for nine years, following four years of marriage, and had been divorced six years prior to the interview. Mr.T said the main causes of the marriage breakdown were his wife's neglect of the children, her drinking, and the arguments it caused. For the first 3 years of their separation by mutual informal consent she had the children, however he said he was increasingly concerned about her care of the children, and when one night the police contacted him because they couldn't find his ex wife, he took the children to live with him and subsequently in court was granted custody with access granted to his wife. At that point he was living with his mother, immediately after being granted custody he was given the tenancy of his present home, a modern terraced council flat, just round the corner from his mothers, in an inner city area. Four weeks ago his son had gone to live with the ex Mrs T following an argument with Mr T; Mr T said that although his son bordered on being 'beyond control' and had been placed in care for 3 days by him because of this, he hoped that a case conference in the near future would decide he should return to him. Social services, who had been involved with the children since their time living with their mother, had told Mr T that he was over physical in his chastisement of his son; Mr T felt that social workers were 'a waste of time... if I can't chastise my own kids there's something wrong.' Mr T has had one or two friendly relationships with women since being separated but felt that a close relationship was to be avoided as 'I've been bitten too many times'. He has lived in the same city all his life, and has worked in the past as a building labourer, but has not worked since he was given custody of the children. He now feels that he's 'too old' to ever get a job. His main source of stress was, he felt, his son's behaviour, although he also found it difficult 'scratching and scraping' on state benefit. He expected the future to be 'the same, unless there's another war, at least I'd get a job then.'

No 21. Ivan U

A 40 Year old father of a girl aged 3½, Mr.U's wife, who had suffered from asthma, had died unexpectedly during the night when their daughter was aged 6 months some 3 years previously. At the time Mr.U, a native of Scandinavia, was working 2 weeks on/2weeks off in the North Sea oilfields. For the following year he looked after his daughter when he was at home, and his ex wife's godmother cared for her when he was away at work. When she had to give up doing this, he got a job locally for 3 months and used a childminder, but since that firm went bankrupt he has not been in paid employment. Mr.U lives in the terraced house he and his wife bought in a small village near a large northern conurbation. He has no relatives in this country, his nearest relatives live 2 days distant by car and ferry, and his ex-wife's relatives are all dead or live a long distance away. He has worked in various parts of the world in the merchant navy or engineering jobs, having been based in the region for 8 years and Scotland for the previous 4 years. As a means of resolving his child care and employment difficulties he was hoping to use some of his dwindling savings to buy a small business or franchise. A regular attender at weekly local Gingerbread meetings, he keenly felt his social isolation, which had recently been increased by the breaking of a relationship he had had with a woman living nearby which had resulted in the birth a year previously of another daughter - he would have wished for the relationship to continue. This loneliness was his major reported source of stress 'not having someone who you can really trust who you can sit down and have a good pow-wow with.' He took great delight in the company of, and caring for, his daughter, but was struggling to see how he could combine child care and paid employment in the future.

No.22. Tony V

A 50 year old father of a girl aged 14 and a boy aged 11, Tony V's wife had died 5 years previously of skin cancer. She had been diagnosed as having cancer 3 years prior to that, and in the intervening period had had 4 operations and periods of chemotherapy. The terminal phase of the illness was 11 weeks, she was in hospital for the last 3 weeks of her life. Mr V was able to continue working with the assistance of his sister-in-law caring for the children after school and in the school holidays. He has lived in the same semi-rural village all his life, and for the past 10 years in the large end terraced house he and his wife bought. He has worked for the past 10 years as a skilled craftsman for the local council. Since his wife's death he has had 3 relationships with women, having had a steady relationship for 3 years with the woman he became engaged to 4 months previously - they intend to marry within the next year or so. Mr.V felt himself to be at the centre of a supportive network of relatives and neighbours, and felt that he was coping well - although he still experienced attacks of loneliness at least twice a week ' when I'm in the house on my own it seems to come over me like a blanket, even now, it lacks a woman in the house.' He was optimistic about the future 'I should be financially better off, and, if she does the housework I'll be a lot happier; if she looks after the house I can get on with the garden and such as that, I'll get back to a routine again.'

No.23. Fergus W

A 46 year old father of a girl aged 11 and a boy aged 9. His wife had died 2½ years prior to the interview, having had cancer for 5 years - whilst he had had worries that she would die for 2 years prior to her death, it was only in the final week of her life that he knew it was a terminal condition. Mr.W is a salesman and a company director, he planned to increase the turnover of his company, and give up the salesmans agency. He and his children live in a large modern detached house on an 'exclusive estate' in a semi-rural setting on the edge of a large town. He had lived in the area all his life, and had only moved once since the birth of the children - they had moved from a larger house on the estate to this house during the course of his wife's illness as they felt she would be able to cope with it better if her health deteriorated. He had a stable relationship of 4 months duration with a woman, and had an optimistic outlook on life, expecting the future to be 'the same or better', believing that it couldn't be worse than it had been - referring to his wife's illness and death.

No. 24 Dick X

A 38 year old father of a boy aged 7 (living with him) and a girl aged 15 (currently living in care having been living with her mother and stepfather and been sexually abused by the latter.) The daughter is the product of Mr X's marriage, which was of 4 years duration and ended 12 years previously, the son is the product of a steady relationship that lasted 6 years, and which ended 4 years previous to the research. Mr X described how he and his wife had split up after they'd both had other relationships. his wife had had custody of their daughter, and had moved to Europe with her new soldier husband. Mr X had subsequently lost contact with his daughter until recently when a social worker had been in touch to update him on her position; he was now possibly intending negotiating to have her to live with him. Two years after his divorce Dick X formed a relationship with Jane, and they began to live together. He had not wanted further children - 'because if anything went wrong I didn't want the hassle' and didn't know that Jane was pregnant until well into the pregnancy. Jane subsequently developed a relationship with a man in the entertainments business, and when he realised what was happening Mr X gave her the choice of staying with him and his son or leaving 'I thought I could do a lot better job with Johnnie than she could, she was a lot younger and didn't want the responsibility.' She left, and she and her partner are now living 300 miles away, seeing Johnnie most school holidays and speaking to him and Mr W twice weekly on the phone. Mr X has a friendly relationship with his ex girlfriend, he would like a friendlier relationship with his ex wife who he has not seen for several years. Mr X lives in a rented private flat in a pleasant suburb of a large conurbation, he has lived all his life in the area and in the flat for the past 12 years. He initially received child care help from his parents and in laws which has steadily declined as his son has got older. His last job was as a semi-skilled worker 9 years ago, since when he has worked intermittently as a driver, but is unable currently to find a job which he feels fits in with his child care responsibilities. He has had several relationships with women since his son's mother left, one serious one which ended against his wishes a few months previously. The ending of this relationship he saw as his major source of stress, he described how he got great satisfaction out of his relationship with his son. He was unsure about the future, but expressed a desire that it would be better, and that he would make it better by getting a job so that he wouldn't brood on his recent broken relationship.

No. 25. John Y

A 45 year old father of girls aged 14 and 18. Mr. Y and his wife separated 8 years previously, he left the home and went to live with his father 4 miles away. During the marriage he said they had both been heavy drinkers, he managed to stop but she became an alcoholic. Twice during the 18 months after the separation he came back to live in the marital home whilst his wife had in patient treatment for her alcoholism, Both times the treatment failed, and eventually 'when I discovered my wife was leaving the children alone at nights to go out drinking I was forced to take them away to live with me.' This was against legal advice, his solicitor told him that by doing this he would be endangering the prospects of getting the custody that he wanted. When the divorce was granted 6 years previously, he was granted custody and 6 months later obtained an injunction to get possession of the matrimonial home. The children visit their mother (who is still an alcoholic), who lives 2 miles away, once a week and once a fortnight respectively, but Mr Y doesn't see her. Mr Y has worked for the past 14 years in a skilled job in manufacturing, he has continued despite some shiftwork difficulties to work whilst caring for the children, with help from relatives. He has always lived in the region, for the past 11 years in the same house - apart from the time at his fathers. He has had 5 or 6 brief relationships and one serious relationship - his current one - with women since separating but does not envisage marriage in the future as 'I wouldn't want to give up my independence, and neither would she hers.' He finds life much less stressful now than when he was married, his major worry is that eventually he will have to repay his wife for the equity in the matrimonial home. Whilst he looked forward optimistically towards the future offering him greater freedom and independence as the children got older, he had found the experiences he had undergone had changed his attitudes 'I had ambitions,I'm not particularly bothered now, I was greedy for money, I don't know why.'

No.26. Chris Z

A 33 year old father of boys aged 12 and 11 and twin boys aged 7. Mr Z and his wife had been divorced 3 years previously, after what he described as a stormy marriage all the way through. The couple had been married for 11 years, and had lived separately for a year after 7 years. Having been reconciled, he discovered her in bed with one of his workmates, he 'kicked her out', she left with all the children, and he sued for divorce immediately. In the 6 months before the divorce was granted the Z's negotiated that she would look after the twins, and he the elder 2 boys, so that they 'wouldn't have to move around too much' and have schooling etc disrupted. She was granted custody of the twins, and joint custody was granted of the 2 older boys with the understanding that they would live with their father. The ex Mrs Z lives nearby, he sees the twins every weekend, and the elder boys see their mother most weekends, albeit at times reluctantly. However, the week following the interview Mrs Z, her new husband, and the twins were moving 300 miles away, which was a source of distress for Mr Z as it would severely diminish his contact with them. Mr Z's mother looks after the older boys in school holidays and when his shift work causes child care problems. Mr Z has been a skilled worker in the coal industry all his working life, and has lived in the same terraced house - which he is purchasing - for the past 5 years. In the previous years of the marriage they had lived in 10 different houses in the area and couldn't feel settled anywhere. Mr Z has had 2 relationships with women since his divorce, and has had a steady relationship for the past 2 years. His main stresses he felt were to do with his younger children's impending move, and more day to day problems like 'finding the boys something new to eat.' Generally, he experienced life as a single father as being much pleasanter and less stressful than when he was married, he has developed more interests including local political activity, and he expected the future to be better, possibly including his remarriage.

No.27.Danny AA

A 29 year old father of boys aged 6 and 5. Mr AA split up with his wife 3½ years previously when they were living in Australia, and returned to England with the children without his wife's permission. He has contact with his wife by letter and 'phone but neither he or the boys have seen her since; she is now remarried with a child and still living in Australia. Mr & Mrs AA were married 7 years ago, and emigrated to Australia the following year. His wife found it hard to settle there and at one point returned to England with the children. When she returned to Australia the couple lived together again for a while, then decided to separate, with Mrs AA caring for the children. Mr AA says he was increasingly worried about her ability to care for the children, and eventually he decided to take them, but felt he would need to bring them back to England as he would need the assistance of his family, particularly his mother, to care for them. Having done a variety of semi-skilled and selling jobs whilst in Australia, Mr AA found it impossible to get a job in his trade when he returned to England, and was unemployed for a year. He subsequently had a variety of jobs locally and elsewhere in the country, during which latter periods his mother cared for the boys. He now sees himself settled in a career as a government skilled worker, a job he has been doing for the past year. Mr. AA lives, with great support from his mother and uncle, in a council house which is located near the centre of the small industrial town where he was born. He has lived there all his life apart from his 4 years in Australia. On returning to England he had a succession of very brief relationships with women, he has had a steady relationship with one woman for the past two years and they are in the process of arranging their marriage and buying a house for themselves, his 2 boys, and her child by a previous relationship. After a period of lack of confidence and stress when he returned to this country, Mr feels that the future is rosey 'It's never been more on the up than it is at the moment, I'm the happiest I've ever been in my life, 2 or 3 years ago I'd never have thought it would happen.'

No.28. Jake BB

A 55 year old father of daughters aged 15 and 17 living with him, and living independently daughters aged 20,22,23, and 28, and a son aged 30 (a 17 year old daughter had died suddenly following a brief illness 2 years previously.) Mr BB and his wife had jointly run a business partnership; gradually her behaviour became more erratic and she became more difficult to live with. 6 years previously, she called a family conference and said that she didn't feel that she had a place in the family - somewhat to her surprise, he feels, he and the children agreed. 3 days later she moved out to the family's country cottage, for the following year she continued to visit the home to discharge her business duties, until the partnership was dissolved and divorce proceedings begun 5 years previously. Both parties sued for divorce, Mr. BB said that his wife was extremely obstructive and constantly changed solicitors, didn't attend hearings etc. When the proceeding finally finished less than 2 years ago Mr BB was granted custody - his children had all wanted him to have custody - and the judge allowed his wife to have limited access but was warned that if her behaviour towards Mr BB didn't improve he would forbid any future access. Mr BB said the divorce and business separation had been personally and financially damaging, he had to pay £15,000 legal fees, but he knew that for his children's sake he had no other choice but to see the process through. He has currently 'zero contact with my ex-wife, which suits me fine' his youngest child visits her mother every 2 weeks 'I think it's partly out of a sense of duty.' Mr BB has lived in the large house from which he also runs his business for the past 27 years, he has lived in the region all his life apart from 9 years as a student and doing National Service. In relation to his children 'I've been very fortunate in that they're all thoroughly sensible, and we have an easy sort of relationship.' Working from home, he has been able to care for them with some assistance from regular longstanding paid domestic help. Life, he felt was much better now than prior to the separation, although the divorce and business separation had been a difficult period, it did not compare to his marriage. He had felt that there was no way out because he and his ex were catholics, but 'I think I'm coping with things pretty well now..(then) life was hell, you never knew what the atmosphere in the family was going to be like.' He has no relatives living nearby, since his divorce he has developed 'a steady relationship at a low level with a woman' but for complicated reasons he feels it will not develop further, although he would wish that it could. He has no worries about the future, and, although he was keen not to look too far ahead, was hoping to take semi - retirement and expecting that the future would be 'no worse'.

No.29. James CC

A 49 year old father of a boy aged 16, with sons of 24 and 22 who live in the Midlands and the South of England. After 20 years of marriage Mr CC's wife left him 6 years ago, following which they were divorced. He had been aware that for 6 months prior to her departure she was becoming attracted to a mutual friend, she told her husband the day before they were due to go on a family holiday that she was leaving to live with this man, 'and that was the last time I spoke to her on good terms.' She left the older 2 children with him to go on the holiday, the youngest child stayed with her for the first month, but Mr CC took him out for the day and then kept him because 'he was so distressed and anxious to come home.' Custody, which was contested, was given to Mr.CC; he hoped his wife would return to him but after 2 years separation she filed for a divorce, which was granted, and she has now married the man she left for. The 16 year old son sees his mother every week at her house, which Mr CC believes is about 10 miles away, when this was younger he and his ex-wife had to make the arrangements, now his son does this & Mr

CC has no direct contact with or knowledge of his wife. Mr CC spent the first 26 years of his life in the Midlands, the next 5 years working in the South, and has lived in the same private semi-detached house in the North since he moved 19 years ago. He is employed in a management position in a local authority. He has had no relationships with women since his wife left, for a long time he hoped for and sought a reconciliation with her, but is now reconciled to that not happening. He is uncertain about the future, feeling that whilst he will take things as they come 'I'll be on my own, and I might start looking around more seriously to get some companionship - but with very great caution.'

No.30. Max DD

A 31 year old father of a boy aged 10 and a girl aged 9. He and his wife had amicably split up and divorced 5½ years, previously following 4 years of marriage, because they were having lots of arguments. For the subsequent year his wife had had the children because that seemed 'natural' and Mr DD saw them every weekend. She then asked him to have the children, he wasn't sure why. He has thus had care and custody of the children for 4½ years, initially whilst living with his mother and father. He has worked as a long distance lorry driver for the past 6 months, prior to which time he was in a garage business for 3 years then a security guard. For the first 2 years after his marriage broke up he was unemployed. He has had a number of short term relationships with women since he and his wife parted, and has had the same steady girlfriend for the past 2½ years. He felt that his mother had more 'charge' over his children than he had expected when he assumed care of them, overall he was content with his current arrangements, and wouldn't want to change things.

No.31. Desmond EE

A 36 year old father of a boy of 11 and a girl of 4, Mr EE's wife, who had suffered from epilepsy, had died suddenly during a 'fit' in the night 2½ years previously - there had never been any expectation that her condition could be life threatening. He had been able to continue working via the use of nurseries, childminders, and relatives' assistance. His employers, a large state owned concern, had proved very considerate in relation to his child care responsibilities. Mr EE has had the same clerical job for 12 years, prior to which he had served in the Forces. The family live in a older upstairs flat, which Mr.EE is purchasing, in a built up area of an industrial town. They have lived in the flat for 6 years, and in the area for another six years, having moved down from Scotland (the children spend school holidays with relatives in Scotland.) Mr EE has neither had nor sought female relationships since his wife's death, but regretted that he had had to cut down on his hobbies of art and long distance running because of his domestic commitments. Whilst he was financially better off since his wife's death, he felt lonely as a single father, we 'toasted in the New Year' - at the end of January - after my interview as he had had no one to do it with before then. Attending a

Cruse group had, he felt, helped him to come to terms with his grief, and he expected that the future would 'undoubtedly get better.'

No.32. Aidan FF

A 52 year old father of girls aged 14 and 13, and boys aged 17 and 19 (the latter is away at University during term times.) Mr FF's wife had died of cancer 9 years previously, having been ill for 18 months (at the start of which she had been told that she had 2 months left to live.) Following her death, for 6 weeks Mr. FF had tried to combine child care and paid employment, but that proved impossible so he was made redundant from his management job with his consent. A year previously he had tried to do a part-time clerical job, but had given it up as he hadn't liked it and had felt unconfident. He has lived in the same privately owned semi-detached house in a residential suburb of a conurbation for 15 years, and in the area all his life. The youngest child has a slight physical handicap and learning difficulties, the others are high achievers at school. As the children have grown older the assistance in caring for them that he had received from relatives has diminished. His main reported sources of stress were financial, he had a keen sense of the house gradually deteriorating around him, and of not being able to afford to repair it, and loneliness 'I can understand the loneliness of being a housewife and of gazing out of the windows now. It's a 7 days a week, 366 days a year job with no breaks.' He has had several close relationships with women since he became a widower, but finished them as the women involved wanted to become 'too serious too quickly.' He currently feels the lack of an intimate, sexual relationship with a woman. He looked back on his paid worklife and 'wonders what it was all about, what it was all for' and saw the future as being 'very depressing -less money, no job, more problems.'

No.33. Kevin GG

A 26 year old father of a girl aged 4, Mr GG and his wife had separated 2 years previously and divorced the following year. He had been unemployed since his daughter was 6 months old, the factory he had worked in in a semi-skilled engineering job having been closed (his wife had continued to work.) After a period of arguments, his wife had left him taking their daughter, he had been concerned that their daughter wouldn't be cared for properly - he had had the major caring role anyway - so had taken his daughter home with him after three days. Although custody was contested and the welfare report to court had recommended that his ex-wife be granted custody, he had been given custody and his ex-wife reasonable access. His daughter stays with her mother at weekends, he described the relationship between himself and his ex as 'cut throat - I'd rather kill her than have her back'. Kevin GG lives in a small modern council house in a pit village in a rural setting, he has lived in the same village all his life, and has moved into his present house - which is exactly what he wanted- since his divorce. He could have a great deal of help from his nearby extended family, but feels that he doesn't need any. Although he has had several intimate relationships with women since he became a single father, he has avoided them becoming more than casual because he felt that his daughter's needs had to come first. Although he felt he could do with more money, he hoped that the future would 'be the same, because I'm doing well now, I like it and I enjoy it'(being a single father.)

No.34. Matthew HH

A 41 year old father of a 12 year old girl, Mr. HH's wife had died 5 years previously. A year prior to her death she had had an operation for breast cancer, which it had been thought was then cured. A month prior to her death she had had a second 'routine' operation from which she had not recovered. Her childless sister and brother in law lived 400 yards away, and she had asked them as she was dying to help 'look after my little girl'. Subsequently, they had cared for her after school and in the holidays to enable Mr H. to continue working. (His daughter could probably look after herself more now, but he doesn't want to offend them by suggesting this.) At the time Mr HH was a mature student at University, and said the student counsellors had been helpful in counselling him re: his bereavement. Since leaving University he has worked for a local authority in a professional capacity, and 2 months prior to the interview had taken a new job with a private firm that involves 80 miles commuting per day. He has lived in the same house for 15 years, and in the region all his life. He has had several close relationships with women since becoming a widower, and currently has a steady girlfriend - he is happy for the relationship to continue as it is. He felt that he had no real problems, although he regretted that his wife had died. He said that he only thought in the short term now, as his wife's death had shown him that the unexpected could happen; he expected that the future probably wouldn't 'be much better in this part of the world'; anticipating further decline in the region.

No.35. Joe II

A 35 year old father of boys aged 9 and 5, Mr II's wife had left him 'exactly a year and 3 days' before, and the divorce had been finalised 3 weeks previously. She had been having an affair with the man with whom she was now living, he had had no inkling, and she had left 2 days after he found out. She had agreed he could have the children, she sees them every day, and works 2 doors away from where they live. Mr II said that he and his ex wife get on better now than before they were separated. Mr II has worked for the past 18 years as a driver. The main child care assistance he gets is from his mother in law who looks after the children after school or who sleeps at the house when his shift work demands it (she had offered to do this to enable him to continue working.) He was bitter that his own mother, who lives 4 miles away, has never offered to help. Mr II has lived in the same house for 14 years, and all his life in the same village - a rural pit village. He has had no relationships with women since he became a single father, and does not wish for any - hoping instead that his wife would return to him. He did not know what to expect of the future, but hoped that it would not get any worse.

Bibliography

Acker, J.(1989), The problem with patriarchy, *Sociology*, vol.23, no.2.

Albrow, M.(1990), English Channel, *Times Higher Education Supplement*, p.20. 20.4.90.

Allcock, P.(1987), *Poverty and State Support*, Longman, London.

Althusser, L.(1971), *Lenin and Philosophy*, New Left Books,London.

Anderson, M. ed.(1980), *Sociology of the Family*, Penguin, London.

Anderson, M.(1980), *Approaches to the History of the Western Family,*Macmillan, London.

Anderson, M.(1983), How much has the family changed? *New Society*, 27.10.1983

Ashen, R.N., ed.(1949), *The Family*, Hayner, New York.

Backett, K.C.(1982), *Mothers and Fathers*, Macmillan, London.

Backett, K.C.(1987), *The negotiation of fatherhood*, in Lewis and O'Brien, eds.

Bailey, R. and Lee, P.eds(1982), *Theory and Practice in Social Work*, Basil Blackwell, Oxford.

Barclay, P.(1982), *Social Workers - their role and task*, NISW, London.

Barker, D. and Allen, S. eds.(1976a), *Dependence and Exploitation in Work and Marriage*, Longman, London.

Barker, D. and Allen, S. eds.(1976b), *Sexual Divisions and Society*, Tavistock, London.

Barker, R.W. and Moran, M.(1990), Prejudice and Abuse, Workbook 6, in *Working with Children and Young People*, Open University, Milton Keynes.

Barker, R.W.(1991), *Lone Fathers, Parenting, and Masculinities*, unpublished Ph.D. thesis, University of Edinburgh.

Barrett, M. and McIntosh,M.(1982), *The Anti-social Family*, Verso, London.

Barron, R.D., and Norris, G.M.(1976), *Sexual Divisions and the dual labour market*, in Barker and Allen, eds, a.

Barry, A.(1979), A research project on successful single parent families, *American Journal of Family Therapy*, Vol.7, pp.65-73.

Bartz, K.W. and Witcher, W.C.(1978), When father gets custody, *Children Today*, vol.7, pp. 2-6.

Beail, N. and McGuire, J. eds.(1982), *Fathers - Psychological Perspectives,* Junction Books, London.

Beattie, S. and Viney, L.L.(1980), Becoming a lone parent, *British Journal of Social and Clinical Psychology,* vol.19, pp.343-351.

Becker, H.S.(1963), *Outsiders - Studies in the Sociology of Deviance,* Free Press, New York.

Becker, H. S. ed.(1970), *Sociological World,* Aldine, Chicago.

Beechey, V.(1977), Some notes on Female Wage Labour in the Capitalist Mode of Production, *Capital and Class,* no.3.

Bell, C. and Roberts, H. eds.(1984), *Social Researching - Problems, Politics, Practice,* Routledge and Kegan Paul, London.

Bell, S.(1988), *When Salem came to the Boro: The true story of the Cleveland Child Abuse Crisis,* Pan, London.

Beresford, P. and Croft, S.(1986), *Whose Welfare?,* Brighton Polytechnic, Brighton.

Berger, P.L. and Luckman, T.(1967), *The Social Construction of Reality,* Allen Lane/Penguin, London.

'Beveridge Report'(1942), *Social Insurance and Allied Services,* Cmnd 6404, HMSO, London.

Biller, H.(1974), *Father Power,* David McKay, New York.

Bleier, R.(1982), *Science and Gender - a critique of biology and its theories on women,* Pergamonn Press, Oxford.

Blumer, H.(1969), *Symbolic Interactionism - Perspective and Method,* Prentice Hall, New Jersey.

Bogdan, R. and Biklen, S.K.(1982), *Quantitative Research for Education: An Introduction to Theory and Methods,* Allyn and Bacon, Boston.

Bott, E.(1957,1971), *Family and Social Network,* Tavistock, London

Bowlby, J.(1951), *Maternal Care and Mental Health,* World Health Organisation, Geneva.

Bowlby, J.(1972), *Child Care and the Growth of Love,* Penguin, Harmondsworth.

Bozett, F.W. ed.(1987), *Gay and Lesbian Parents,* Praeger, New York.

Bradley, H.(1989), *Men's Work, Women's Work,* Polity Press, Cambridge.

Bradshaw, J. and Morgan, J.(1987), Budgeting on benefit, *New Society,* 6.3.1987.

Brannen, J. and Wilson, G. eds.(1987), *Give and take in families,* George Allen and Unwin, London

Brent, London Borough of(1985), *A Child in Trust - Report on the death of Jasmine Beckford,*London Borough of Brent.

Brittan, A.(1989), *Masculinity and Power,* Basil Blackwell, London.

Brod, H. ed.(1987), *The Making of Masculinities,* Allen and Unwin, Winchester.

Brook, E. and Davis A. eds.(1985), *Women, the Family and Social Work,* Tavistock, London.

Brophy, J.(1989), Custody Law, Child Care and Inequality in Britain, in Smart and Sevenhuijsen, eds.

Brownmiller, S.(1976), *Against our will: Men, Women, and Rape,* Penguin, London.

Brown, G. and Harris, T.(1978), *Social Origins of Depression,* Tavistock, London

Brown, R.(1976), *Women as employees: some comments on research in industrial sociology,* in Barker and Allen eds, b.

Bryman, A., Bytheway, B., Allatt, P. and Keil, T. eds.(1987), *Rethinking the Life Cycle,* MacMillan, London.

Bryman, A.(1988), *Quantity and Quality in Social Research,* Unwin Hyman, London.

Burden, D.S. and Gotlieb, N.(1987), *The Woman Client,* Tavistock, London.

Burgess, R.G.(1982), *Field research: A sourcebook and field manual,* George Allen and Unwin, London.

Burgoyne, J. and Clark, D.(1984), *Making a Go of It - A study of stepfamilies in Sheffield,* RKP, London.

Burgoyne, J., Ormod, R., and Richards, M.(1987), *Divorce Matters,* Penguin, London.

Burgoyne, J.(1987), *Rethinking the Family Life-Cycle: Sexual Divisions,Work and Domestic Life in the Post-War Period,* in Bryman, Bytheway, Allatt and Keil, eds.

Burns, T. (1967), Sociological Explanation, *British Journal of Sociology,* vol.XVIII.

'Butler Schloss',(1988), *Report of the inquiry into child sexual abuse in Cleveland, 1987,* HMSO, London.

Byrne, D.(1989), *Beyond the Inner City,* Open University Press, Milton Keynes.

Campbell, B.(1988), *Unofficial Secrets,* Virago, London.

Cannell, C.F. and Kahn, R.L.(1968), *Interviewing,* in Lindzey and Aronson, eds.

Carrigan, T.,Connell, B. and Lee, J.(1987), *Towards a new sociology of masculinity,* in Brod, ed.

Cashmore, E.E.(1985), *Having To - the world of one parent families,* Counterpoint/Unwin Hyman, London.

Chapman, R. and Rutherford, J. eds.(1988), *Male Order - Unwrapping Masculinity,* Lawrence and Wishart, London.

Child, J. ed.(1973), *Man and Organisation,* Allen and Unwin, London.

Clarke, Hall, and Morrison (1972), *Child Care Law,* Oyez, London.

'Collins'(1989), *Concise Dictionary Plus,* William Collins, London.

Conan Doyle, A.(1981), *The Penguin Complete Sherlock Holmes,* Penguin, London.

Connell, R.W.(1987), *Gender and Power - Society, the person, and sexual politics,* Polity Press, Cambridge.

Cotgrove, S.(1967), *The Science of Society,* George Allen and Unwin, London.

Dale, J. and Foster, P.(1986), *Feminists and State Welfare,* Routledge and Kegan Paul, London.

Dale, P. with Davies, M., Morrison, T. and Waters, J.(1986), *Dangerous Families,* Tavistock, London.

Daniel, W.W.(1973), Understanding employee behaviour in context, in Child, ed.

272

Davidoff, L.(1976), *The rationalisation of housework,* in Barker and Allen, eds, a.

Davis, G., McLeod, A., and Murch, M.(1982), Divorce:Who supports the Family?, *Family Law,* Vol 13 pp.217-224.

Davis, L.(1985), Female and Male Voices in social work, *Social Work,* pp.106 - 112.

Delamont, S.(1980), *The Sociology of Women,* George Allen and Unwin, London.

Delphy, C.(1985), *Close to Home: A materialist analysis of women's oppression,* Hutchinson, London.

Dennis, N., Henriques, F., and Slaughter, C.(1969), *Coal is our Life,,,* Tavistock, London.

Department of Health and Social Security(1982), *Child Abuse - A Study of Inquiry Reports 1973-1981,* HMSO.

Department of Health(1988), *Working Together,* HMSO, London.

Dingwall, R.(1980), Ethics and Ethnography, *Sociological Review,* Vol.28, no 4.

Donzelot, J.(1980), *The Policing of Families,* Routledge and Kegan Paul, London.

Draper, H.(1970), Marx, Engels, and Women's Liberation, *International Socialism,* pp.20-29, July-August.

Ehrenreich, B,(1983), *The Hearts of Men,* Pluto, London.

Ennew, J.(1986), *The sexual exploitation of children,* Polity Press, Cambridge.

Erikson, E.(1977), *Childhood and Society,* Penguin, London.

Ferri, E.(1986), *Growing up in a one-parent family,* NFER/NCB,London.

Finch, J. and Groves. D. eds(1983), *A Labour of Love: Women, work and caring,* Routledge and Kegan Paul, London.

Finch, J.(1984), *'It's great to have someone to talk to': the ethics and politics of interviewing women,* in Bell and Roberts, eds.

Finkelhor, D.(1986), *A Sourcebook on Child Sexual Abuse,* Sage.

Firestone, S.(1974), *The Dialectic of Sex,* Morrow, New York.

Ford, J., Keil, E.T., Beardsworth, A.D., Bryman, A.(1982), How employers see the public employment service, *Employment Gazette,* Vol.91, no.11.

Frankenberg, R.(1976), *In the production of their lives, men?,* in Barker and Allen eds, b.

Franklin, C.W.(1984), *The changing definition of masculinity,* Plenum Press, New York.

Foucault, M.(1976), *The History of Sexuality,* Penguin, Harmondsworth.

Gamarnikow, E. and Purvis, J.(1983), *The Public and the Private,* Heinemann, London.

Gasser, R. and Taylor, C.(1976), Role adjustment of single parent fathers with dependent children, *The Family Coordinator,* vol.25, pp.397-401.

The Guardian, p.20, 28.12.1989

The Guardian, p.24, 9.4.1990.

The Guardian, p.1, 18.1.1990.

George, V. and Wilding, P.(1972), *Motherless Families,* Routledge and Kegan Paul, London.

Gersick, K.E.(1979), *Fathers by Choice,* in Levinger and Moles, eds.

Gerstein, I.(1973), Domestic work and capitalism, *Radical America,* vol 7, no.5, pp.101-128.

Giddens, A.(1989), *Sociology,* Polity Press, Cambridge.

Gilligan, C.(1982), *In a different voice: Psychological theory and women's development,* Harvard University Press, Cambridge, Mass.

Gittins, D.(1985), *The Family in Question, Macmillan,* Hampshire.

Glaser, B.G. and Strauss, A.L.(1967), *The Discovery of Grounded Theory,* Aldine Press, Chicago.

Glaser, D. and Frosh, S.(1988), *Child Sexual Abuse,* Macmillan, London.

Goffman, E.(1967), *Interaction Ritual,* Doubleday Anchor, New York.

Goffman, E.(1971), *Relations in Public,* Allen Lane, London.

Goffman, E.(1969), *The Presentation of Self in Everyday Life,* Penguin, London.

Graham, H.(1983), *Caring: A labour of Love,* in Finch and Groves.

Greif, G.(1985), *Single Fathers,* Lexington Books, Massachusetts.

Greenwich, London Borough of(1987), *A Child in Mind - Report on the death of Kimberley Carlile,* Greenwich, London.

Griffiths, M.(1990), The split difference is that the women are forking out, *The Sunday Correspondent,* 7.1.1990, p.23.

Gross, A.E.(1989), *The Male Role and Heterosexual Behaviour,* in Kimmell and Messner, eds.

HMSO(1968), *Report of the Committee on Local Authority and Allied Personal Social Services, London,*Cmnd 3703, London.

HMSO(1974), *Report of the Finer Committee on One Parent Families,*Cmnd 5629, London.

HMSO(1988), *Report of the Inquiry into Child Abuse in Cleveland 1987,* Cmnd 412, London.

Hadley, R. and Hatch, S.(1981), *Social welfare and the failure of the State,* George Allen and Unwin, London.

Hakim, C.(1986), *Strategies and Choices in the design of Social Research,* Allen and Unwin, London.

Hale, J.(1983), *Feminism and Social Work Practice,* in Jordan and Parton, eds.

Hanmer, J. and Maynard, M.eds.(1987), *Women, Violence and Social Control,* Macmillan, Hampshire.

Hanmer, J. and Statham, D.(1988), *Women and Social Work,* Macmillan, Hampshire, 1988

Hargreaves, J.(1989), *The problems and possibilities of women's leisure,* in Rojek, ed.

Harris, C.C.(1983), *The Family and Industrial Society,* George Allen and Unwin, London.

Hart, N.(1976), *When Marriage Ends,* Tavistock, London.

Haskey, J.(1986), One Parent Families in Britain, *Population Trends,* no. 45, HMSO, London.

Haskey, J.(1989), One Parent Families and their children in Great Britain, *Population Trends,* no.55, HMSO, London.

Hearn, J.(1987), *The Gender of Oppression: Men, Masculinity, and the Critique of Marxism,* Wheatsheaf, Brighton.

Hearn, J.(1990), *Child Abuse and men's violence,* in Violence children study group, eds.

Hetherington, E.M., Cox, M. and Cox, R.(1976), Divorced fath *Family Coordinator,* vol.25, pp.417-428.

Hicks, C.(1988), *Who cares - looking after people at home,* Virag\ London.

Hillery, G.A.(1955), Definitions of community, *Rural Sociology,* vol.20, pp.111-123.

Hipgrave, T., (1978), *When the Mother is Gone - Profile studies of 16 lone fathers with pre-school children,* Unpublished M.A. thesis, University of Nottingham.

Hipgrave, T.(1982), *Lone Fatherhood: a problematic status,* in McKee and O'Brien, eds.

Hill, M.(1987), *Sharing Child Care in Early Parenthood,* Routledge and Kegan Paul, London.

Hoggart, R.(1957), *The Uses of Literacy,* Penguin, London.

Holland, J.(1982), Social class and changes in orientation to meaning, *Sociology,* 15(1), pp.1-18.

Holman, R.(1972), *Unsupported Mothers and the care of their children,* Mothers in Action, London.

Horna, J. and Lupri, E.(1987), *Fathers' participation in work, family and leisure: a Canadian experience,* in Lewis, C. and O'Brien, M.

House of Commons(1985), *Hansard - Written answer,* 3rd April, column 636.

Howell, M.C.(1986), *Women, Production, and Patriarchy in Late Medieval Cities,* University of Chicago Press, Chicago.

Hoyles, M.(1979), *Changing Childhood,* Writers and Readers, London.

Hudson, A.(1985), Feminism and Social Work, *British Journal of Social Work,* vol 15, p.635-655.

Hudson, A.(1989), *Changing perspectives: feminism, gender and social work,* in Langan and Lee, eds.

Hudson, R.(1986), *Producing an industrial wasteland,* in Martin and Rowthorne, eds.

Hunt, A.(1973), *Families and their needs with particular reference to one parent families,* HMSO, London.

Ingham, G.(1984), *Capitalism Divided?,* Macmillan, London.

Jackson, B.(1982), *Single Parent Families,* in Rapaport, Rapaport, and Fogarty, eds.

Jensen, J.(1989), *The talents of women, the skills of men: flexible specialization and women,* in Wood, ed.

Jordan, B. and Parton, N. eds.(1983), *The Political Dimensions of Social Work,* Basil Blackwell, Oxford.

Jordan, B.(1984), *Invitation to Social Work,* Martin Robertson, Oxford.

Joshi, H.(1986), *Gender Inequality in the Labour Market and the Domestic Division of Labour,* in Nolan and Paine, eds.

Kane, E.(1985), *Doing your own research,* Marion Boyars, London.

Katz, A.(1979), Lone Fathers, *Family Coordinator,* vol.28, pp.521-528.

Kelly, J.R.(1983), *Leisure Identities and Interactions,* George Allen and Unwin, London.

Keshet, H.F. and Rosenthal, K.M.(1978), Fathering after marital separation, *Social Work,* vol.23, pp.11-18.

Kimmel, M.S.(1987), *The contemporary 'crisis' of masculinity in historical perspective,* in Brod, ed.

Kimmell, M.S. and Messner, M.M.(1989), *Mens Lives,* Macmillan, New York.

Kubler Ross, E.(1970), *On Death and Dying,* Tavistock, London.

La Fontaine, J.S.(1985), Anthropological perspectives on the family and social change, *Quarterly Journal of Social Affairs,* Vol 1, No.1.

La Fontaine, J.S.(1988), *Child Sexual Abuse: An ESRC research briefing,* ESRC, Swindon.

La Rossa, R. and La Rossa, M.M.(1980), *Transition to Parenthood,* Sage, London.

Lamb, M.E. ed.(1982), *Nontraditional Families: Parenting and Child Development,* Lawrence Erlbaum Associates, Hillsdale, New Jersey.

Lamb, M. E.and Sagi, A. eds.(1983), *Fatherhood and Family Policy,* Lawrence Erlbaum Associates, Hillsdale, New Jersey.

Lambeth, London Borough of(1987), *Whose Child? - Report on the death of Tyra Henry,* Lambeth, London.

Land, H.(1985), *The Introduction of Family Allowances,* in Ungerson, ed.

Langan, M. and Lee, P. eds.(1989), *Radical Social Work Today,* Unwin Hyman, London.

Laslett, T.P.R.(1969), *The World We Have Lost,* Cambridge University Press, Cambridge.

Laslett, T.P.R.(1977), *Family Life and Illicit Love,* CUP, Cambridge.

Lerner, G.(1986), *The Creation of Patriarchy,* Oxford University Press, Oxford.

Levinger, G. and Moles, E. eds.(1979), *Divorce and Separation,* Basic Books, New York.

Lewis, C. and O'Brien, M. eds.(1987), *Reassessing Fatherhood,* Sage, London,1987.

Lindzey,G. and Aronson, E. eds.(1986), *Handbook of Social Psychology,* vol.II, Addison-Wesley, Reading, USA.

Lippert, J.(1989), *Sexuality as Consumption,* in Kimmell and Messner, eds.

Litwak, E.(1960), Geographical mobility and extended family cohesion, *American Sociological Review,* Vol.25, no.3, pp.385-394.

Loether, H.J. and McTavish, D.G.(1974), *Descriptive Statistics for Sociologists,* Allyn and Bacon, Boston.

Lowe, N.V.(1982), *The legal status of fathers: past and present,* in McKee and O'Brien, eds.

Marchant, H. and Wearing, B. eds.(1986), *Gender reclaimed : Women in Social Work,* Hale and Leimonger, Marickville, New Zealand.

Marsden, D.(1969), *Mothers Alone,* Penguin, London.

Marsh, P.(1987), *Social work and fathers - an exclusive practice?,* in Lewis and O'Brien, eds.

Marshall, G., Rose, D., Newby, H., and Vogler, C.(1988), *Social Class in Modern Britain,* Unwin Hyman, London.

Martin, R. and Rowthorne, B. eds.(1986), *The Geography of Deindustrialisation,* Macmillan, London.

Mead, G.H.(1934), *Mind, Self and Society,* University of Chicago Press, Chicago.

Mendes, H.A.(1975), *Parental Experiences of Single Fathers,* Unpublished doctoral dissertation, University of California at Los Angeles.

Mendes, H.A.(1976), Single Fatherhood, *Family Coordinator,* Vol.25, pp. 439 - 444.

Mercer, K. and Julien, I.(1988), *Race, Sexual Politics, and Black Masculinity - A dossier,* in Chapman and Rutherford, eds.

Merton, R.K.(1957), *Social Theory and Social Structure,* Glencoe Free Press, New York.

Metcalf, A. and Humphries, M.(1985), *The Sexuality of Men,* Pluto Press, London.

McConchie, H.(1982), *Fathers of mentally handicapped children,* in Beaill and McGuire, eds.

McCintosh, M.(1987), *Sex, Gender, and the Family,* in Worsley..

McKee, L. and O'Brien,M. eds.(1982), *The Father Figure,* Tavistock, London.

McKee, L. and O'Brien, M.(1983), *Interviewing Men: Taking Gender Seriously,* in Gamarnikow and Purvis, eds.

McLeod, E. and Dominelli, L.(1982), *The Personal and The Apolitical,* in Bailey and Lee, eds.

McLeod, E. and Sagara, E.(1988), Child Sexual Abuse, *Feminist Review,* vol.28.

Millar, J.(1989), *Poverty and the Lone Parent Family,* Avebury, Aldershot.

Mitchell, A.(1982), *Children in the Middle,* Tavistock, London.

Mitterauer, M. and Sieder, R.(1982), *The European Family - Patriarchy to partnership from the Middle Ages to the present,* Basil Blackwell, Oxford.

Morgan, D.H.J.(1975), *Social theory and the Family,* Routledge and Kegan Paul, London.

Morgan, D.H.J.(1981), *Men, Masculinity and Sociological Enquiry,* in Roberts, ed.

Morgan, D.H.J.(1985), *The Family, Politics and Social Theory,* Routledge and Kegan Paul, London.

Morgan, D.H.J.(1987), *Masculinity and Violence,* in Hanmer and Maynard, eds.

Morgan, D.H.J.(1988), Two faces of the family: the possible contribution of sociology to family therapy, *Journal of Family Therapy,* 10, pp.233-253.

Morgan, D.H.J.(1990), *In search of post-modern man,* paper presented to BSA conference, 2-5th April, University of Surrey.

Morgan, S. and Righton, P.(1989), *Child Care - concerns and conflicts,* Open University Press, Milton Keynes.

Morris, L.(1987), *The life cycle and the labour market,* in Bryman et al.

Morris, L.(1990), *The Workings of the Household - A US -UK Comparison,* Polity Press, Cambridge.

Moser, C.A. and Kalton, G.(1971), *Survey Methods in Social Investigation,* Heinemann, London.

Mount, F.(1982), *The Subversive Family - An alternative history of love and marriage,* Unwin Paperbacks, London.

Murch, M.(1973), Motherless Families Project, *British Journal of Social Work,* Vol.3, No.3, pp.365-376.

Nelson, S.(1987), *Incest: Fact and Myth,* Strathmullion, Glasgow.

Newson. E., Newson, J. and Lewis, C.(1982), *Father participation through childhood and it's relation to career aspirations and delinquency,* in Beaill and McGuire, eds.

Norman, J. ed.(1985), *Marital Violence,* Routledge and Kegan Paul, London.

Norusis, M.J.(1983), *SPSSx - Introductory Statistics Guide,* SPSS Inc., Chicago.

Nye, F.I.(1976), *Role Structure and Analysis of the Family,* Sage, Beverley Hills.

Oakley, A.(1974), *The Sociology of Housework,* Martin Robertson, London.

Oakley, A.(1982), *Subject Women,* Fontana, London.

O'Brien, M.(1982), *Becoming a lone father: differential patterns and experiences,* in McKee and O'Brien, eds.

O'Brien, M.(1984), *Fathers without Wives - A comparative study of married and separated fathers,* unpublished Ph.D. thesis, University of London.

O'Brien, M.(1987), *Patterns of kinship and friendship amongst lone fathers,* in Lewis and O'Brien, eds.

Olson,D.H. and Markoff, R. eds.(1981-83), *Inventory of marriage and family literature,* Vol. viii, ix and x, Beverley Hills and London.

OPCS(1993), *1991 Census Report for Great Britain,* vol.1, HMSO, London.

Orthner, D., Brown, T., and Ferguson, D.(1976), Single parent fatherhood: an emergent lifestyle, *Family Coordinator,* vol. 25, pp.429-437.

Parkinson, L.(1987), *Divorce and separation,* Macmillan, London.

Parker, S.(1976), *The Sociology of Leisure,* George Allen and Unwin, London.

Parsons, T.(1949), *The Social Structure of the Family,* in Ashen, ed.

Parsons, T. and Shils, E.(1951), *Towards a General Theory of Action,* Harper Torchbooks, Harvard.

Parsons, T.(1956), *Family, Socialisation, and Interaction Process,* Routledge and Kegan Paul, London.

Parsons, T.(1980), *Reply to his critics,* in Anderson, ed.

Parton, C.(1990), *Women, Gender Oppression, and Child abuse,* Violence against children study group, eds.

Parton, N.(1990), *Taking child abuse seriously,* Violence against children study group, eds.

Pichinto, J.C.(1983), Profile of the single father: a thematic integration of the literature, *Personnel and Guidance Journal,* pp.295 - 299.

Polsky, N.(1971), *Hustlers, Beats, and Others,* Penguin, Harmondsworth.

Popay, J., Rimmer, L. and Rossiter, C.(1983), *One Parent Families: Parents, children and public policy,* The Study Commission on the Family, London.

278

Portelli, A.(1981), The peculariaties of oral history, *History Workshop*, No.12, August.

Punch, M.(1986), *Ethics and Social Research*, Sage, USA.

Ramazanoglu, C.(1989), Improving on sociology: the problems of taking a feminist standpoint, *Sociology*, vol. 23, no.3, pp. 427 - 442.

Rapaport, L.(1970), *Crisis intervention as a mode of brief treatment*, in Roberts and Nee, eds.

Rapaport,R.N., Rapaport, R. and Strelitz, Z.(1977), *Fathers, Mothers, and Others*, Routledge and Kegan Paul, London.

Rapaport,R.N., Fogarty,M.P., and Rapaport, R. eds.(1982), *Families in Britain*, Routledge and Kegan Paul, London.

Roberts, H. ed.(1981), *Doing Feminist Research*, Routledge and Kegan Paul, London.

Roberts, R.W. and Nee, R.H.(1970), *Theories of Social Casework*, University of Chicago Press, Chicago.

Rojek, C.(1989), *Leisure for Leisure*, Macmillan, London.

Russell, G.(1983), *The changing role of fathers*, Open University, Milton Keynes.

Rutter, M.(1967), A child's behavioural questionnaire, *Journal of Child Psychology and Psychiatry*, vol.8, pp.1-11.

Rutter, M.(1972), *Maternal Deprivation Reassessed*, Penguin, Harmondsworth.

Sainsbury, E., Nixon, S. and Phillips, D.(1982), *Social Work in Focus*, Routledge and Kegan Paul, London.

Santrock, J. and Warshak, R.(1979), Father custody and social development in boys and girls, *Journal of Social Issues*, vol.35, 4, pp.112-125.

Schofield, R.(1986), *Did the mothers really die?*, in Bonfield and Smith, eds.

Scott, S.(1984), *The personable and the powerful: gender and status in sociological research*, in Bell and Roberts, eds.

Seccombe, W.(1974),The housewife and her labour under capitalism, *New Left Review*, no.83.

Segal, M.(1990), *Slow Motion - changing masculinities, changing men*, Virago, London.

Seidler, V.(1988), *Fathering, Authority and Masculinity*, in Chapman and Rutherford, eds.

Sharrock, W.W., Anderson, R.J., and Hughes, J.A.(1987), *Classic Disputes in Sociology*, Unwin, London.

Shaw. M.P.(1994), *Women and Political Action*, unpublished Ph.D.thesis, University of Durham.

Sinclair, P.J.N.(1987), *Unemployment - Economic Theory and Evidence*, Basil Blackwell, Oxford.

Smart, C.(1989), *Power and the politics of child custody*, in Smart and Sevenhuijsen, eds.

Smart, C. and Sevenhuijsen, S. eds.(1989), *Child Custody and the Politics of Gender*, Routledge, London.

Smith, G.(1990), The crisis of fatherhood, *Achilles Heel*, no.9, pp. 7-11.

Smith, H.W.(1981), *Strategies of social research*, Prentice Hall, New Jersey.

279

Smith, R.M. and Smith, C.W.(1981), Child rearing and single parent fathers, *Family Relations,* vol.30, pp.411 - 417.

Stacey, J.(1974), *And Jill Came Tumbling After,* Dell, New York.

Stacey, M.(1969), The Myth of Community Studies, *British journal of Social Work,* vol.20, no.2, pp.134 - 147.

Stark, E. and Flitcraft, A.(1985), *Woman battering, child abuse, and social heredity - what is the relationship?* in Norman, ed.

Stock Whitaker, D. and Archer, D.(1989), *Research in Social Work,* CCETSW, London.

Stockard, J. and Johnson, M.(1980), *Sex Roles - Sex Inequality and Sex Role Development,* Prentice Hall, New Jersey.

Sunday Times, The Sunday Times Magazine, 2.4.1989.

Tedder, S.L., Libbee, K.M., and Sherman, A.A.(1981), A community support group for single custodial fathers, *Personnel and Guidance Journal,* vol.60, pp.115-119.

Thane, P.(1978), *The Origins of British Social Policy,* Croom Helm, London,

Thompson, E.P.(1968), *The Making of the English Working Classes,* Penguin, London.

Tiger, L. and Fox, R.(1974), *The Imperial Animal,* Paladin, London.

Todres, R.(1975), *A Study of 72 Motherles Families in the Metropolitan Toronto Area,* Occasional Papers in Social Work, University of Toronto, Toronto.

Tolson, A.(1977), *The limits of masculinity,* Tavistock, London.

Townsend, P.(1957), *The Family Life of Old People,* Routledge and Kegan Paul, London.

Townsend, P.(1987), *Poverty in the United Kingdom,* Penguin, Harmondsworth.

Tremblay, M - A.(1982), *The key-informant technique: a non-ethnographic application,* in Burgess, ed.

Triseliotis, J.(1973), *In Search of Origins,* Routledge and Kegan Paul, London.

Tufte, V. and Myerhoff, B. eds.(1979), *Changing Images of the Family,* New Haven, London.

Ungerson, C.(1987), *Policy is Personal: Sex, Gender, and Informal Care,* Tavistock, London.

Violence Against Children Study Group, (1990), *Taking Child Abuse Seriously,* Unwin Hyman, London.

Walby, S.(1986), *Patriarchy at Work,* Polity Press, Cambridge.

Walby, S.(1989a), Theorising Patriarchy, *Sociology,*Vol.23, no.2, London.

Walby, S.(1989b), *Flexibility and the changing sexual division of labour,* in Wood, ed.

Wallerstein, J.S. and Kelly, J.B.(1980), *Surviving the Breakup,* Grant McIntyre, London.

Wallerstein, J. and Kelly, B.(1990), *Second Chance - Men, Women, and Children after Divorce,* Bantam, London.

Walton, R.(1975), *Women in Social Work,* Routledge and Kegan Paul, London.

Walvin, J.(1985), *A Child's World,* Penguin, London.

Warren, C.A.B.(1988), *Gender Issues in Field Social Work,* Sage, London.

Waters, M.(1989), Patriarchy and Viriarchy: An exploration and reconstruction of concepts of masculine domination, *Sociology,* Vol.23, no.2.

Weeks, J.(1986), *Family Studies-Information needs and resources,* Library and Information Research Report 43, The British Library, London.

Weeks, J.(1989), *Sex, Politics, and Society,* Longman, London.

Weller, S. and Kimball Romney, J.(1988), *Systematic Data Collection,* Sage, Beverley Hills.

Wheelock, J.(1986), *Unemployment, Gender Roles, and housework Strategies on Wearside,* EEC.

Wheelock, J.(1990), *Husbands at Home - the domestic economy in a post-industrial society,* Routledge.

Whitehead, A.(1976), *Sexual antagonism in Herefordshire,* in Barker and Allen, eds, b.

Williamson, B.(1982), *Class, Culture, and Community,* Routledge and Kegan Paul, London.

Willis, A.(1988), Working with fathers in the inner city, *Social Work Today,* 18.12.1988, pp.12 - 13.

Wood, S. ed.(1989), *The Transformation of Work?,* Unwin Hyman, London.

Worden, J.W.(1983), *Grief Counselling and Grief Therapy,* Tavistock, London.

Worsley, P. ed.(1970), *Introductory Sociology,* Penguin, London.

Worsley, P. ed.(1987), *The New Introductory Sociology,* Penguin, London.

Wynn, M.(1964), *Fatherless Families,* Michael Joseph, London.

Young, M. and Wilmott, P.(1957), *Family and Kinship in East London,* Penguin, London.

Young, M and Willmott, P.(1973), *The Symmetrical Family,* Routledge and Kegan Paul, London.

Zaretsky, E.(1976), *Capitalism, the Family, and Personal Life,* Pluto Press, London.